RELIEF CARVING IN WOOD

RELIEF CARVING IN WOOD

A PRACTICAL INTRODUCTION

Chris Pye

Guild of Master Craftsman Publications Ltd

First published 1998 by
Guild of Master Craftsman Publications Ltd,
166 High Street, Lewes, East Sussex, BN7 1XU

All photographs by Christopher J. Pye except where otherwise stated
All drawings by Christopher J. Pye
Cover photograph by Andrew Southon

ISBN 1 86108 096 4

Designed by Christopher Halls at Mind's Eye Design, Lewes

Set in Trajan and Goudy

Colour origination by Viscan Graphics (Singapore)

Printed and bound by Kyodo Printing (Singapore) under the supervision of MRM Graphics, Winslow, Buckinghamshire, UK

Measurements

Although care has been taken to ensure that metric measurements are true and accurate, they are only conversions from imperial. They have been rounded up or down to the nearest whole millimetre, or to the nearest convenient equivalent in cases where the imperial measurements themselves are only approximate.

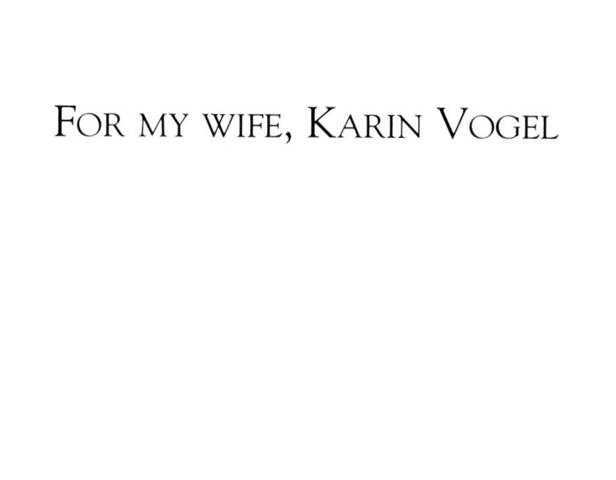

For my wife, Karin Vogel

CONTENTS

ACKNOWLEDGEMENTS

It has been well said: 'To teach is to learn twice': I would like to thank all those students who have helped me over the years to learn more about woodcarving – when all the time they thought I was helping *them*. In particular I would like to thank those students, now to be called carvers, who allowed me to photograph their fish and subsequent relief carvings which appear in the gallery: Beryl Thompson, Bill Grice, Christine Tutt, Eileen Kemp, Geoff Tutt, Glyn Jones, Graham Alcock, John Daines, Ken Wilce, Mick Botten, Roger Pickford, Sue Locke, and Vivien Wallace.

I would like to thank the following for help with photographs: Don Dennis; Geoff Brown of BriMarc Associates; Tormek AB, Sweden; Axminster Power Tools; and David Lloyd.

Thanks also to Liz Inman for unwavering confidence in my writing; to Stephen Haynes for overseeing the production of this book in such a relaxed and professional manner, for his many useful suggestions and keen eye; and to Chris Halls, the book designer, who magically transformed my unlikely-looking bundle of papers into a fine-looking book.

In my mind I have always titled this 'The Book of the Fish'. It is with pleasure that I dedicate it to someone referred to in a previous book as 'the loveliest catch of all': my wife Karin Vogel, as always a great source of encouragement and support.

Finally, an apology: to all fishes, everywhere.

CHAPTER ONE

INTRODUCTION

This is a different kind of carving book. Rather than proceed through a large number of projects superficially, there are only two, treated in great depth.

The projects are meant to be followed closely. I explain exactly what I am doing at any particular point in the carving, and why I am doing it. By the end of the practical work the student will have acquired a range of essential woodcarving skills and be able to apply them intelligently, not only to relief carving but to other work as well.

This book is based directly on teaching, both absolute beginners and those with some woodcarving experience. I have asked more students than I care to think about to carve the fish projects on which this book is based, and I know this short course works extremely well. A small gallery of students' subsequent relief carvings is shown in Chapter 8 (pages 137–49). I must emphasize that these are 'next' carvings – projects which directly follow on from the fish and are aimed at consolidating what the students have learned. It is only fair to say that I am hovering in the background with advice and encouragement, but it is the students who have done the work and demonstrate their carving skills.

Every student coming to my workshop starts here – carving a fish: first in low relief, then the *same design* in high relief. The fish itself is irrelevant, a red herring: it is only a vehicle for acquiring woodcarving skills. No knowledge of fish is required!

The two projects in this book are attainable by beginners without too much difficulty; the skills needed are graded as the work proceeds. Both projects can be completed with a simple set-up and a very useful set of 11 carving tools which I specify.

In writing this book I have continually referred to the notebooks I keep on students' questions and problems, my replies and suggestions. In my mind I would recall particular instances and students along with issues which recurred frequently. So the tone of this book is one of addressing students directly, almost as if they were there.

This is my first carving book of a broader nature, and is meant as an introduction to woodcarving in general, and relief carving in particular. This book does *not* include:

- pierced relief;
- applied carving;
- lining or stamping techniques;
- finishing with colour and so on;
- mixing these techniques into complicated designs;
- relief carving that involves building up areas;
- joining up panels;
- the use of machinery such as routers, and so on.

To do this would be to invite the superficial treatment I am trying to avoid, and I hope in future books to look at more advanced relief carving and work in the round, and to include many other techniques and options.

As I write more books, I find there is a delicate balance to be struck between repeating myself – tedious for me and for those who have read my other books – and giving adequate information necessary for newcomers. In particular, I recommend my first book, *Woodcarving Tools, Materials & Equipment* (GMC Publications, 1994), as a reference manual for all the bits and pieces which are not direct carving but will fill out much of the background to what is presented here.

My own teacher, the late Gino Masero, said once that carving 'was a sort of joy'. This is absolutely so.

Within the frustrations and sheer hard work that are often to be found in woodcarving, there is also a delight; I hope this book puts you on the right path to finding it.

HOW TO USE THIS BOOK

- Start by browsing through to get a general idea of the contents and where to find things.
- Set up for the projects, as described in Chapter 2. This chapter contains some check lists to help you:
    - Gather your carving tools;
      pages 10–13 list of tools;
      pages 156–8 list of sources
    - Make sure that they are sharp enough;
      pages 14–15 how to check tool sharpness;
      pages 156–8 list of suppliers of sharpening equipment; pages 15–22 sharpening
    - Prepare your wood;
      pages 5–8 selecting wood;
      page 8 dimensions of the wood used in the projects
    - Hold your wood safely;
      page 9 notes on holding;
      pages 9–10 holding devices
- If you are not familiar with carving tools or wood, go through Chapter 3, Basics, carefully and try the exercises described there.
- Begin with the low relief project (Chapter 4), following the method carefully step by step.
- Go on to the high relief project (Chapter 5).
- Design a relief carving to consolidate what you have learned (Chapter 7, Next Steps).

Both high and low relief are used together to create the passion and drama in this detail from the door of the Asamkirche, Munich (built c. 1733–46). The subject is the martyrdom of John of Nepomuk.

CHAPTER TWO

SETTING UP

Newcomers to woodcarving often put a simple, practical question: *How do I start?*

At its simplest, to carve wood you need:

- a place to work;
- a suitable piece of wood;
- some safe and convenient way of holding what you are carving;
- a selection of carving tools;
- the means of sharpening them;
- a workable idea.

It is these various practical needs that I will look at in this chapter. For further information and advice I would recommend my book *Woodcarving Tools, Materials & Equipment*.

At the beginning, when you are unsure how far you might want to pursue woodcarving, a balance needs to be struck between having a decent opportunity to find out, and keeping costs down.

As to the opportunity: by following closely the two fish projects at the heart of this book, you should begin to understand how straightforward carving is. I hope of course that you will then feel confident to start your own work – so becoming happily hooked by woodcarving.

In terms of cost: I have always considered that, relative to other major crafts, woodcarving is inexpensive. However, you cannot avoid a certain amount of outlay, if you mean to give yourself a fair chance to enjoy it. The projects are based on what I consider to be a minimum number of specific (but ever-useful) carving tools, and a simple set-up. If you can start off as I recommend, not only will you best follow the projects and learn most from them, but you are giving yourself a good start for future work.

I am including check lists of specific requirements as we go along, with a summary at the end of the chapter of what is necessary to follow the projects.

So, what further questions do I usually get asked?

A PLACE TO WORK

What sort of mess does woodcarving make?

Woodcarving *can* create a lot of mess: a large piece of wood, a machine like an Arbortech flinging woodchips across the workshop, power-sanding ... very messy! And, to me, unpleasant.

However, at the level of simple relief to which we will be working here, carving wood is a remarkably clean craft. You will produce larger chips and shavings of wood to begin with, as the rough waste is removed, and end with fine, small shavings as the carving is finished (Fig 2.1).

Fig 2.1 *Sweepings from a carving class: the sort of easily managed mess woodcarving makes.*

It is perfectly feasible to carve in the corner of a living room, protecting the carpet – I did this when I started carving. As we will *not* be sanding, there is hardly any dust. The work area can be cleaned easily with a dustpan and brush, and vacuumed after if necessary.

It is the sharpening of tools, usually involving oil, that can create dirt and mess. I strongly advise you to keep the sharpening area *separate* from the carving area. After sharpening you must wash your hands to prevent dirtying the freshly cut wood.

If your tools are of good quality and you are carving the sort of medium-hard wood we use in the projects, once you have your tools sharp you will not need to go to the sharpening stones for a long while. This is provided you strop the cutting edge regularly (see pages 21–2).

After a session of carving with clean wood and tools you should find that your hands will hardly need washing.

CHECK LIST

To keep your work area clean you use:

- bench brush;
- dustpan and brush;
- vacuum;

and for yourself:

- facilities for washing hands.

How much space does woodcarving need?

For the two projects in this book I am using a small bench, 2ft (60cm) square (Fig 2.2). This is about the minimum size which allows the workpiece to lie at the front while tools are placed in a row at the rear. You will of course need to work *around* your bench, but you can see that you only need quite a small area to carve in.

To start with you can use a strong table. The problem is in the *working height*. I will say a little more about this, and about benches, later (page 9).

Sharpening must be kept separate, so it helps if you have another place for this. However, use the same work area if you must; but try and 'fence it off' (in time or space) from the wood and take care not to transfer grime to the carving from your hands.

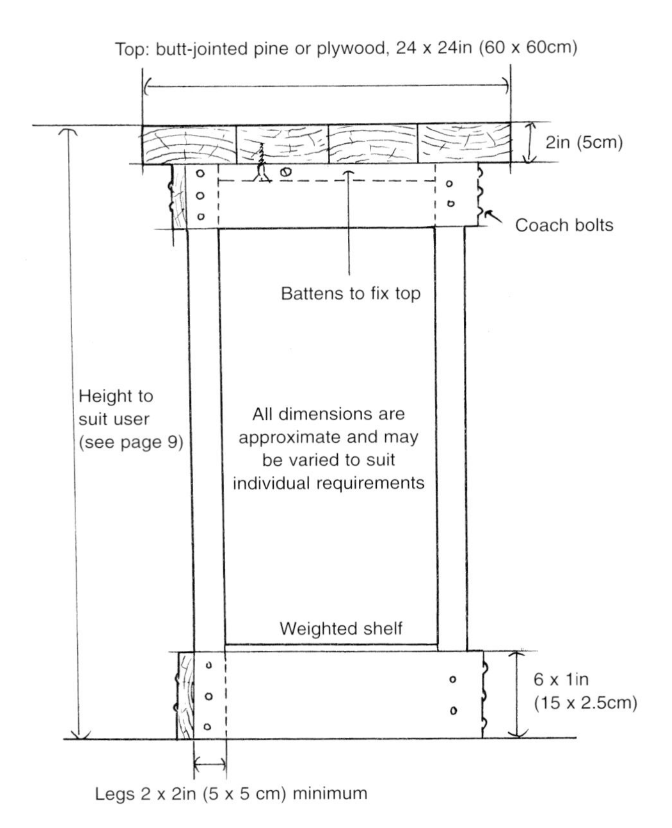

***Fig 2.2** A simple bench, to the size used by me for the projects. The underframe can be made without joints, using coach bolts or screws, as long as the horizontal rails are wide enough to give rigidity.*

CHECK LIST

You need room for:

- the carving;
- placing the tools;
- moving around the carving;
- sharpening.

What else do I need?

Comfort: I think the workplace should be one you like going to and enjoy being in. Make it pleasant and physically comfortable – and this includes making it warm enough.

The back of the garage, or a garden shed, is often the only option for some students who cannot (or are not allowed to!) take over a corner of the spare room or kitchen table. Garage or shed is fine – but take the trouble to make a place you enjoy being in, not one to which you feel exiled.

If you have an area dedicated to carving, you can leave your tools out – provided the atmosphere is dry. Woodcarving tools are not rustproof and will corrode if subjected to damp. If in doubt, or if your carving area is temporary, then store your tools carefully, and somewhere dry. Take care not to knock their sharp edges together. Rolls for carving tools are easy to make (Fig 2.3); or for quicker access, tools may be hung in racks or kept neatly in drawers (see *Woodcarving Tools, Materials & Equipment*, pages 96–8).

Lighting is very important. Carving of any depth is about nothing if it is not about light and shadow (Fig 2.4). You need two sources of light: a main light to illuminate the work area generally, and an adjustable lamp to angle across the work to bring out the light and shadow.

CHECK LIST

In the workplace think about:

- carver comfort (pleasant, warm enough);
- how dry the atmosphere is;
- caring for your carving tools (tool rolls, drawers, racks);
- lighting (main light and adjustable side light).

A PIECE OF WOOD

What's the best wood for carving?

I have to say this clearly: wood, the right wood, is *extremely important* to you as a carver. You will spend a lot of time and energy on a single carving – even on the projects in this book. I am continually surprised at what poor offerings students appear with, based solely on the wood being free; either given to them or found. Some are fortunate and have acquired a decent piece to work with; but, even so, the fortuitous nature of the material usually radically alters their ideas and they carve what they can, rather than what they wanted to.

Never skimp on your material; always get the best wood you can; and be careful of compromising your ideas and desires. This means both making a deliberate point of learning all you can about wood, and having a choice to hand.

Which wood a carver needs for a particular job depends really on what they want to carve. They will be thinking about how easily it carves; its size, availability, cost, colour, figuring (surface pattern) and so on – in relation to the idea they have.

I am averse to giving students long lists of possible carving woods. This never addresses what

Fig 2.3 *Your tools must be looked after carefully. Tool rolls like this are easy to sew up. Note the cork protecting the vulnerable point of the skew chisel.*

Fig 2.4 *Ostensibly acanthus leaves on the end of a pew in Southern Germany, this carving is nothing less than an exercise in movement, light and shadow.*

Fig 2.5 *A selection of 'classic' carving woods: (top) walnut; (second row) mahogany, oak and pear; (bottom left) lime. All show tight, dense, fairly bland grain.*

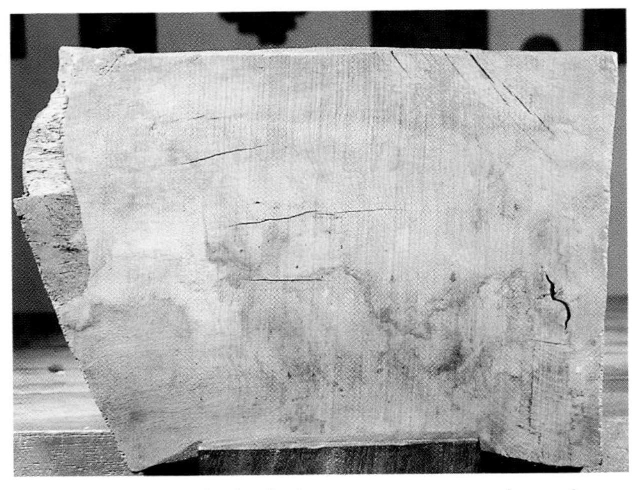

Fig 2.6 *This panel of oak shows grain rising to the surface (shown by the bark to the left); shakes (cracking); a large knot (right); associated irregular grain distribution – definitely 'trouble'!*

happens in real life. I suggest you begin with just one or two well-known 'carver-friendly' woods. Then look around at other carvings, both old and new, in books and magazines, and (ideally) the real thing. Make notes of what wood is being used by the carver and how successfully. Although it is worth trying as wide a range as you can, most students eventually settle down to a few favourite woods and stick to them.

We will be using **jelutong** – this carves easily but may have latex channels. It is an excellent wood for a first carving like our projects. Other woods suitable for the projects, and in general to start carving with, are lime, English or Japanese oak, fruitwoods such as pearwood, mild (Brazilian) mahogany, and walnut (Fig 2.5).

Since mahogany is connected with deforestation and similar important issues, I never buy it. However, it is still widely used by joiners and useful offcuts can often be salvaged from them.

Beech, (European) sycamore and maple are readily available but tend to be very hard and 'hang on' to the chisel: avoid these to begin with. In the USA, butternut and basswood are used a lot for carving.

Almost any wood can be carved, but it may not be desirable to do so! So much depends on what you want to carve. Besides the actual species you need to look at its quality.

The best carving wood is:

1 **Close-grained**: the annual rings are tightly packed – dense and evenly distributed;

2 **Coloured evenly**: most traditional carving woods are bland, because patterns can disrupt the light and shadow (figuring is best left for the smooth surfaces of more abstract carvings);

3 **Clean**: without knots, disfiguring streaks or marks, and with straight, regular grain;

4 **Crack-free**: unless you can put any splits in the waste area of your design.

When you visit a timberyard you can remember this list as the 'four Cs'. If you select your material well you will avoid a lot of trouble (Fig 2.6).

CHECK LIST

- Examine the wood for the 'four Cs': Close grain, Colour even, Clean and Crack-free.
- Study what other carvers use, what for, and how.
- Use seasoned (dried) wood only.
- Try lime, English oak, walnut, Brazilian mahogany, jelutong.

Fig 2.7 *Many students don't relate 'wood' to 'trees', but this is it: where you start, your raw material.*

Fig 2.8 *The wedge in this experiment was originally cut at right angles from the section of tree. As the wood dried, a gap of about 20° developed, but the wood itself has hardly any cracking and would provide useful carving wood.*

Fig 2.9 *A section of a newly cut whole log. The shrinkage gap in Fig 2.8 will be distributed throughout the log as splits – probably rendering it useless for carving.*

Where does wood come from?

Of course there is an obvious, facetious, answer to this question – which I'm afraid I can never resist. Actually the student is really asking another question, about where wood can be got; but I use my poor quip to make a point.

Wood comes from trees (Fig 2.7). The problem is that you can't (or can only with certain woods) just take a lump of tree and carve it without it splitting. Trees are very wet inside. Cut into logs, they will loose their water until they reach the amount of water in the surrounding atmosphere. In losing water, wood shrinks: different parts of a log shrink by different amounts and at different speeds, this creates tension within, and the wood splits. If you have carved the wood first, it is highly likely to take the carving with it, disastrously, as the experiment below suggests.

EXPERIMENT

1 Cut two thin (say 3/4in or 20mm) slices from a newly cut log or branch – any diameter.

2 From one, saw out an exact right-angled wedge that touches the centre, and replace it.

3 Leave both slices somewhere to dry.

After a few months you will see how the wedge has shrunk and no longer fits (Fig 2.8). When fully dry, the gap represents the amount the wood has shrunk. A similar amount is distributed unevenly, in the form of splits, around the uncut slice (Fig 2.9).

This experiment demonstrates:

- how much wood needs to shrink as it dries;
- that by removing some wood, adjustment is possible as the material shrinks, lowering tension between parts and minimizing or eliminating cracking.

Controlling the drying of wood – the way water is lost and the wood shrinks – is the purpose of the process called **seasoning**. Seasoned wood is much more stable and trustworthy, although the downside is its smaller dimensions. Nevertheless, seasoned wood is what you should use for carving.

Fig 2.10 *Boards 'in stick' (stacked with spacing sticks between) and air-drying in a timberyard. (Photograph by Don Dennis)*

Trees are cut into pieces and dried, either in kilns or in the air, in timberyards (Fig 2.10) – which are a main source of wood for carvers. You can season boards yourself by air-drying (see *Woodcarving Tools, Materials & Equipment*, page 301) if you have space and time. Elm and yew are two woods which, having interlocking grain, can be used as whole logs with the smallest amount of cracking.

You may spend days, even weeks, on a carving. It is reckless not to make sure your material is as safe as possible. This means using *seasoned* wood. If in doubt, wait and get another piece. It really is very frustrating, and sad, to have your work self-destruct.

CHECK LIST

- Learn about wood, about your material: you can save yourself a lot of time, effort and money.
- Use seasoned (dried) wood.

Where do I get wood?

The answer is vague: when and where you can. Once you are carving regularly, and people know about it, you will find wood widely available and you will even be given it. One piece will often last a long time, so the material costs can be very low over a long period.

Don't wait until you need wood. Try and build up a store, even a small one, so that you have material to hand – both to try out ideas, and to inspire them. Keep the wood in a dry, cool, airy place where you can easily see what you've got.

For particular projects you can approach timberyards for offcuts. Carvers can often use wood that no one else wants. If you buy wood, buy a bit extra for your store.

Barring timberyards, check out your local joiners, cabinet-makers, turners, restorers and tree surgeons. Many magazines for woodworkers (including *Woodcarving*) carry adverts from wood suppliers.

If you can link up with other carvers you can share planks and larger billets, and swap wood.

Scavenging and reclaiming wood can turn into a profitable hobby: skips, old furniture, fence posts, driftwood.

Exactly what your store of wood will consist of will depend on your carving interests and your experience of dealing with wood as a material. I suggest you begin with decent, seasoned wood from a timberyard and branch out later with your experience as your guide.

CHECK LIST

- Build up your own small store of wood.
- Start with seasoned wood obtained from timberyards or other woodworkers, or through magazines or *Yellow Pages*.
- Is there anyone else carving in your area?
- Unseasoned wood will need converting and drying.

What wood do I need to follow the projects in this book?

The wood used in the projects is jelutong, and the size required is 11 x 6$^1/_2$ x 1$^3/_4$in (280 x 165 x 45mm). I like to start with at least the top surface planed smooth; this helps me make a clearer drawing and a clean start. Avoid sanding, as this leaves grit in the wood, dulling the cutting edges. My sample is also planed around the edges and back to give a well-finished carving.

A SAFE AND CONVENIENT WAY OF HOLDING THE CARVING

Do I need a bench?

No doubt the best way to carve is using a proper bench. Benches can be seen as 'work stations' to which fixed and adjustable vices, jigs and other fixtures (lights, drawers etc.) can be added. Essentially, though, a bench is just a very strong table. It might even be a shelf, fixed at both ends in an alcove.

You need space to fix the carving and space for tools, lamp and so on. I use a bench for the projects which is 2 x 2ft (60 x 60cm); longer, at 3ft (90cm) or even 4ft (120cm), is better.

You *can* carve the projects in this book on an actual table, provided it is strong enough and won't move. This may be a good idea if you are not willing to invest in a bench at such an early stage.

The problem is the height. *Unless you physically cannot, always stand to carve:* you are much freer to move behind the carving tool. Normal tables, and even carpentry benches, Workmates, etc. are far too low and will soon give you backache.

A good height for your work surface is *a little below your elbow height, when you are standing upright.* If you are to avoid sitting down to work, this may mean either lifting the table onto blocks or preparing a false top to work on (Fig 2.11).

Whatever your 'bench' is, it literally and figuratively supports your woodcarving and is worth preparing well.

CHECK LIST

You need to provide yourself with:

- a strong, fixed table or bench;
- a work area for carving, with space for tools and adequate light;
- a surface of the correct working height;
- a false top to raise the height if necessary.

How do I hold the carving?

The most useful equipment for holding relief carvings to your bench is a pair of G-clamps (C-clamps) (Fig 2.12). The 'quick action' ones are best. Some have plastic pads to protect the wood

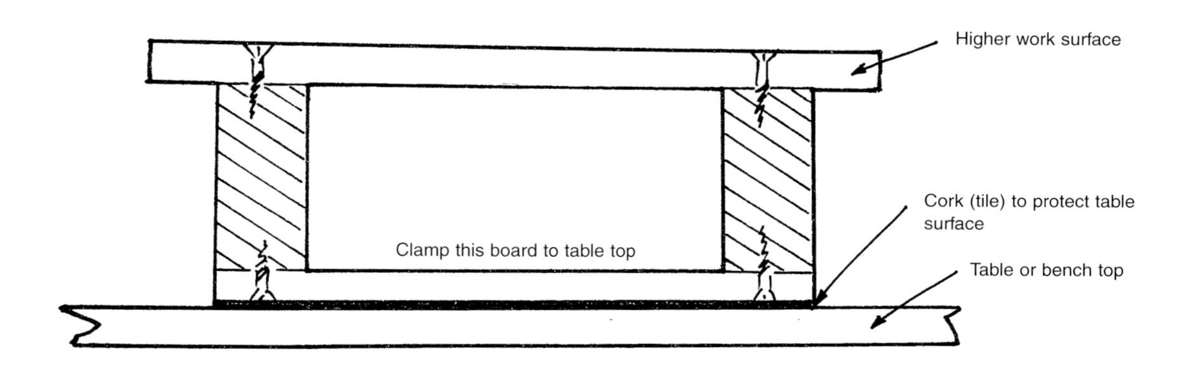

Fig 2.11 (above) *A simple false top to raise the work surface to a more comfortable level, made from plywood and offcuts of timber. The new top must be firm; it may be boxed in at the back to resist movement.*

Fig 2.12 (left) *An assortment of G-clamps (C-clamps) for holding panels to a bench. The two on the right are 'quick action', with a bar on which the arm slides. Of these, the left one has a simple handle. The clamp at far right (by Record) is the best, with an easy toggle-joint handle for good pressure which can swing out of the way after use.*

surface from bruising; if not, some pads of thin ply or hardboard will do (Fig 2.13).

Fig 2.13 *Protecting wood from crush marks with a pad of wood beneath the clamp head.*

As the clamps are used, the handle is invariably screwed further in than the amount it is loosened: the screw thread works its way to the end and jams. The user then thinks they have gripped the carving when in fact they haven't; the clamp falls off later, endangering toes. Before using clamps get into the habit of winding back the thread nearly to its end each time, and you will avoid this problem.

If the clamps are *directly* gripping the carving they are liable to get in the way at times and will need moving. The projects in this book use an *indirect* method of clamping them to the bench top. The wood is fixed to a board with fences and wedges, made from scrap wood (Fig 2.14), the whole board being clamped to the bench top. This allows the wood to be removed and turned around easily while keeping the clamp heads out of the way. You can even screw this board directly to your workbench, saving the cost of clamps altogether!

Fig 2.14 *Holding the block of wood with simple fences and wedges enables it to be lifted out and turned round quickly and easily. A wedge angle of about 10° gives a good 'bite'.*

Another way of holding a small relief carving is to glue it to a flat board, sandwiching newspaper or brown paper in between. Dilute the glue and keep clamped or under pressure until dry. The paper can be split later with a spatula and the carving released from the board.

You may be able to screw through a board into the back of the project wood: or you might be able to grip it in a vice if you have one large enough.

The important point is that the carving *must be fixed safely*, and in no danger of moving. You must be able to get at your work conveniently, and adjust it easily whenever you want to.

CHECK LIST

Project carving:

- Make up the wedge and fence board.
- Clamp to bench.
- Is the carving fixed safely?
- Can I get at the carving easily?
- Can I adjust it freely?

A SELECTION OF CARVING TOOLS

What tools do I need for carving?

Another vague answer, I'm afraid: what tools you need, and how many, really depends on what you actually want to do. If you don't know what you want to do – and after all this may be the first time ever you have worked with wood – then you must start with a small number of tools which carvers use frequently and build up from there.

I have selected a toolkit for the two fish projects in this book. These are very common, useful carving tools. As your own designs get more complicated, or bigger, or smaller, so you will need more. However, many students carve for a long time with just these 11 tools. A few of the carvings in the Gallery are quite complicated, and some students have bought additional tools where they have felt the need.

However, this applies to only a small fraction of the total work accomplished, and has involved bent or smaller versions of the tools in the basic list, students basing their choice on their experience with the tools used so far. I would advise you not to buy a boxed set of tools, since the compiler will know even less of what you want to do than yourself!

There is a wide (and for the beginner, confusing) range of carving tools, but they fall into three main categories:

1 **Gouges**: These are the primary carving tools. They remove wood; shape, flatten and texture it; cut neat outlines and patterns. Most gouges are arcs of circles in cross-section, and the curve in cross-section is called the **sweep**.

   U-shaped gouges have straight side walls and cut deep channels or **flutes**.

2 **Chisels**: Straight chisels are not very useful in general carving work, which requires few straight lines; although they will smooth off rounded surfaces. The **skew chisel**, however, which has a pronounced corner, is essential.

3 **V-tools**: This is like two chisels joined at an angle; the most useful angle is 60°. It is used to draw lines and cut grooves, or to separate one area from another – again an essential tool for the carver.

All carving tool sweeps and widths may be had in **bent** forms for cutting within hollows (Fig 2.15); or in **fishtail** shape for light finishing or getting into corners (Fig 2.16). But for now, stick to a few straight 'regular' carving tools such as the ones I suggest and you will not go far wrong, no matter what carving you do in the future.

You will see the tools being used in a variety of ways – these projects demonstrate this as one of their aims. When you move on to your own projects you will find that by now you have an idea of what you need: perhaps something wider, or deeper, or bent. You can then go to tool catalogues and select, using the illustrations they contain.

Which are the best tools to buy?

There are many excellent makes of woodcarving tools on the market, at varying prices: Auriou, Ashley Iles, Bristol Design, Henry Taylor, Kirschen, Lamp Tools (USA), Pfeil, Stubai – to name a few. Each firm has its strengths and weaknesses in shaping and supplying, and it is worth sampling them all eventually. Some suppliers are listed on pages 156–8; send for their catalogues, and file them.

Old tools are sometimes to be had, and can be better than new ones, if not too corroded or worn. Restoring old tools is dealt with in *Woodcarving Tools, Materials & Equipment*, pages 92–5.

Fig 2.15 *The same width and sweep of gouge in (from left) regular, longbent, shortbent and backbent profiles.*

Fig 2.16 *Regular and (right) fishtail flat gouges. The fishtail is a lighter tool, excellent for finishing, which gets its corners into recesses well.*

Of the firms mentioned above, I suggest newcomers start with Pfeil or Ashley Iles tools, which come with the sharpening reasonably started off. Check them against the sharpening advice on pages 14–22.

Unfortunately there is no one standard numbering system for tools, although the 'Sheffield List' is as near to one as any. Use the table on pages 150–1 to compare the sweeps of different makes.

What tools do I need to start?

Here we come to the specific toolkit for the projects in this book.

To follow the projects and get the most out of them you need to have the following 11 tools, or something close to them (Fig 2.17). I am using the Sheffield List numbering, which is shown in the table on pages 150–1.

1 no. 3 (flat gouge)	x 1/4in (6mm)
2 no. 3 (flat gouge)	x 1/2in (13mm)
3 no. 3 (flat gouge)	x 3/4in (19mm)
4 no. 6 (medium gouge)	x 1/4in (6mm)
5 no. 6 (medium gouge)	x 1/2in (13mm)
6 no. 6 (medium gouge)	x 3/4in (19mm)
7 no. 9 (semicircular gouge)	x 1/4in (6mm)
8 no. 9 (semicircular gouge)	x 1/2in (13mm)
9 no. 9 (semicircular gouge)	x 3/4in (19mm)
10 no. 2 (skew chisel)	x 3/8in (10mm)
11 no. 39 (60° V-tool)	x 3/8in (10mm)

If your chosen manufacturer does not make exactly the same specification or size, then choose the nearest.

Pfeil tools use a somewhat different numbering system and are labelled in metric sizes only; the nearest equivalents are:

1 cut 2 (flat gouge)	x 5mm
2 cut 2 (flat gouge)	x 12mm
3 cut 2 (flat gouge)	x 20mm
4 cut 7 (medium gouge)	x 6mm
5 cut 7 (medium gouge)	x 14mm
6 cut 7 (medium gouge)	x 20mm
7 cut 9 (semicircular gouge)	x 5mm
8 cut 9 (semicircular gouge)	x 13mm
9 cut 9 (semicircular gouge)	x 20mm
10 cut 1S (skew chisel)	x 8mm
11 cut 12 (60° V-tool)	x 8mm

Fig 2.17 *The basic set of carving tools used in the two projects (from left): three deep, three medium and three flat gouges in wide, medium and narrow sizes; 60° V-tool; and skew chisel.*

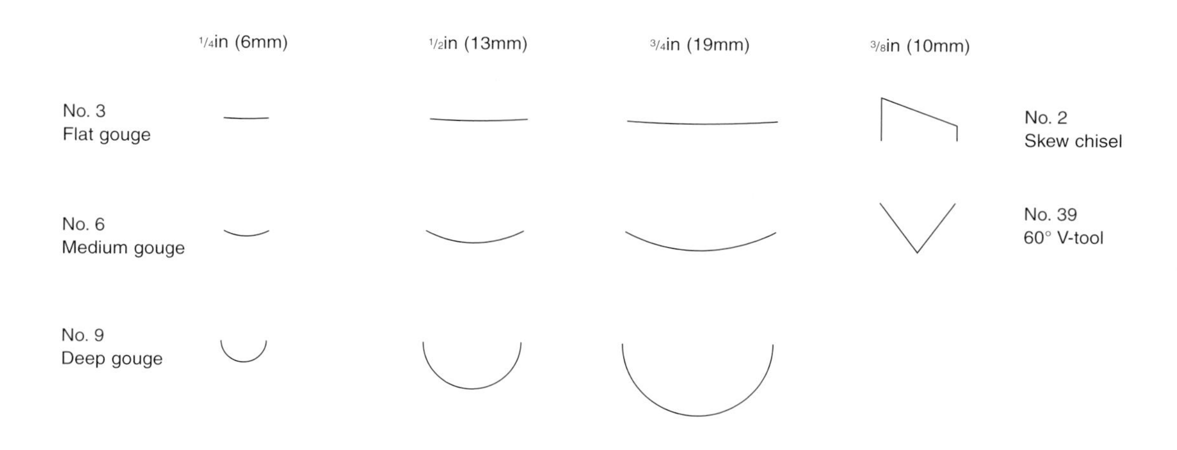

Fig 2.18 *Sweeps of the 11 tools which make up a good starting set, used for both projects.*

When you have the tools, offer them up to the Sheffield List chart to see how they fit into the overall scheme. You will see that they scatter across the chart and cover a broad area of size and shape (Fig 2.18).

Whatever make you choose, *it is not crucial to have exactly the same tools as I use*. You will most likely be designing your own project, using mine only as a guide, and this may involve using some tools more or less than I do; and in any case, as we shall see in the next chapter, one tool can be used to cut a variety of different curves.

Additional tools?

Besides regular carving tools you will need (Fig 2.19):

- **Mallet**: This should be a round woodcarver's mallet, weight about 1½lb (700g), although many carvers have two: a lighter 1lb one (450g) and a heavier one at 2lb (900g).
- **Marking gauge**: Not essential, but used for drawing a depth line to which to work our relief carving.
- **Carving brush**: something like an emulsion or horse brush for brushing away wood chips and keeping the carving clean.
- **Pencil, paper,** etc.

Fig 2.19 *Additional tools: mallets, clamps, marking gauge, try square and carving brush.*

A MEANS OF SHARPENING YOUR CARVING TOOLS

How important is sharpening?

It may not be evident to you at this stage in the book that the projects are left *straight from the cutting edge*, without subsequent sanding. This is not the only way to leave a wood surface, but it has many advantages. It is also the way I usually carve, and the way I teach carving. In the projects I will be showing you how to carve directly with the carving tools, and leave the surface without further work. In order to get crisp edges, fresh lines and clean surfaces your carving tools must be perfectly sharp, at all times.

The analogy is fair: *sharpness goes with carving wood, as tuning strings goes with playing the guitar.* Whether you like it or not, whether it takes a long time or short, it has to be done. If you are at all serious about carving, then you must be serious about sharpening.

How do I know if the tool is sharp and cutting as well as it should be?

Differentiate between a 'sharp' tool and one which is 'cutting well'.

Sharpness relates to the actual cutting edge. This must leave the cut surface perfectly smooth. As the heel (see Fig 2.20) follows the cutting edge, pressing down on the surface, the wood beneath will be burnished and the tool will leave a polished, even shiny, facet behind. If there is torn grain, evidenced by pale, matt streaks or tears – 'snail tracks' – this means that the cutting edge is nicked or otherwise blunt at these places, and work must be done to restore the edge (Fig 2.21).

Cutting well refers to the way the leading part of the blade – from the cutting edge to the heel, including the bevel – cleaves the wood. A gouge can be sharp, but cutting badly. The bevel is a wedge, which prises the fibres apart as they are cut. It must be the right shape, which (except for special purposes) is flat. The usual reason for a tool cutting badly is that the bevel is at too big an angle – which is often because it is rounded. For the tool to cut better, the angle must be lowered, or a rounded bevel flattened.

Fig 2.21 *A 'snail track' (top) produced by a blunt area which would show up as a white spot on the cutting edge. This must be corrected straight away, as the surface of the carving will be left without further work (such as sanding).*

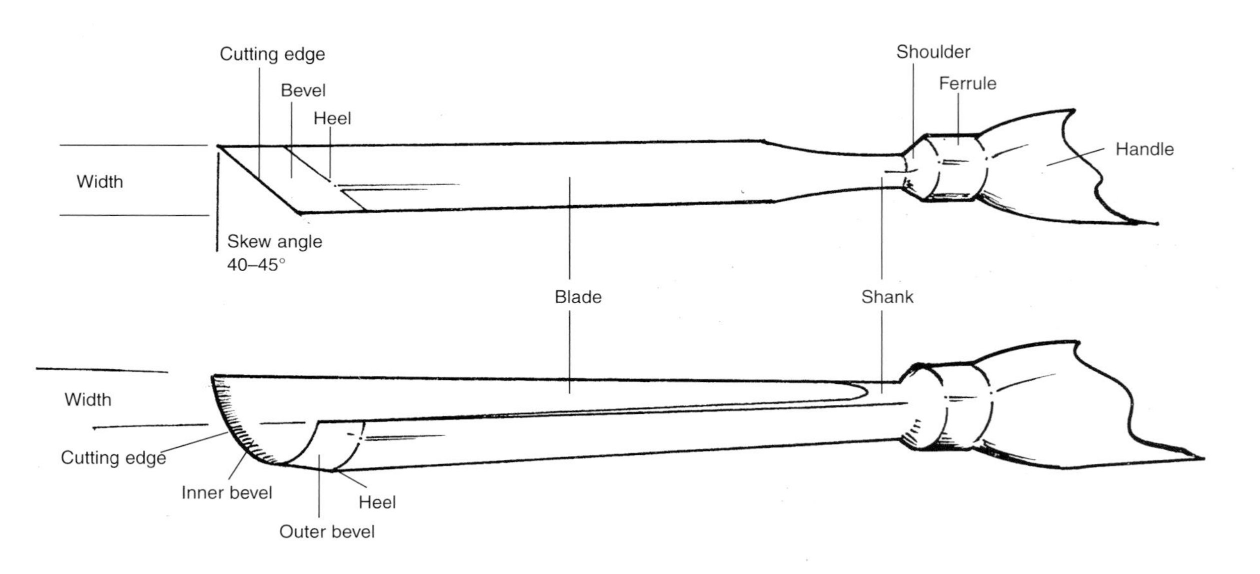

Fig 2.20 *Named parts of carving tools: skew chisel (above), and gouge (below).*

TO CHECK THE CUTTING EDGE

1 Carve along and across some medium-density carving wood.

2 Look for 'snail tracks' and torn grain.

3 Look to the cutting edge itself – the defects in the cut will usually appear as white spots or lines on an otherwise invisible edge.

Correct these straight away using the fine Arkansas bench- or slipstone, as described below.

TO CHECK THE BEVEL

1 Place the tool horizontally on the bench, or on a piece of scrap board.

2 Move it slowly forward, lifting the handle as you do so (Fig 2.22).

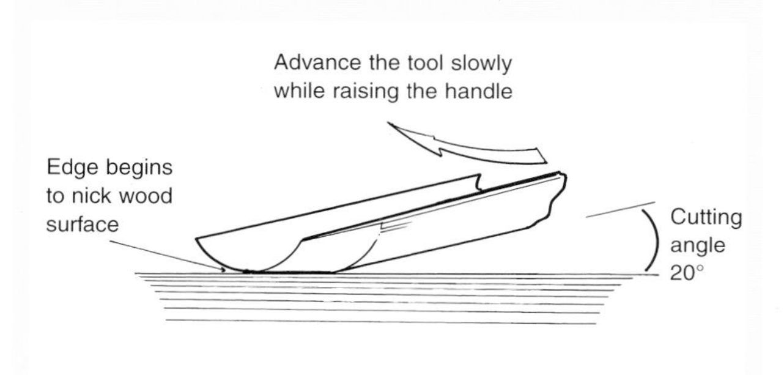

Fig 2.22 *Checking the cutting angle.*

3 At some point you will feel the cutting edge start to nick the bench surface: stop.

The angle at which the tool starts to cut as you push it forward slowly, raising the handle, is the **cutting angle**. It should be about 20° – just enough to clear the knuckles of the front hand in the low-angle tool grip (see page 25).

If it is higher, look to see if the bevel is rounded: flatten it just up to, but not including, the cutting edge – which you have already sharpened – on the coarse benchstone or grinding wheel. Finish off with the fine Arkansas stones (see below). However, if the bevel is already flat and the gouge is still not cutting well, the bevel must be too short. Lengthen it to give a lower angle with the coarse benchstone or grinding wheel. As for the rounded bevel, avoid grinding the actual cutting edge and finish with the fine Arkansas stones.

CHECK LIST

- Check sharpness: shiny, clean facets appear as wood is cut.
- Check cutting angle: about 20°, so as to clear knuckles in low-angle grip.

What do I need to sharpen my tools?

I always advise newcomers against using fast electrical sharpening devices until they feel at home with slower hand methods and really know what is needed to make the most efficient carving tool.

These machines have both strengths and weaknesses, and sometimes it is doubtful who is in control. There is a real danger of losing the valuable corners of the cutting edge, or in other ways destroying the shape. But once you know exactly how to sharpen tools, and what they should look like, some sharpening machines are available which can help with some of the work.

If you buy ready sharpened tools, such as those by Pfeil, then you only need to touch up the bevel and cutting edge now and then, but almost certainly you will need to add the inside bevel (see page 17). For this you must have (Fig 2.23):

- a fine Arkansas benchstone;
- fine Arkansas slipstones;
- light (bicycle) oil for the stones.

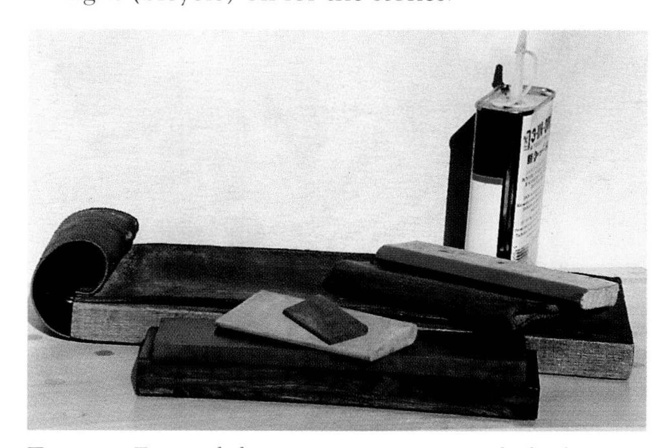

Fig 2.23 *Essential sharpening equipment: at the back, a benchstrop and slipstrops for the insides of gouges and V-tools; at the front, fine Arkansas benchstone and two sizes of Arkansas slipstones.*

Fine ceramic stones (1200 grit) are an alternative. *These, unlike Arkansas stones, must be used dry*. Any oil on their surface will eliminate their cutting properties. Some carvers find Japanese water stones a satisfactory alternative.

If, however, you need to take more metal away to reshape the bevel, then you need:

- a coarse Carborundum benchstone;
- coarse Carborundum slipstones;
- light (bicycle) oil.

But if you have a *lot* of metal to remove then you need to have, or have access to, a bench grinder.

For beginners, and students who are unfamiliar with machines, the ordinary electric grinder is often a bit frightening. It goes very fast and sends out sparks. An alternative is a water-cooled grinder, which is a lot slower and more friendly. Tormek have now made changes to their standard machine (Fig 2.24) to make it more suitable for carvers – for example, reversing the flow of water to the blade so that visibility is much better. Although expensive for occasional use, it takes the fear out of having to grind a carving tool – which you will have to do sooner or later if you pursue carving.

Check list

(Suppliers are listed on pages 156–8)

- Fine Arkansas benchstone, 8 x 2in (20 x 5cm);
- fine Arkansas slipstones (large 4 x 1in (10 x 2.5cm) 'knife blade' slip and 4-piece small slipstone set);
- coarse Carborundum benchstone, 8 x 2in (20 x 5cm);
- coarse Carborundum slipstones (same sizes as Arkansas);
- light (bicycle) oil;
- bench grinder.

How do I sharpen my carving tools?

My book *Woodcarving Tools, Materials & Equipment* is a sort of workshop manual. Chapter 3 on sharpening woodcarving tools is 90 pages long; it covers everything you need to know about the subject – although not everything that *can* be known! Please refer to this book; here there is only space to summarize guidelines and some basic principles. There are exceptions to all rules, but they are not relevant now.

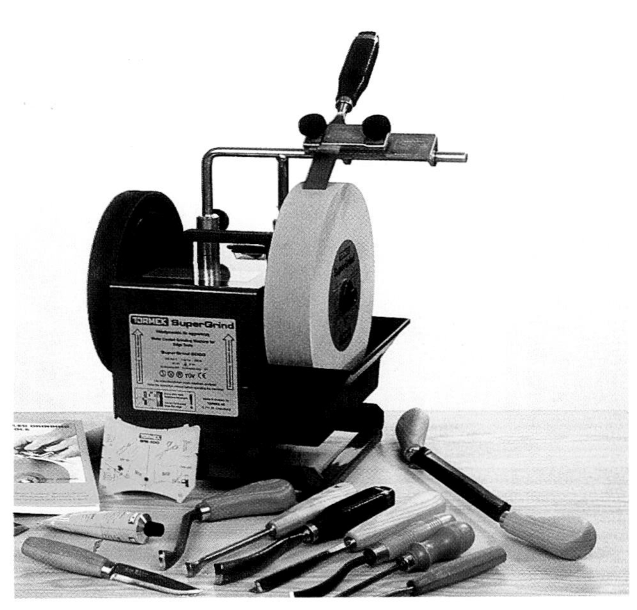

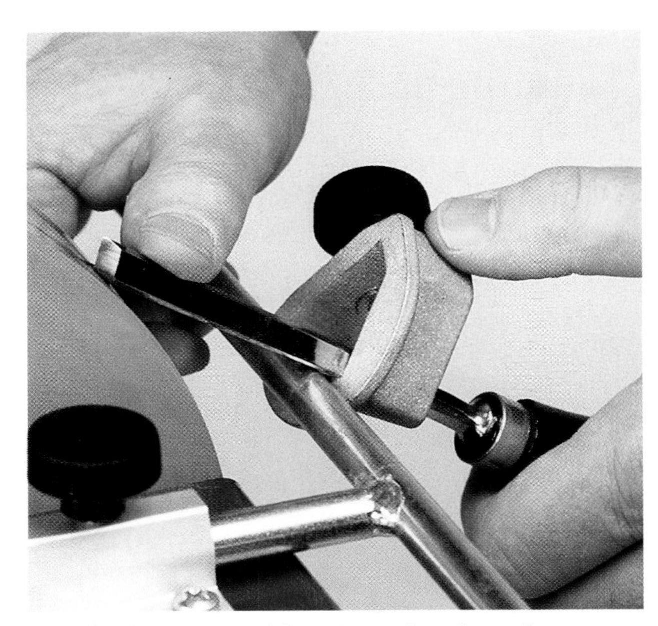

Fig 2.24 *In the Tormek grinder the cooling water runs away from the edge for greater visibility. Quiet, friendly, with jigs to help grind edges and bevels accurately, this grinder finds favour with many carving students. (Photographs by courtesy of Tormek AB, Sweden)*

All correctly shaped carving tools have four principal features (Fig 2.25):

1 **flat bevels** from edge to heel – no secondary bevel;

2 **unrounded corners**;

3 edges in a **straight line** between corners;

4 edges at **right angles** to the axis of the blade (except in the case of a skew chisel).

The bevel angle

This should be around 20° (15–25°).

Essentially this means presenting the tool to the benchstone at the same angle as it is presented to the wood.

Inside bevels

Even if it is only 5% of the length of the outer one, an inside bevel added to a gouge greatly improves tool control and cutting when the tool is used in the 'upside down' position, with the concave side presented to the wood.

Pfeil tools come with a small secondary (micro) bevel on the outside which increases the cutting angle, and no inside bevel. If you use a fine Arkansas slipstone to create an inside bevel, you will find this draws the edge back so that the secondary bevel on the outside disappears.

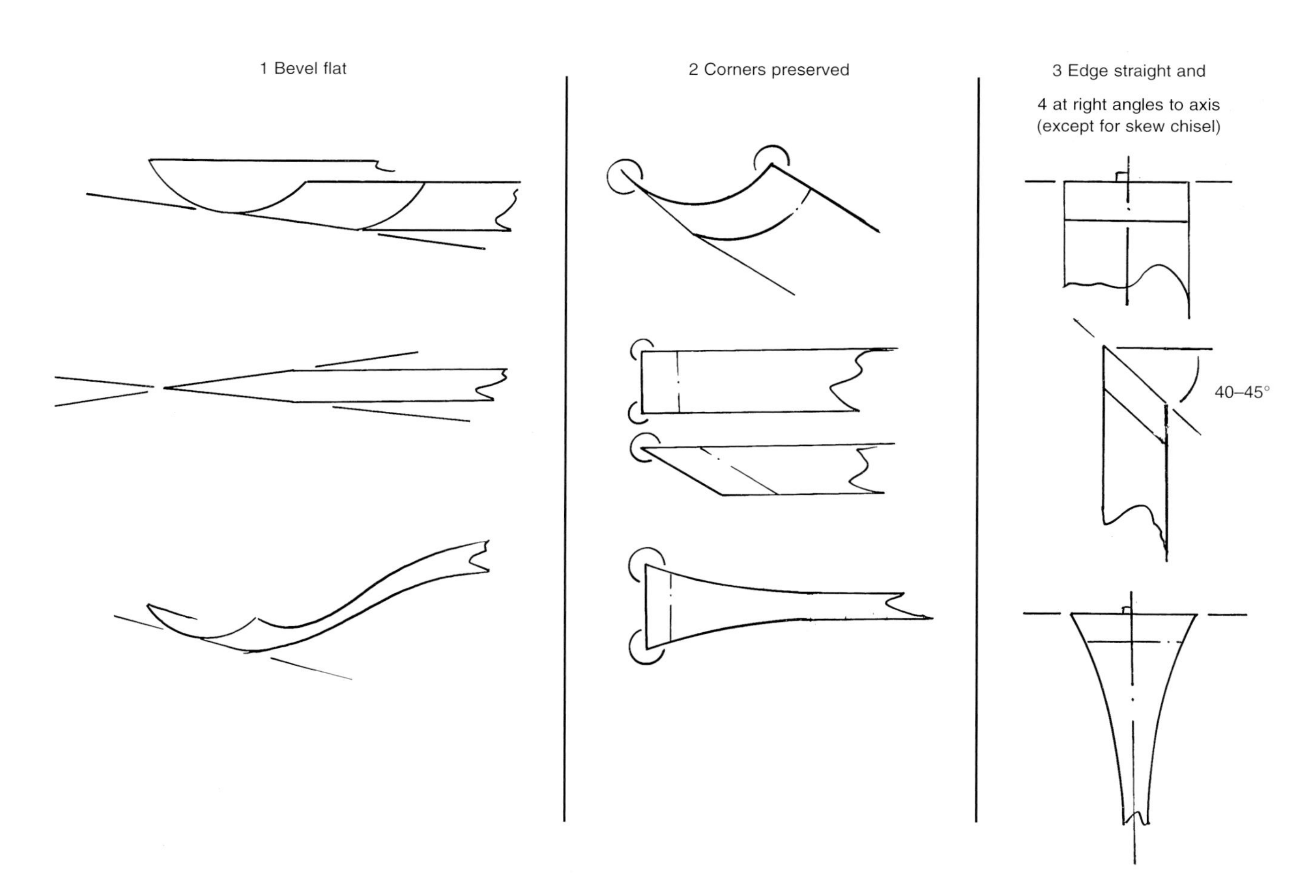

Fig 2.25 *Unless there is a specific reason, carving tools have four principal features: flat bevels; proper corners; and edges which are straight and at right angles to the axis of the blade.*

SHARPENING SEQUENCES

The stages are summarized in Fig 2.26. Gouges are rubbed from side to side on the benchstone (Figs 2.27 and 2.28), keeping the bevel flat at all times. The inside bevel is then formed with a slipstone (Fig 2.29), which simultaneously removes the burr (or 'wire edge') formed as the outside bevel is rubbed on the benchstone.

Chisels, skew chisels and V-tools are rubbed *along* the stone (Fig 2.30), keeping the bevel flat at all times. The apex of the V (Fig 2.31) is treated like a very small gouge.

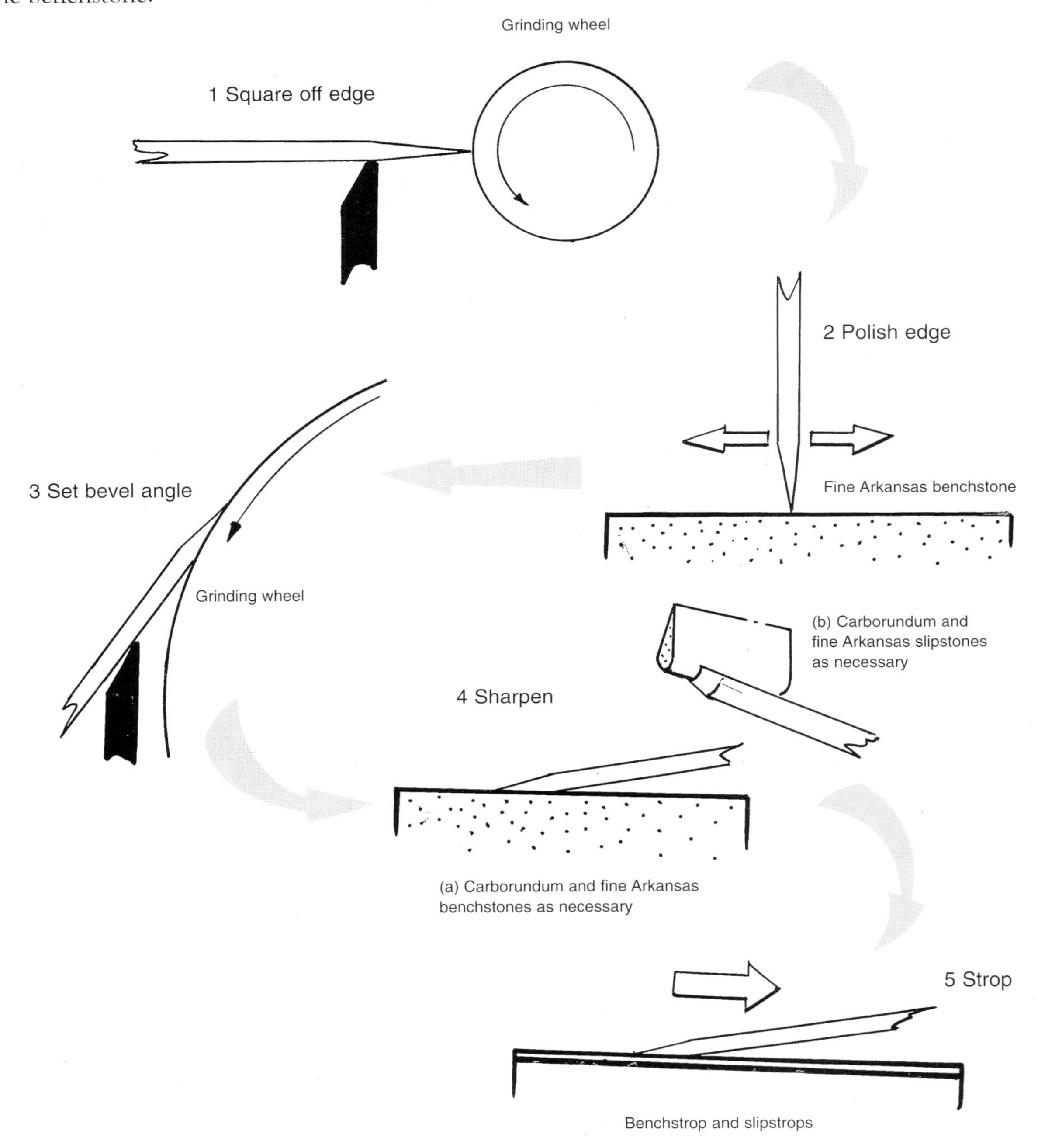

Fig 2.26 *General steps in the sharpening of carving tools. For further details see my* Woodcarving Tools, Materials & Equipment.

The two guides to sharpening are:

1 a **white line of light** along the edge itself. This is seen in a blunt tool with a good cross light, and disappears when the edge is sharp;
2 the **scratches on the bevel**. Where and what they are will depend on the grit of the stones and how you orientate the tool to their surface. They should be continuous across the bevel if it has been laid flat on the stone.

The secret of successful sharpening is to be continually guided by the white line and the bevel scratches: thin the white line *evenly* until it disappears, while checking that the bevel has remained flat. If the white line becomes thinner at any place, leave it alone and work on the thicker parts to regain evenness.

Fig 2.29 *Slipstones create the important inner bevel. Keep a constant angle of about 5–10°.*

Fig 2.27 *Gouges are presented to the stone side-on, and the bevel is kept flat as the tool is moved from end to end of the stone, rotating it as shown in Fig 2.28.*

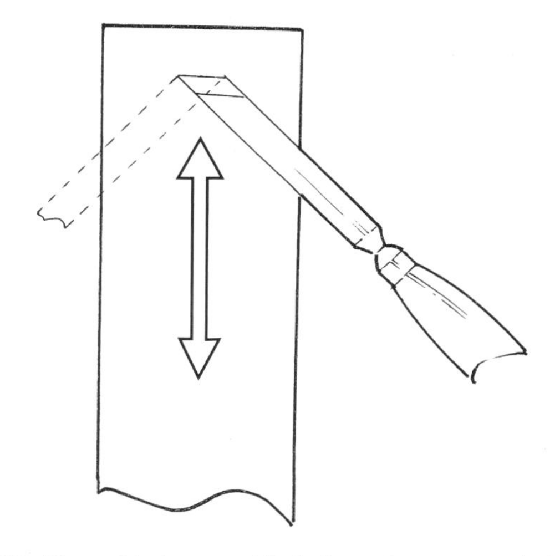

Fig 2.30 *Skew chisels are rubbed along the stone with the cutting edge at right angles to the length of the stone. V-tools are treated in the same way, like two conventional woodworking chisels; the angle of the V is then treated like the gouge in Fig 2.27.*

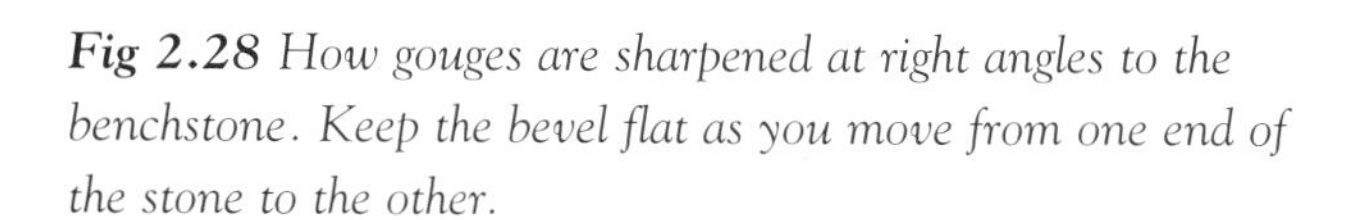

Fig 2.28 *How gouges are sharpened at right angles to the benchstone. Keep the bevel flat as you move from one end of the stone to the other.*

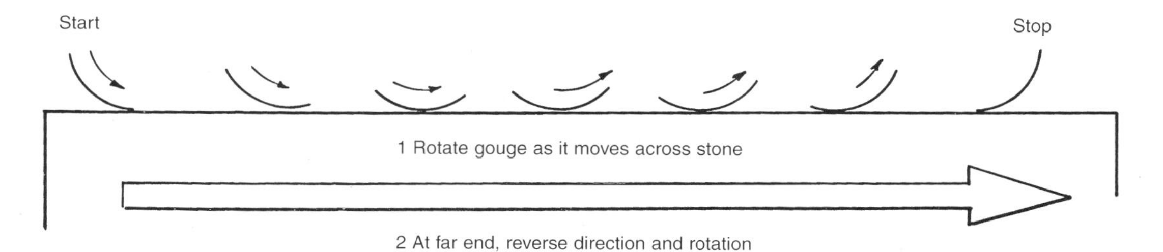
Start
Stop
1 Rotate gouge as it moves across stone
2 At far end, reverse direction and rotation

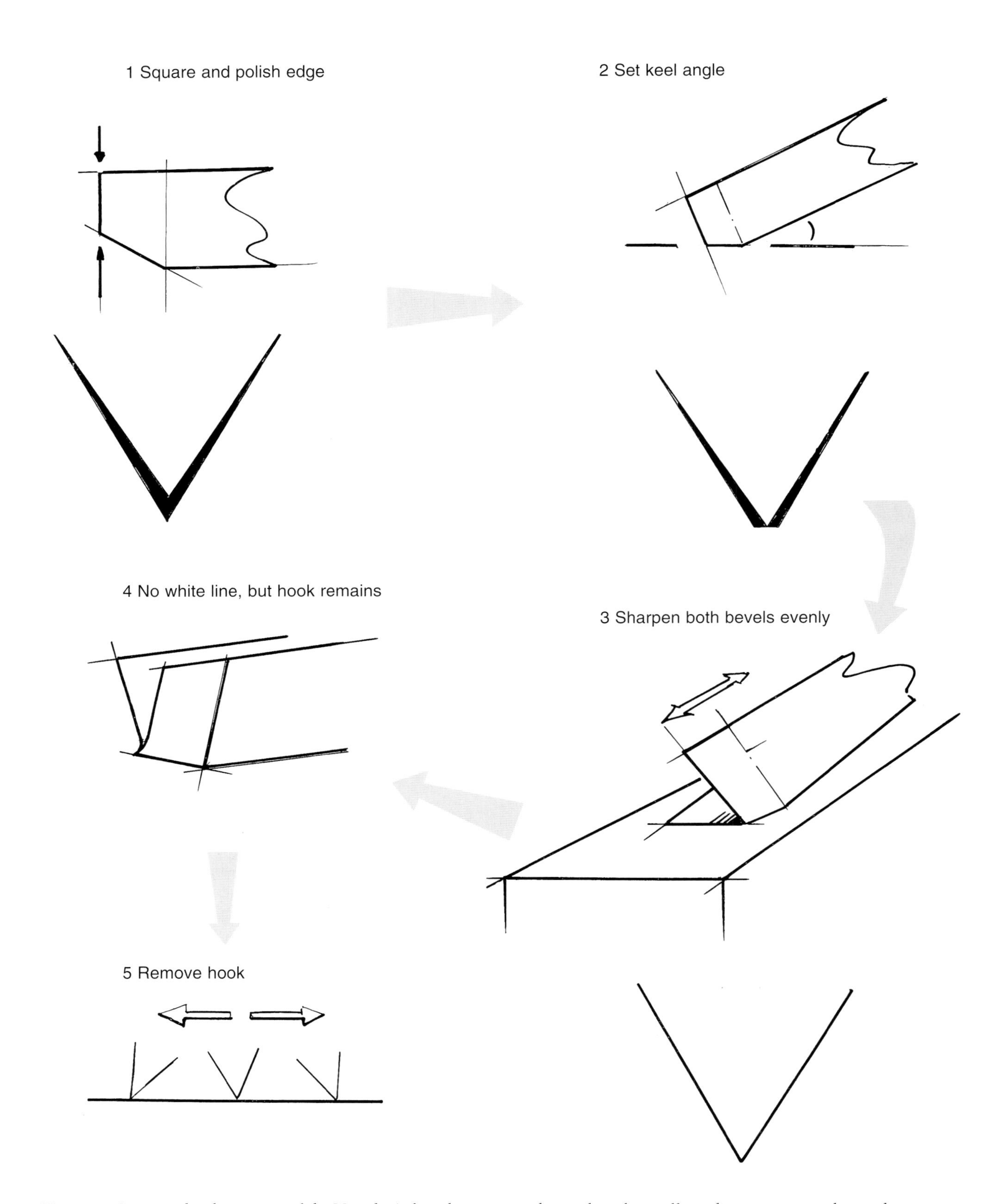
1 Square and polish edge
2 Set keel angle
3 Sharpen both bevels evenly
4 No white line, but hook remains
5 Remove hook

Fig 2.31 *Steps in the sharpening of the V-tool. A fine slipstone can be used to clean off any burr arising on the inside.*

CHECK LIST

Check cutting edge:

- corners?
- square?
- straight?
- inner bevel?
  Square off on fine benchstone; add inner bevel with fine slipstone.

Check bevel – test cutting angle (page 15 – it should be about 20°):

- too high?
- rounded bevel?
- flat but too short?

Reset bevel:

- resharpen following the flow diagram (Fig 2.26). Monitor by white line on edge and bevel scratches.

Check tool cut in wood:

- blemishes, snail tracks?
  Check for white dots or lines of light at cutting edge. These indicate blunt spots; touch up with fine bench- or slipstone.

How often do I need to sharpen carving tools, and how do I keep them sharp?

Good quality tools, cutting through clean medium-density wood without levering or scraping, will keep their edges for a long time *if stropped regularly*.

Make yourself a benchstrop, and a slipstrop for gouges and the V-tool (Fig 2.32), and keep them to hand all the time you are carving.

You can dress the leather with proprietary strop paste (available from Tiranti's and others; see Resources, pages 156–8) or a mixture of tallow and any fine abrasive: valve grinding paste, or a metal polish such as crocus powder, Autosol or Brasso. The hard blocks of polishing compound sold for use on polishing and sharpening machines can also be melted in with the tallow, which makes the compound soft enough to cling to the leather.

Fig 2.32 *Strops and slipstrops: present on the bench at all times and used frequently for keeping edges keen.*

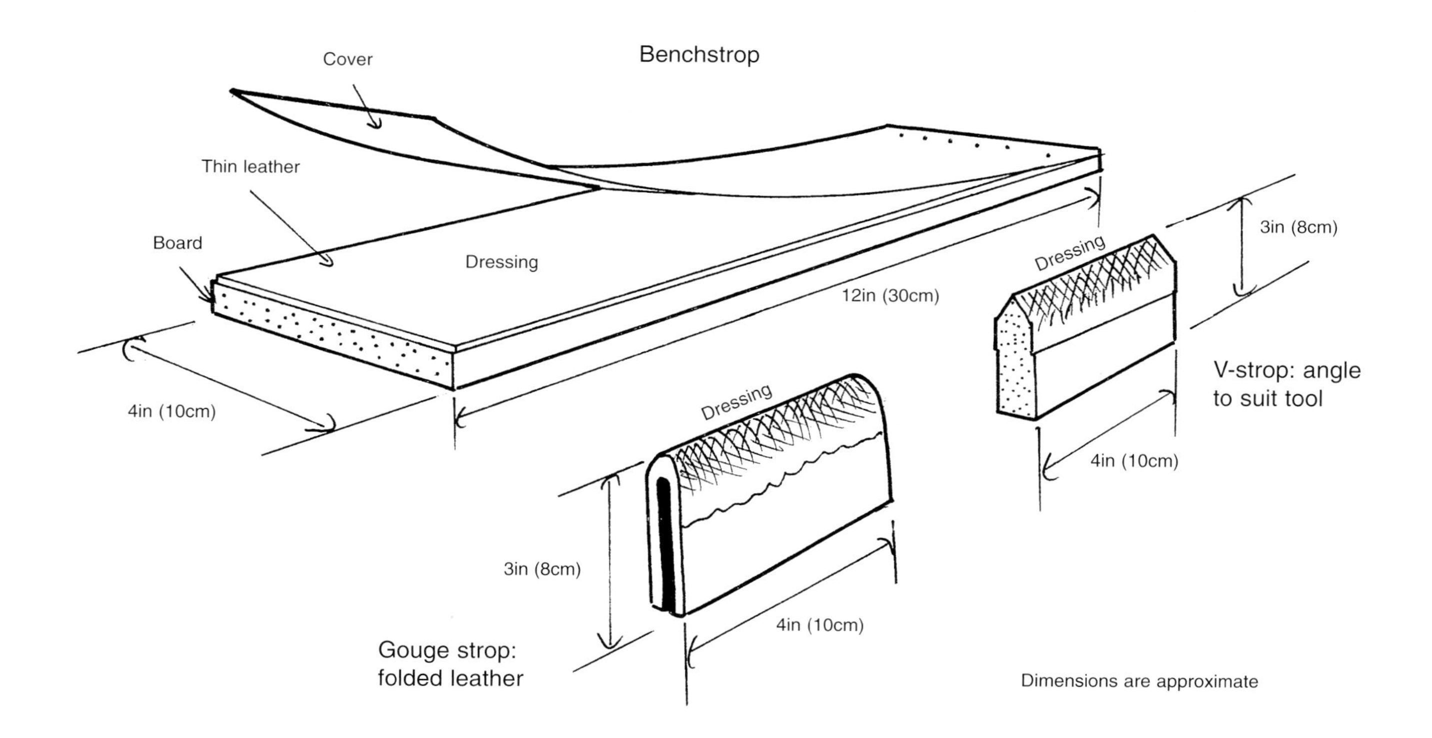

Fig 2.33 *All edges must be* pulled back *along the leather strop so as not to cut into it. Keep the bevels flat and at the correct angle; rotate gouges to cover the whole bevel.*

Keep the bevel of the tool flat on the benchstrop (Fig 2.33) so that the leather moves *away* from, and is not cut by, the sharp edge. Push the slipstrop *out* from the inside of the gouge or V-tool for the same reason.

Occasionally you will find blemishes in the tool cut. Deal with these straight away with the fine stones and re-strop.

The major cause of tools cutting poorly is a rounded bevel, leading to an increased cutting angle, which often arises unnoticed. Check your bevels regularly and flatten the bevel on the benchstone if you find it noticeably 'bellied'.

Don't be too ready to resort to the grinder. Grinding means major metal removal. You normally need to do this only when putting a new tool into commission.

CHECK LIST

- Benchstrop
- Slipstrop
- V-tool slipstrop
- Strop dressing

A SUITABLE IDEA

What should I carve?

The range of what *can* be carved seems excitingly, and intimidatingly, boundless.

Most students, in the beginning at least, have ideas that go beyond their skills. One of my jobs as a teacher is to balance what I think a student can manage with a stimulating degree of challenge; to order the student's imagination so as to avoid disappointment or frustration, while taking advantage of successes.

Besides a student's skill it is also necessary to consider:

- the feasibility of translating an idea into wood (say from a painting or cast model);
- the amount of research or drawing required;
- the availability of the right sort of wood;
- the adequacy of tools;
- the means of holding the work; and such like.

So how do you select projects when you are starting out?

Obviously, to begin with, I am asking you to start here: following closely through the two projects in this book with the minimum of tools and equipment. See the projects as well-tested exercises for you to learn carving skills. If you visited my workshop to learn carving I would ask you if you had any ideas. But then, invariably, I would get you to do these exercises anyway!

After the fish carvings I suggest you go on to a larger relief carving to consolidate your understanding and skill. You need to deepen your understanding of wood: what can you do with it; how it works with a design; what you can make the tools do; and so on. This does take time, and practice.

Whatever projects you undertake in the beginning – relief or three dimensions proper – my advice is to keep everything *simple* and take a path of regular steps: a lot of simple projects rather than one big complicated one; a consistent pattern of practice, rather than haphazard bursts.

Check list

- Start with the two projects in this book.
- Read Chapters 6 and 7.
- Study your material and your tools.
- Try to anticipate problems, ask yourself: Have I done adequate research? How will I hold the workpiece? Have I adequate tools? Is the wood working with the design or against it? – and so on.

Summary

(For suppliers, see pages 156–8)

You have found a place to carve, a strong work surface with good lighting. This book will provide the 'idea'. So, specifically, you need:

Wood

- Jelutong, lime, mild oak, mahogany, sweet chestnut, etc.
- Size: 11 x 6½ x 1¾in (280 x 165 x 45mm)

Holding work

- Strong, fixed table or bench;
- work area for carving, tools, light;
- wedge and fence board – clamp or pin to bench;
- two G-clamps (C-clamps).

Carving tools

- No. 3 (flat gouge) x ¼, ½, ¾in (6, 13, 19mm);
- no. 6 (medium gouge) x ¼, ½, ¾in (6, 13, 19mm);
- no. 9 (semicircular gouge) x ¼, ½, ¾in (6, 13, 19mm);
- no. 2 (skew chisel) x ⅜in (10mm);
- no. 39 (60° V-tool) x ⅜in (10mm).

Or, if using Pfeil tools:

- cut 2 (flat gouge) x 5, 12, 20mm;
- cut 7 (medium gouge) x 6, 14, 20mm;
- cut 9 (semicircular gouge) x 5, 13, 20mm;
- cut 1S (skew chisel) x 8mm;
- cut 12 (60° V-tool) x 8mm.

Additional tools

Besides regular carving tools you will need:

- mallet, 1½lb (700g);
- marking gauge, pencil, paper etc. – a square and a ruler may also be useful;
- carving brush (e.g. emulsion or horse brush).

Sharpening

- Fine Arkansas benchstone, 8 x 2in (20 x 5cm);
- fine Arkansas slipstones (large 4 x 1in (10 x 2.5cm) 'knife blade' and 4-piece small slipstone set);
- coarse Carborundum benchstone, 8 x 2in (20 x 5cm);
- coarse Carborundum slipstones (same sizes as Arkansas);
- light (bicycle) oil;
- bench grinder;
- benchstrop;
- slipstrop;
- V-tool slipstrop;
- strop dressing.

CHAPTER THREE

BASICS

The previous chapter looked at the tools and equipment, the bits and pieces, you need to begin carving wood; in particular, what is necessary to follow the exercises and projects in this book. This chapter is more concerned with certain key *knowledge*.

You'll come across most of this book's practical information as you tackle the carving projects themselves, with some important points enlarged on in Chapter 6, Further Techniques. There are, however, some essential aspects of woodcarving to absorb before we actually put steel to wood:

- how to hold and manipulate carving tools;
- what you can actually do with them;
- grain – understanding what it is and how to work with it;
- the basic carving process – how a carver thinks and proceeds;
- relief carving – what it is and how it 'works'.

So you could say that the projects start here. You will need your carving tools and some waste wood to try out the exercises.

HANDLING WOODCARVING TOOLS

Woodcarving is fundamentally about holding and handling the carving tools correctly in order to realize your vision as a carver in the best way possible.

There are, without doubt, 'good', 'not-so-good' and 'bad' ways of holding carving tools, and you want to get into the best habits right from the beginning; these include the safest possible ways of working.

CORRECT GRIPS

What you are trying to do? A good, correct, way of holding a carving tool gives you:

- maximum control – you make the cuts you want, not those you get by default;
- an ability to start and stop the cut at will;
- the means to exert a wide range of pressure – putting (body) weight behind the tool;
- a wide option of cuts, from a broad range of positions;
- a relaxed way of working that is not tiring to the fingers, hands, wrists, arms, shoulders and neck;
- safety from the sharp cutting edge.

A good grip is characterized by a balance between strength and flexibility. A poor grip is weak in either of these factors.

TWO RULES

Any good grip will involve the two basic rules for holding carving tools which maximize control:

1. With the exception of mallet work, all carving tools must be held in *both* hands.
2. The hand gripping the blade – or the forearm – must *always* rest on the wood being carved (or the bench, clamp, etc.).

I teach students two excellent tool grips with which to start. There are variations on these themes, which I find students quite naturally develop, incorporating them into their own good ways of working.

TWO PRINCIPAL CARVING TOOL GRIPS

The 'low-angle' grip

(Figs 3.1–3.3)

This is a powerful grip, used whenever you want to cut at a low angle (say, below 45°) to the wood. Most people will find it easier to use their dominant hand as the 'back' hand, but, from the beginning, *you should learn to use this grip with hands in the reversed position*. This means that you can carve from either direction without difficult body postures.

METHOD

1 **Front hand**: wrap around the middle of the tool so that part of the hand covers the blade, and part the handle (Fig 3.2). (The front hand adopts the same grip when the tool is being struck with the mallet.)

2 **Back hand**: hold the handle comfortably, something like a screwdriver (Fig 3.3).

3 Extend the thumb of the front hand along the handle – this gives added control.

4 Bring the elbow of the back hand in to your body.

5 Rest the heel of the front hand on the wood surface.

This is the basic low-angle grip.

6 Now swap hands and hold the tool in the reverse direction.

To use the low-angle grip:

- Back hand pushes the tool forward against the resistance of the front hand, and rotates the handle as necessary.
- Front hand controls the forward push of the back hand, tensing, or braking, against it and sliding along the wood to advance the cut.

It is extremely important to understand that the front and back hands *work together*, controlling the cut in a precise way: the back hand propels the tool forward, the front hand acts as a brake. There is a continual, fluid balance between the two. Both hands work to rotate, raise or lower the carving tool, start and stop the cut, and direct the tool along the wood.

By keeping your elbows in you can put your weight behind the cut.

Fig 3.1 *This is the basic low-angle grip, where the tool is offered at a shallow angle to the wood surface. Both hands work together: pushing from the back and braking from the front.*

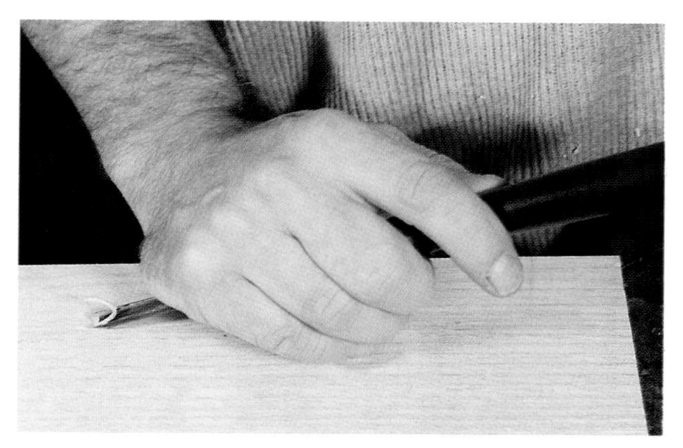

Fig 3.2 *To form the grip: front hand resting on wood, thumb along the handle; ...*

Fig 3.3 *... back hand gripping handle. In general, keep your elbows in and use your body behind the cut.*

As you try to present the tool at a higher angle you will see how the back hand and elbow must be raised awkwardly. As it becomes uncomfortable so this hand shifts to the blade, turning the low-angle grip into:

The 'pen and dagger' grip

This is the grip to use if you want to carve with the tool at a high angle (say above 45°), for setting in, paring downwards, stabbing, and corner work (Fig 3.4).

The pen and dagger grip can mostly be used without reversing hands. I assume right-hand dominance in my description; left-handers can reverse the instructions. The name I use for this grip describes the look of it.

METHOD

1 **Right hand**: hold the blade somewhat like a pen, as follows:

- Middle finger: place the tip behind the bevel and heel of the carving tool (Fig 3.5). This finger runs along the wood with the tool but *never goes beyond the cutting edge*, supporting and guiding the cutting edge from behind.
- Index finger and thumb: grip the sides of the blade.
- Remaining fingers: tight in to the middle finger to support it (Fig 3.6).
- The lower knuckles, backs of fingers, and edge of the blade hand (or parts or combinations of these) rest on the wood.

Fig 3.4 *The basic 'pen and dagger' grip when the tool cuts at higher angles. Both hands co-ordinate to control the cut.*

Fig 3.5 *The middle finger of the blade hand supports the bevel (or the 'inside' of the gouge if the tool is turned round).*

Fig 3.6 *Bring the other fingers to support the middle one; index finger and thumb grip the blade.*

2 **Left hand**: grip the tool handle like a dagger. The thumb can be placed on the top of the handle (Fig 3.7).

Fig 3.7 *Grip the handle comfortably with the other hand. Putting your thumb on the top is an option.*

To use the pen and dagger grip:

- The blade hand controls the immediate and precise cutting of the edge, particularly by pivoting on the thumb.
- The upper hand sets the angle of the handle to the wood and rotates it as necessary.

Again it cannot be overstressed that both hands *act together* and balance forces in order to control the movement and power of any cut.

It is easy to adapt the pen and dagger grip for cutting at low angles (Fig 3.8), but not to use the low-angle grip for cutting at a high angle.

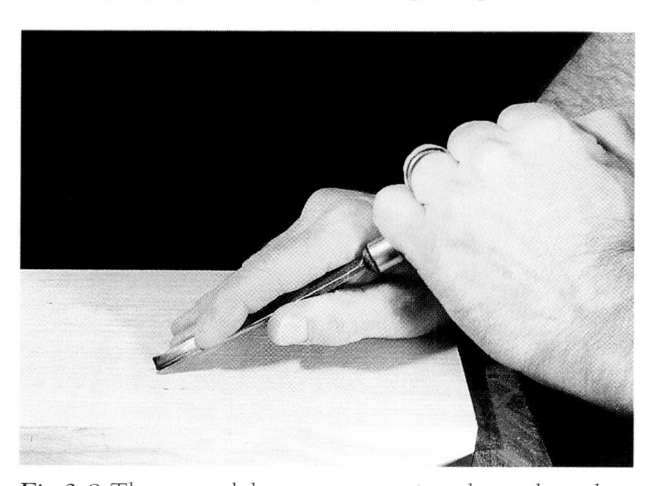

Fig 3.8 *The pen and dagger can sometimes be used at a low angle rather than switching to the low-angle grip proper.*

If the pen and dagger grip is to be used for heavy cutting, as in stabbing cuts or strong, downwards paring cuts, put your weight behind the blade by bringing the handle in towards your right shoulder and body – *keeping your elbows in*. There is quite a strain on the arms and elbow joints, if you keep your elbows away from the body.

These are by no means the only ways to hold carving tools, but they are a good place to start.

POOR WAYS OF HOLDING CARVING TOOLS

A poor carving grip is one in which the strength in the hands and wrists is weak and the grip relatively inflexible. It gives unsatisfactory tool control, or may simply be dangerous.

Such ways of holding tools often arise in carvers who have taught themselves, remaining as a matter of habit. When such carvers write books, these grips appear in publications.

Here are three poor grips:

The 'back crank'

The front hand is cranked back and grips the blade palm-uppermost. One or more knuckles may rest on the wood (Fig 3.9).

Fig 3.9 *The 'back crank': a relatively poor grip, weak and inflexible.*

Fig 3.10 *The 'snooker cue': another poor way of holding carving tools. The front hand exercises little control, particularly as regards braking against the forward push.*

Fig 3.11 *'Look, one hand': a dangerous way of carving, with little control.*

The 'snooker cue'

The blade slides forwards and backwards under a loose front hand. Essentially the tool is only being controlled by the back hand, rather than both (Fig 3.10).

'Look, one hand'

One hand is holding the wood, the other pushing the tool. There is no control over the forward movement of the tool, which can jerk forward out of the cut suddenly (Fig 3.11). This is not the same as proper whittling and carving grips that appear one-handed but in fact brace the blade safely between thumb and fingers.

Compare these ways of holding with the two grips described before and you will immediately see the difference in strength and control.

Manipulating carving tools

There are many ways of using the tools with these correct grips, which can only really be appreciated in practice. I will make a few introductory comments, however; bear these in mind while cutting on some practice wood.

Low-angle grip

- Control comes through both hands working together: pushing opposing braking.
- The moving body can give authority to the cut by following behind.
- The heel of the leading (blade) hand can be made to act as a pivot around which to carve a smooth arcing cut; so can the elbow.
- Reversing hands allows you to pivot smoothly in the opposite direction. For a professional carver it is hard to underrate the importance of some degree of ambidexterity: reversing hands and being able to cut in the opposite direction fluidly.

Pen and dagger grip

- The *thumb* of the blade hand is vital for pushing and controlling the cutting edge.
- The thumb is often used as a pivot.
- In this grip you can often have a sense of using the cutting edge and corners like a knife.
- Move your body over so that the opposite shoulder (to the hand gripping the handle) is brought to bear on the handle. By leaning over the tool you can put your full weight behind a more vertical cut.

Fig 3.12 *With both corners clear of the surface, the shaving comes away cleanly.*

Fig 3.13 *Drop the corner below the surface and wood fibres are burst out by the wedge action of the bevel beneath.*

Fig 3.14 *The fibres at the edge of the wood are unsupported and break away. Always work* into *supported wood.*

Fig 3.15 *A carving tool enters the wood and stops, then the handle is lowered: the grain splits in front of the tool, and the delicate cutting edge might be damaged. To cut, the tool* must *be moving forwards.*

WAYS OF CUTTING

For both these and other correct grips there are some principles which can act as guides to cutting in sympathy with the wood. These are best seen if you make a little experiment on a piece of practice wood, using a medium gouge.

EXPERIMENT

1 Start running a shallow groove, but then rotate the gouge so one of the corners drops beneath the surface of the wood (Figs 3.12 and 3.13). Observe what happens.

2 Run the cut out over the edge of the wood (Fig 3.14). Observe what happens: this is known as **breaking out**.

3 Enter the cutting edge into the wood as if starting a cut. Stop; then lower the handle (Fig 3.15). Again, observe what happens.

You should easily see that there is a loss of control over the wood, and reach the following conclusions:

- Don't bury the whole cutting edge when taking a shaving, but always *keep the corners clear* of the wood. This way the fibres are cut, not torn.

- Work *in* from an edge – the wood fibres are supported in this direction, but not when working out.
- Cuts have three parts: in, through, out. To make a cut the tool *must be moving forwards all the time*, no matter how slightly. Otherwise you are levering instead of cutting: the wood fibres are prised up and not severed.

Bear these points in mind as we work through the projects.

Yet other poor ways of handling carving tools come up regularly in students' classes, so often that they have ended up with names:

'The wiggle-waggle'
The tool handle is agitated rapidly from side to side or up and down as it is pushed along. It is better to make confident, simple cuts. Waggling is not the same as 'rocking' the tool through its cut (see page 32) to put a slice on it.

'The piston'
Rapidly shunting the tool backwards and forwards under a loose blade hand. Again, simple, sure cuts are quicker and more controlled.

'The crowbar' (wrecking bar)
Using the blade as a lever to break off wood. This can also damage the cutting edge.

'The scrape'
Dragging the cutting edge across a surface in an attempt to clean it. Scraping leaves a less clean surface than cutting, and blunts the cutting edge. A proper scraper is occasionally needed in very difficult recesses to clean up (see *Woodcarving Tools, Materials & Equipment*, pages 220–1).

WHAT CARVING TOOLS DO

The first thing they may do is to cut *you* – unless you pay attention to safety.

Working safely

- Keep your fingers *behind* the cutting edge at all times. Only the very edge can cut, less than 1% of the tool! No other part can cut you.
- Never push the tool directly towards another part of your body.
- Keep *both* hands on the tool, except when using the mallet.
- Always keep carving tools *razor sharp*: blunt tools need more force to push them through the wood, making them *more* dangerous, not less.
- Never try to catch a falling tool; wear shoes tough enough to protect your feet against such an accident.
- Place tools down carefully when you have finished with them – in a line, flat at the back of the bench. Never allow their edges to project over the bench or workpiece.
- The workpiece must *always* be fixed securely.
- Brush or vacuum away dust or woodchips; never blow them, which risks getting bits in your eye.
- Keep the bench and work area tidy: avoid trailing electrical wires; sweep up after work and put away tools and finishing materials.
- Rags used with oil (both for sharpening and finishing) are particularly inflammable and should be kept in a metal tin and disposed of away from house or workplace.

Have a first-aid kit to hand. I am happy to say that in the classes I have run over many years, the most serious accidents have been nicks and small cuts – usually had when getting tools out or putting them away.

Cutting with carving tools

Again, knowledge of how to use the carving tools to cut the wood will grow with practice, but a few introductory points can be made. For example, do you really appreciate what great value you are getting when you buy a carving gouge? You get seven tools for the price of one!

With a gouge you can

1 cut with the tool in the 'normal' position (for producing hollows);

2 cut with the tool 'upside down' (for rounding edges);

3 stab down fully across the edge with the tool vertical to the wood (as when setting in);

4 vary the stab cut made by a gouge of any particular sweep by varying the angle at which the tool enters the wood (see Fig 3.16).

5 cut with just the corner, like a knife (at junctions between surfaces, for example);

6 cut with any part of the edge between the corners – for example, a big, deep gouge can be made to cut a narrower, flatter shaving by using only a small part of its sweep (Fig 3.17);

7 vary the sweep by winding the tool through its cut while holding it vertical (see page 33 and Fig 3.25).

Try these seven cuts with one of your larger gouges.

Fig 3.16 *Both these cuts were made with the same gouge; the angled cut on the right is 'quicker' (of smaller radius) than the vertical cut at left.*

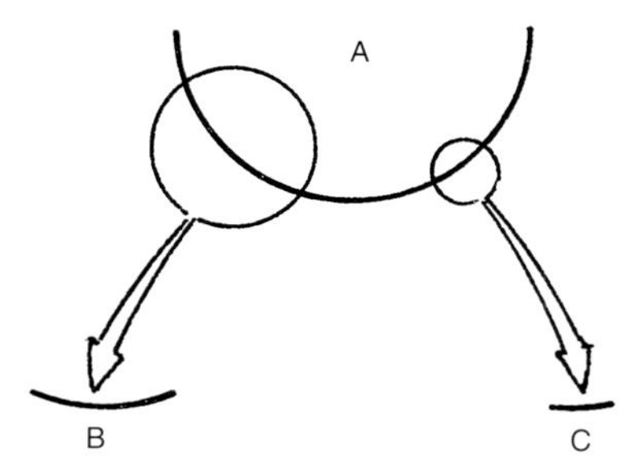

Fig 3.17 A *is the sweep of a 1¼in (32mm) semicircular gouge (no. 9). If you cut with only part of its edge you can get, for example, the equivalent of a ½in (13mm) no. 4* (**B**)*, or a ¼in (6mm) no. 3* (**C**).

You will practise orientating the tools in most of these ways in the projects. In addition, there are ways of cutting with carving tools which are repeated often enough to be given names by carvers. These cuts appear again and again in the projects. We can list them here so you can practise them before starting in earnest.

Basic cuts

STABBING AND STOP CUTS

In a **stop cut** the whole edge, or just a corner, is pushed into the wood with the pen and dagger grip to control the splitting of fibres from a subsequent, or previous cut (Figs 3.18 and 3.19).

You may need to use a mallet; or to put weight behind the tool with your shoulder.

The **stab cut** is a cut, normally vertical, into the wood with a gouge or chisel *without* the blade taking out a chip or shaving (Fig 3.20). It may be used either for decorative reasons or as a stop cut.

Push with the hand, or use a mallet; the edge goes straight in and out to leave an incision.

At times the stop cut and the stab cut will be identical, but at other times they will look quite different: stabbing may be done with the whole edge to make a pattern (such as fish scales), whereas a stop cut may be done with only a corner of the cutting edge, as at the end of a V-groove when lining in.

Fig 3.18 A **stop cut** *with a skew chisel (or any other carving tool) severs fibres in order to control their splitting.*

Fig 3.19 *The shaving then falls away when the V-tool meets the stop cut.*

ROCKING, SLICING AND SWEEPING CUTS

These are rather similar in principle. Practically all my carving cuts have an element of **rocking** to them. As the tool is pushed forwards, the handle is given a twist, 'rocking' the tool through its cut. The wood chip is removed almost with a flick. Rocking cuts are easiest with medium to deep gouges, and remove wood with less effort, and far more cleanly, than simply pushing the tool straight along.

Practice rocking to the left and the right; avoid burying the corners. There are two types of rocking cut:

Slicing works best with flat gouges. The cutting edge moves to the side as it is pushed forward. The edge passes through the wood more cleanly and with less effort than when pushed straight ahead. Particularly good for smoothing surfaces.

Fig 3.20 A **stab cut** *with a gouge may function as a stop cut, or may be decorative.*

Use the low-angle grip. Drift the blade to the side (left or right – giving you two options), while rotating the handle *slightly* so that the shaving is drawn across the edge as it moves forward (Figs 3.21, 3.22 and 3.23). The shaving is pared away as cleanly as when you pull the knife back as you cut a slice of cucumber.

The **sweeping** cut works best with 'quicker' or deeper gouges. It is a type of slicing cut in which the blade rotates around the **sweep** (that is, along the arc of a circle which forms the cross section of the blade) as it moves (Fig 3.24). It is used for setting in and for 'rocking' cuts – see above.

It is possible to make a gouge cut a curve or circle which is tighter than its own sweep (Fig 3.25), but not a wider one – try it!

Fig 3.21 *The extremely important* **slicing cut***. As the gouge moves forward the tool is rotated so that the shaving is drawn across the cutting edge. The corners are kept clear. The slice starts with the shaving to one side of the blade.*

Fig 3.22 *The handle is rotated slightly as the gouge pushes forwards.*

Fig 3.23 *The shaving reaches the other end of the cutting edge and is released before it reaches the far corner. You can also draw the shaving in the opposite direction.*

Fig 3.24 *The* **sweeping** *(or* **sweep***)* **cut** *makes full use of the inner curvature or sweep of a gouge. Note how the leading corner must clear the wood surface to prevent ploughing up the fibres.*

Fig 3.25 *A gouge can be made to cut the circle of which its sweep is an arc. By rotating the handle and lifting the leading corner, tighter curves are readily possible; but not wider ones.*

RUNNING CUTS

In the low-angle grip, long grooves can be made by holding the tool at a fixed angle and sliding the front hand along the wood surface, without rocking the cut.

This is the prime way of lining in (see page 48), which is done with the V-tool or with a U-shaped gouge. Control is particularly necessary from the front, braking, hand.

This is by no means a complete list, but will give you some idea of the versatility of carving tools.

USING THE MALLET

When the wood is hard (or the carver feeling particularly weak) a mallet is needed.

Don't choose a mallet which is too heavy: about 1½lb (700g) is a good weight to begin with for most people. *Try, right from the start, to use it in either hand;* this way you can work from either the left or the right without awkward body contortions.

Stand somewhat side-on to the carving so that you can swing the mallet without your body getting in the way. Keep your elbows in (Fig 3.26).

If you can rest the forearm of the blade hand on the wood, or on the bench, you will find you can position the tool more steadily.

PALM MALLETS

There is always the temptation to thump the tool handle with the palm of your hand. There is a real danger of damaging nerves and tendons in the carpal tunnel of the wrist, so avoid this for all but the lightest of blows.

If this is a way you would like to work, or if you find your palms becoming sore or blistered from pushing the carving tools, then invest in a palm mallet (Fig 3.27). This is a pad containing an impact-absorbing gel – far more protective than leather alone – which you can wear without affecting the normal holding of carving tools.

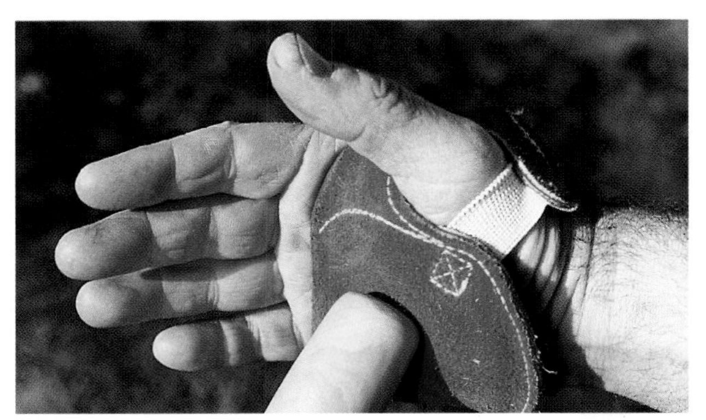

Fig 3.27 *A palm mallet, containing a shock-absorbent gel, will protect the sensitive parts of the hand.*

Fig 3.26 *Using the mallet: keep the elbows in and the body to one side of the work. If you can rest the tool arm or hand on the bench or on the work, control is increased.*

GRAIN

'Grain' is a word which fills some newcomers with trepidation and gives rise to a lot of confusion.

Part of the problem is that different people use 'grain' to mean different things; for example, any of: the arrangement, direction or size of the wood fibres, or the patterning of the wood.

Something about wood in general was said in the last chapter, and I encouraged you to learn about your material. This includes how trees grow and what wood consists of, and so on (see *Woodcarving Tools, Materials & Equipment*, chapter 8, pages 289–332).

If you want to talk about the *appearance* of the wood surface – how it is patterned – I suggest you use the term 'figure'. Otherwise, what we are interested in here is the lie of the *wood fibres* that made up the original tree.

Fig 3.28 *'Grain' is nothing less than conductive (carrying water and nutrients) and skeletal (non-conductive) wood fibres which run up the tree and connect leaves with roots.*

UNDERSTANDING GRAIN

The long tough fibres which conduct water up and down a tree lie all in one direction: upwards along trunk and stem, towards the leaves (Fig 3.28). When the tree is cut down and converted into a piece of wood for carving, these fibres are still there, all going in one direction.

In our piece of wood, the direction in which the original long fibres lay is said to be **with the grain** or **along the grain**; in other words, 'with the grain' means *with* the wood fibres. This is, mechanically, the strongest direction. In designing a carving we want to 'lead' the fibres into weak parts; we make them stronger by making the fibres longer. So, **long grain** means the fibres are long.

Conversely, **short grain** means the wood fibres are short. Mechanically, short fibres have the least strength: they tend to break away, or separate from each other easily. In a carving we would want to make the areas where grain is weak in this way either bulky or attached to a stronger part, such as the background.

A last term, **end grain**, refers to any part of the wood where the fibres have been cut *across*. As these fibres are like straws, their open ends absorb more stain or oil than the sides of the fibres; this will affect the final colour of a carving when finish is applied.

EXPERIMENT

1 Take a long, thin but broad piece of wood cut with the length running in the original direction of the tree (all planks and battens are cut like this). This means the wood fibres run along its length.

2 Bend it lengthwise into an arc (Fig 3.29).

3 Bend it across its width (Fig 3.30).

You will find that you can bend the wood lengthwise into an arc, possibly even a circle, and it will try to spring back. But bend it *across* the lie of the fibres and the wood is easily split. This demonstrates how the direction of the fibres is important to the strength of the wood: stronger along the fibres, weaker across them.

WORKING WITH THE GRAIN

English can be confusing. As we shall see, 'with' here can mean cutting 'in the direction of' the fibres; whereas what I actually mean is 'in relation to' and in particular 'in co-operation with' the wood fibres. This manner of speaking often misleads students, and you need to be clear what it is you mean to say. Here we are discussing working with regard to the wood fibres.

As you might expect, if you carve in the direction of the wood fibres you are working **with the grain**, with the fibres; the cut is at its cleanest and usually requires least effort.

If you carve at a right angle to the direction of the wood fibres you are carving **across the grain**. Depending on the wood and the sharpness of the cutting edge, this way is normally quite successful too.

However, you wouldn't be able to carve much if you stuck to these two directions! We normally carve every which way; working exactly along or across the grain is unusual, and then answers a particular need, such as flattening the background. In addition, the fibres don't often lie in neat straight lines; there may be knots, curly areas or forking into branches.

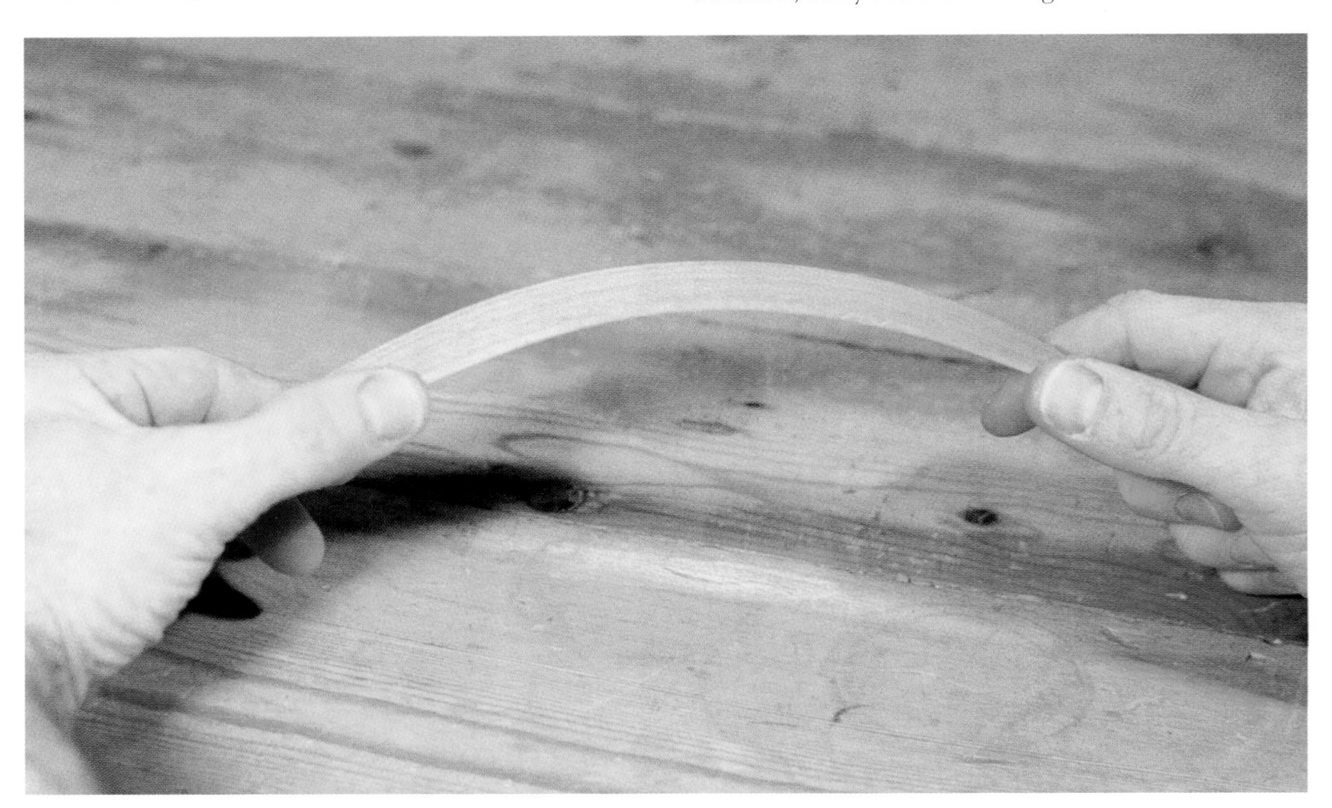

Fig 3.29 *Bending in the direction of the fibres demonstrates wood's strength and flexibility . . .*

Fig 3.30 . . . *but bending across the fibre direction demonstrates its inherent weakness.*

As I said a little earlier, there is another sense in which we can say we carve 'with' the grain, and that is when we carve sympathetically. In practical terms this means carving in *any direction in which the fibres are supported* and do not tend to pull up when they are cut.

EXPERIMENT

1 Make a small bundle of dried spaghetti. For a less impressive experiment use a dozen straws, or pencils, etc. Stagger the ends to make a slope.

2 Run your fingers *down* the slope (Fig 3.31).

3 Run your fingers *up* the slope (Fig 3.32).

The spaghetti or straws represent wood fibres. Moving *down* the slope, the shorter fibres are supported by the longer ones beneath. If we were cutting in this direction the fibres would resist the cutting edge and be severed cleanly. This would be carving *with the grain*, and the result would be the cleanest possible facet left behind by the carving tool.

Conversely, in running *up* the slope, the shorter fibres are *not* supported by longer ones at their ends: they tend to break off. If we were cutting in this direction, the wood fibres would tend to tear away before they were cut, leaving a torn, jagged surface to the gouge cut. This is what happens when you carve *against the grain*. 'Going against the grain' is unpleasant and usually thwarting.

The spaghetti experiment above shows that carving with the grain is effectively carving 'downhill', and against the grain 'uphill'. At the same time, in our experiment you could still carve directly *across* the bundle of fibres. This would be carving *across the grain*, and the result would be somewhere in between. With sharp tools and light cuts the surface can be almost as good as when cutting with the fibres.

Fig 3.31 *A simple experiment with straws representing wood fibres. As you run your fingers 'downhill' (to the left), the straws flex and support each other. This is the equivalent of cutting with the grain.*

Fig 3.32 *Running your fingers 'uphill' (to the right) is hardly possible: the unsupported straws flex without support, and so are pushed up and kink or break. This is the equivalent of cutting against the grain.*

Sometimes you have to carve with and against the grain at the same time. Try this:

EXPERIMENT

1 Take the 1/2in (13mm) deep gouge and a flat board of practice wood. Use the mallet or the low-angle grip.

2 Run some grooves, as long as possible, *along* the grain; first in one direction, then the other.

3 Run some more grooves, *across* the grain.

4 Make final cuts diagonally in one direction, and then diagonally in the other, across the wood (Fig 3.33).

You will usually find one direction is still better than the other, even though you start cutting along the grain, because, although you cannot see it, the fibres lie in three dimensions and may be rising to the surface against the direction you are going. If you cut against fibres, they will always tend to tear (Fig 3.34).

When you cut across the grain the fibres will break up quickly and come off in bits rather than long shavings. But, usefully, this is *always* so, and we will find later that this predictability comes in handy in the preliminary roughing-out stages of our carvings (see page 51).

When you cut diagonally, one side of the gouge can't help but carve with the grain (downhill) and the other against it (uphill). The groove will therefore have a smooth ('good') side and a rough ('bad') side (Fig 3.33). We will see in the projects (see page 49) how to accommodate this by always putting the bad side to the waste.

It is very important to work 'with regard to' the wood fibres, cutting wood with awareness. At the end of the day, although I have tried to give you a concept of the grain to work with, the answer lies in working with your material – a lot. Quite quickly, after lots of mistakes, you will find that you can tell the best direction to be cutting, simply by looking at the wood. It will feel instinctive. But even the best carvers can be stumped for a moment and have to think occasionally.

If I can give you one rule to work with in the beginning it is this:

> If you find yourself working against the grain (the fibres tearing), *don't persist*! Stop. Reverse direction – swapping hands if you can.

Fig 3.33 *A furrow cut with a gouge in the direction of the arrow, diagonally to the wood fibres (grain). One side of the cut is clean – with the grain – the other is against it and torn.*

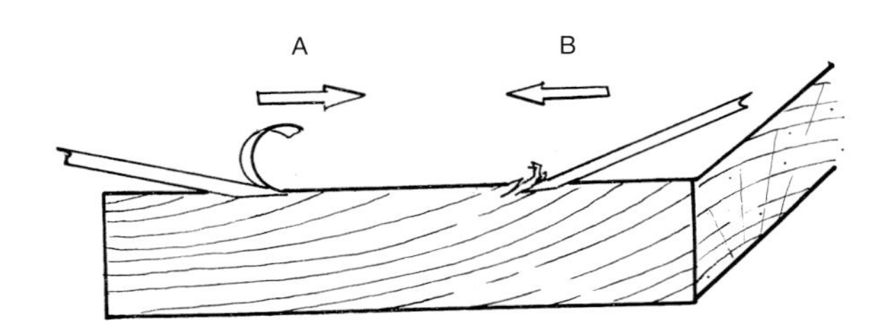

Fig 3.34 *In carving, fibres lie three-dimensionally in ways that are sometimes difficult to predict. Carving in the direction* **A** *is 'with' the grain and would give a clean, shiny cut. Direction* **B** *is 'against' the grain and the fibres will be torn up – once you notice this happening you must not persist, but reverse direction immediately.*

THE CARVING PROCESS

When we come to carving the fish projects it will soon be evident that there is an order of working. The process of turning a blank of wood into a carving is pretty much the same, whether it is a relief carving or sculpture ('work in the round').

However, grasping the way of going about things is often a problem for newcomers. A student question:

I have much trouble in the beginning, roughing-out stage. Confused, I wonder where to begin. I try to start detailing before I have done with the roughing stage. I'd like to know about the mind-set of the carver: how thoughts should be organized. What thoughts are going through your head?

The first thing to realize is that carving can be seen as consisting of *stages*. I encourage students to keep them distinct to begin with – this is how the projects in this book are treated. Later on the edges of the stages become more blurred as one's carving becomes more fluid; but it helps to start by thinking in stages.

The second point is that *each stage lays the foundation for the next*. The student has a sense of this in the original question: details put in too soon are in the wrong place at the wrong time and end up being carved out.

In the carving you are working *from the bigger to the smaller*. In other words you make the big, underlying, lumps first, then divide out smaller ones, and so on down to the details. The stages are summarized in Fig 3.35.

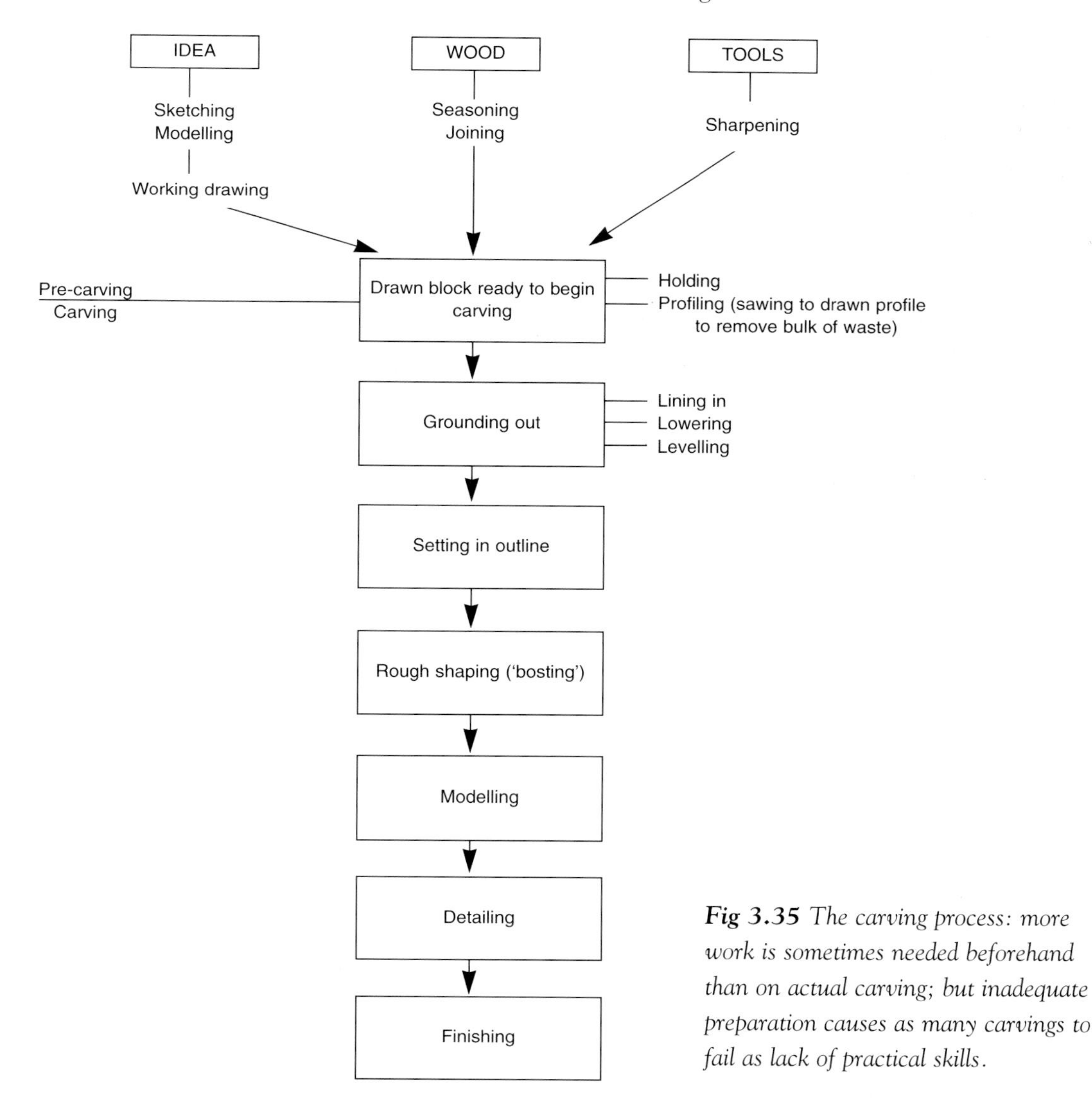

Fig 3.35 *The carving process: more work is sometimes needed beforehand than on actual carving; but inadequate preparation causes as many carvings to fail as lack of practical skills.*

What is the first stage in a woodcarving? Not *carving* – but working out, in your mind, what you are aiming at; being clear, with research, drawings and models, what it is you want. Most students fall down right here (see Chapter 7, Next Steps). The more complicated the idea, the more information is needed, and the more preliminary work. Only with abstract 'playing' can you really be successful – and then usually only accidentally – without this vital stage.

Then you need to match the idea to the wood: this entails preparing the wood; finding a way of holding it properly; perhaps there is some sawing to be done, and so on. Only then does actual carving begin, with properly sharpened tools.

Roughing out (which in a relief carving includes **grounding out** and **setting in**) is the first 'tools-on' stage in every carving, except for shallow work. In this stage the basic forms and movements are established relative to each other. It usually takes students a while to understand that roughing out is *the most important stage* – without any doubt – in the carving. It lays the foundation for all the forms which follow.

As a general principle you should:

- use the largest tool you can;
- use it for as long as possible before changing it;
- work with a mallet where you can;
- work methodically.

If the roughing out is successful, the next stage is to refine the forms, dividing while still maintaining the sense of the whole. You will begin to see your vision appearing, but the carving will have a sense of being 'unfocused'.

At the **middle (modelling) stage** of the carving you still want to include a degree of fluidity – an ability to change what you've got. The mistake is usually to fix things irrevocably too early, particularly by undercutting. Every part has a bearing on every other. Although you have now set the main masses and have less freedom than before, at this stage you should still be able to alter the flow and feel of many items and adjust their positions.

As the forms are refined, wood is removed in smaller amounts, the final surface begins to appear, and the carving starts to become 'focused'.

Only now, towards the end as the underlying forms are fixed, is it time to think of the **details**. Invariably these will take care of themselves.

There is a logic to the carving process which I hope will become really evident in the fish projects. Following it, the carver arrives at the underlying forms first, without having to undo work later, and can disregard many problems – such as detail – until their proper time. But, as always, what starts as 'logic' turns into more of a feeling, intuitive approach with practice.

The projects are designed to give you an entry into relief woodcarving; but I hope you are encouraged to explore all aspects of carving, where you will find the process similar in many ways.

WHAT IS RELIEF CARVING?

Many students start by not being quite sure what relief carving actually is, so here are a few introductory thoughts.

The essence of relief carving is that *the depth dimension is reduced* from what it would be if the subject was rendered true to life, or 'in the round'. So, for example, a relief carving of an apple is not simply half an apple stuck onto a background.

What happens is that there is an unequal 'squashing' of the object in order to trick the eye into seeing more of the depth, more three-dimensionality, than there really is.

Relief carvings involve a bit of trickery, in the same way as a drawing or a painting fools the viewer into thinking there are three dimensions when there are really only two.

A relief carving has only *one viewpoint*. In other words, there is one place to look at it, from which the carving 'works'. If you move to the side, what may have been an entirely convincing appearance starts to fail, to distort (Fig 3.36). Wood carvings in the round – sculpture – can be seen from any direction and read true, even if the back is not so interesting as the front.

Fig 3.36 *A relief carving has only one viewpoint from which it 'works', and a certain amount of visual trickery is needed to get the right effect. A relief will appear distorted if viewed from any other point, as in this side view of the frog in John Daines'* Heron *relief* *(see page 141)*.

The lower the depth, the nearer the relief is to drawing. But it would be wrong to see relief carving as a sort of glorified painting (or cut-down sculpture). In relief we can create landscapes and hang objects in space in ways which would be impossible or impractical in either drawing or sculpture, and in this way relief carvings inhabit their own world, with their own rules, somewhere between painting and fully three-dimensional sculpture.

There is an extremely important sculptural point to grasp here. We normally draw objects by putting lines around them (which say 'space here, mass there'). In reality objects, or forms, have no lines around them.

If you look at any rounded form there is a horizon, beyond which you cannot see. I have coined the phrase **form horizon** to mean this sort of soft edge; as opposed to genuine, hard edges. Move your position, and the form horizon also changes; an *edge* will stay more in the same place. We choose the particular viewpoint for a certain relief carving and place the edges and form horizons appropriately.

So, as an example, when we come to the high relief carving the profile of the fish will actually end up something like Fig 3.37. There are edges and form horizons which will appear to be the mid-line of the fish where the fins lie, and beyond which we cannot see. Behind these edges the wood of the fish is undercut at a tighter angle, to give the effect of more of a body behind the fish than there really is.

'Low' and 'high' relief are loose terms, and both are often present in the same carving (Fig 3.38).

They describe the relationship between the highest point in the carving and the background. The two fish projects demonstrate the differences, but they also demonstrate how high and low relief are usually combined within one piece of work. Indeed, if you look at your hand you will see that even though it can be carved fully in three dimensions, the relation between shirt cuff and wrist is one that requires relief carving.

There are other forms of relief carving, and many other things which can be said about how they 'work', which will have to wait for a later book.

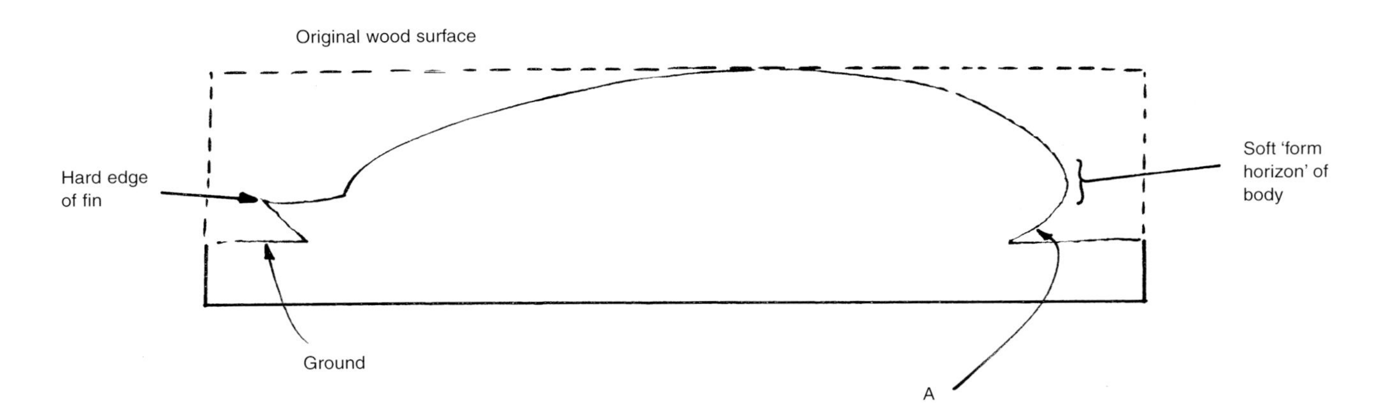

Fig 3.37 *A section through our high relief carving shows the hard and soft edges beyond which wood is undercut. By making the undercutting a little tighter than the curve of the body leading into it (**A**), a greater sense of 'lift' from the background is felt, giving the illusion of there being more body behind.*

Fig 3.38 *High and low relief very often appear together in any one carving, as in this detail from the background of Mick Botten's high relief (see page 139). There is a lovely sense of depth, with the river passing behind the hill and the hermit's hut nestling in the recess, yet the carved depth is only around $^1/_8$in (3mm).*

CHAPTER FOUR

LOW RELIEF CARVING PROJECT

When you have completed the carving project in this chapter (Fig 4.1) you will have practised a range of low-relief skills and techniques that are absolutely invaluable for any woodcarving in the future.

I have listed some of these at the end of the chapter and you can have a quick glance now. The list is surprisingly long to some people, but it should not be seen as complete.

Forget about this list for now. The point is that our exercise here is designed to demonstrate some basic skills of woodcarving and allow you to practise them. You are quite likely to end up with a decent carving at the end, and you should try your best to do so. However, do relax and remember that it is only a piece of wood!

Fig 4.1 *The low relief fish carving project, using the same drawing as in the high relief version.*

GETTING READY TO START

You should have wood, tools and everything else you need to begin (Fig 4.2), as described in Chapter 2.

I hold the workpiece in this project with fences and wedges, as described on page 10. However, if you are starting with thinner wood than that shown here, the fences and wedges must be correspondingly thin so as to lie *below* the level down to which we are going to take the background of the carving. Alternative methods are discussed in Chapter 2, pages 9–10.

You will need to make a drawing of the fish on paper first, then transfer the drawing to the wood.

DRAWING THE FISH

Although I am describing a particular carved fish, and show my working drawings, in fact I would like you to draw one of your own. All my students do this, and so far all their fish have been carved using the basic tools I've specified.

I will give you guidelines for your own drawing; you should find this straightforward, even if you feel you lack artistic skills. It is actually an advantage to know nothing about fish – except perhaps their having a head at one end and a tail at the other.

It is inevitable that your fish will have a unique character – you can see this in the Students' Gallery: the fish of one may be said to look somewhat startled, another broody. Exactly what this says about the student carvers is humorously debated. Not a debate I get involved in: I think my fish looks a bit gormless.

Do relax about the drawing and have fun.

METHOD

1 Read through my guidelines below.
2 Make a few rough sketches first;
3 then a full-size working line drawing.
4 Check your drawing against the guidelines to make sure you are not going to give yourself trouble.
5 Transfer the fish to the wood (see page 46).

Remember you only need an outline and the main lines; there is no need for shading or details.

If you must use my drawing then you will need to enlarge it on a photocopier to fit the wood. When you have finished this carving and are feeling more comfortable about the work, do try another fish of your own, following the guidelines below: you will find it ultimately, and personally, more satisfying.

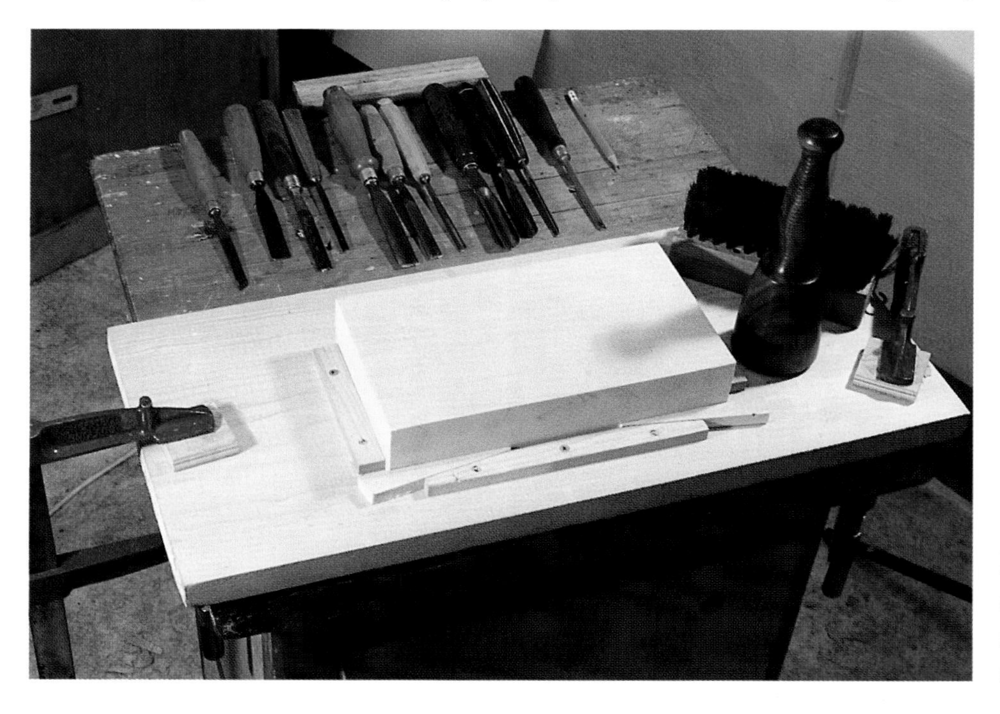

Fig 4.2 *Ready to go: carving block held securely; tools safely at the back; mallet and carving brush ready.*

Guidelines for drawing the fish

(Fig 4.3)

I try to make this low relief exercise simple. Students find there is a lot to learn in the beginning, and what we are trying to do here is to limit the number of problems. These will appear in their own good time as you continue carving! So these are the points to bear in mind:

- Make your fish very basic: a side view with head, tail, eye, gill, a few fins, a mouth if you like. It can point in either direction but it may help to orientate it as mine.
- Use simple, flowing lines for all the parts, including the fins.
- Fill the available space, but leave a gap of 1/2in (13mm) all round between the fish and the edge of the wood to allow you room to work.
- Where an outer fin meets the body of the fish, keep the angle around 90°; more is better. If you make these angles acute (tight), you will have problems working within them. The 'inside' fin, as in my drawing, can be at a somewhat tighter angle – it is quite shallowly carved and much more easily dealt with.
- The fibres of the wood (see 'Grain', pages 35–8) must be kept long for strength. Don't swerve the tips of fins across the grain as this makes the fibres short and weak, leading to that part of the carving breaking off.

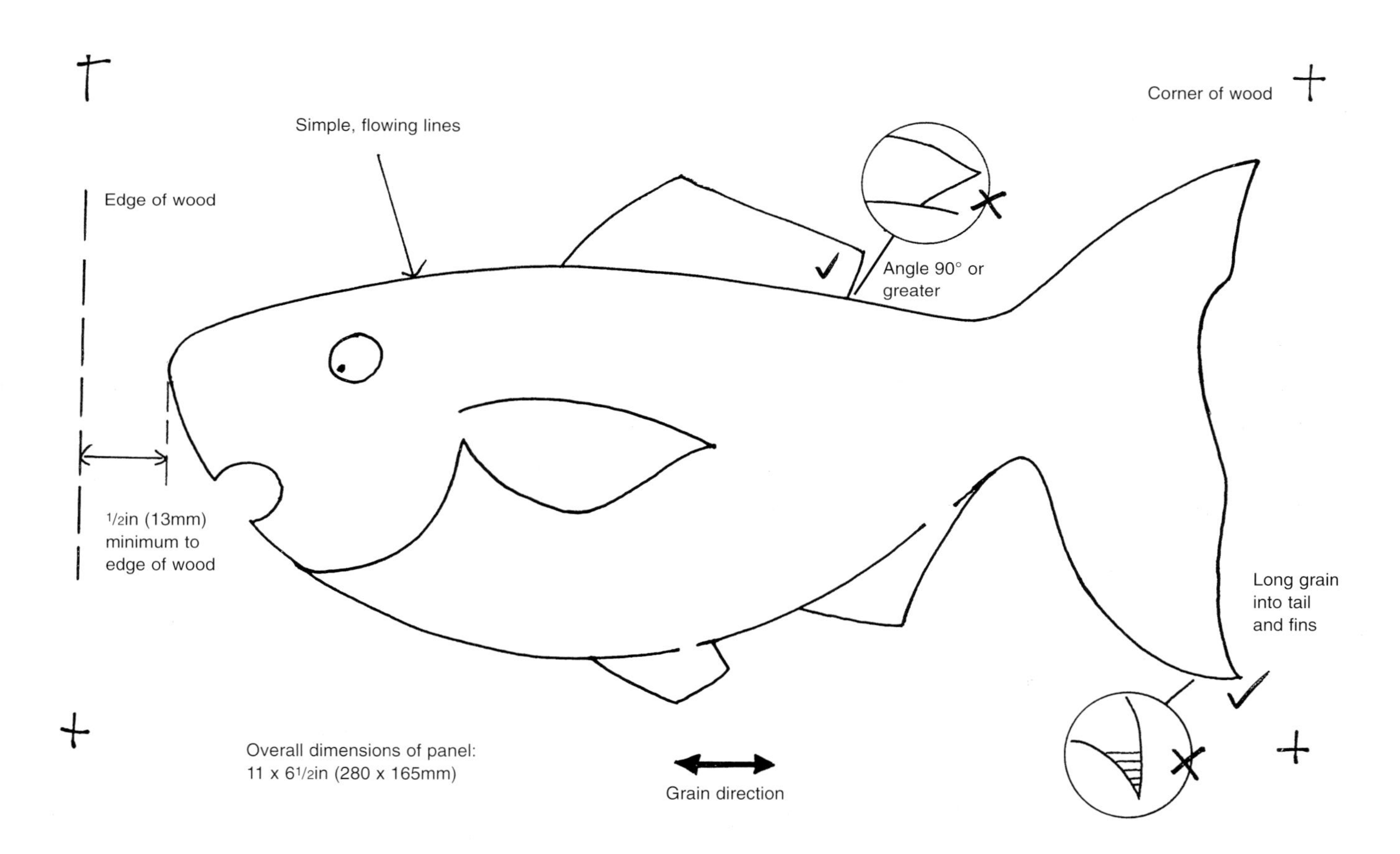

Fig 4.3 *The working drawing for both projects includes features which challenge, yet don't make the carving too difficult. Feel free to use this drawing if you wish to follow the projects exactly; but repeat the project with a design of your own.*

I have included some background line details in my demonstration carving. By all means work out your own on paper and keep the drawing until the final stages. Don't bother drawing them on the wood as they will immediately be cut away with the background.

TRANSFERRING THE DRAWING TO THE WOOD

There are several ways, of which the first is my preferred method for soft wood such as jelutong. It is also the cleanest, and allows you to refine lines on the wood.

METHOD

Either

Tape or pin the drawing in position and press through the paper with a ballpoint pen to mark the wood (Fig 4.4). You can easily see the indentations with a cross light when the paper is removed. Then firm up the drawing with a pencil, keeping the lines as smooth and flowing as you can.

Or

Use carbon paper. This tends to rub and smear. However, masking tape over the ink lines will stop this; you can still see the lines and can carve through it.

Or

Rub the back of the paper with a pencil before lining it up and going over the drawing.

Or

Prick through the drawing and join up the resulting holes in the wood.

Or

If you feel confident enough, draw the fish directly on the wood. Remember: clear, simple outlines only – anything else will be carved away.

Figure 4.5 shows my piece of wood with the drawing firmed up.

Fig 4.4 *Pressing through the drawing will mark the soft wood enough, without the need for carbon paper; note aligning marks where I originally creased the paper to the size of the wood.*

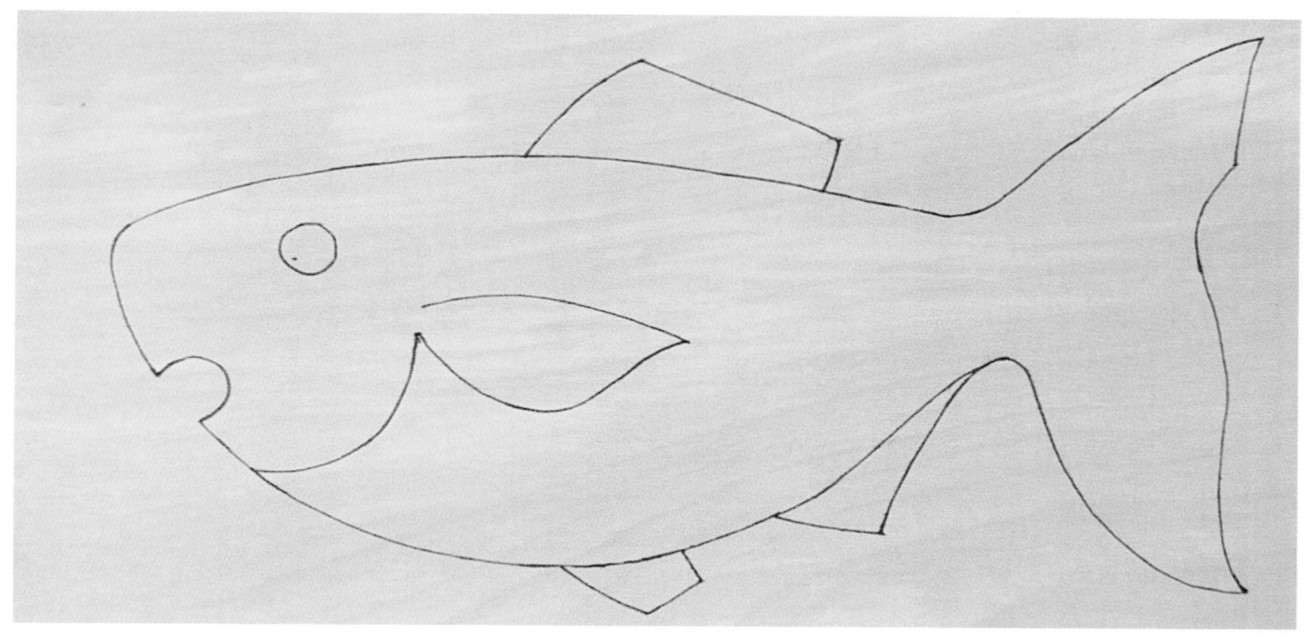

Fig 4.5 *Fish drawn on the wood and ready to go!*

DEPTH OF BACKGROUND

Before we actually start the carving there is one more useful thing we can do: set the depth of the background to which we want to work. In this low relief the depth of background will be no more than 1/8in (3mm).

Fig 4.6 *A scored line to the correct depth gives us an accurate level to which to finish neatly. The marking gauge runs along the face of the wood and scores the edge with the point of its pin.*

Because we have left the edge free, we can mark this depth on the side of the carving with a gauge. (See pages 119–22 for a discussion of 'enclosed grounds', where there are no free edges.)

Without the marking gauge you can use a pencil and ruler, but the real advantage of the gauge is that it gives you a neat, scored line to which the depth can be brought. A pencil line is more vague, although quite adequate in these circumstances.

METHOD

1. Set the depth of the gauge to 1/8in (3mm).
2. Hold the gauge in whichever hand is comfortable, as shown in Fig 4.6. You can hold the wood in a vice if you have one.
3. Tilt the gauge so that the pin drags behind as you push it away from you. *Make sure the face of the gauge remains firmly up against the face of the wood* – the side with the drawing on it – as you mark its edge.
4. Make a light scoring pass first, then strengthen it with a few further passes. Too deep an initial pass and the pin of the gauge may be pulled out of true by the wood grain.
5. Work your way around all four sides of the wood in the same way.

CARVING

Before starting, please make sure you are familiar with Chapter 3, and in particular:

- the correct ways of holding the carving tools (pages 24–8);
- grain, and in particular how the V-tool cuts a trench with a 'good' side and a 'bad' side (pages 35–8).

We will carve the fish in seven distinct stages.

Briefly:

1 **Lining in:** here the subject – our fish – is roughly outlined, separated from the surrounding waste wood.

2 **Grounding:** the waste around the fish is removed down to a chosen background level (sometimes called by carvers simply the **ground**).

3 **Setting in:** the outline of the fish is defined.

4 **Modelling:** the fish is shaped, given some form, and undercut.

5 **Detailing:** finally the details are added to the fish, which may be either decorative or anatomically necessary.

In addition we have two other tasks:

6 **Background:** this is optional, and here consists of simple lines representing reeds and bubbles.

7 **Finishing:** sealing and polishing the fish, fixing a hanger – perhaps even signing it!

For 'fish' here you could substitute any low-relief carving: a leaf, flower, whatever. The pattern of working will be similar (see Chapter 3, pages 39–40).

By dividing the work into these stages we have a chance to see the basic, logical, carving process in action. You will find, however, that as you become more competent and proficient at carving wood, your approach becomes more fluid, and that this pattern of working and division into stages do not apply so neatly.

> Please read through the instructions carefully before beginning any section, as there are usually several points to juggle with at the same time!

So, with your wood (on which the fish is drawn and the depth level marked) held safely; tools sharp and neatly arranged; mallet, bench- and slipstrops, and carving brush to hand (Fig 4.2), we can begin the first stage.

1 Lining in

In this stage the V-tool is run around the fish, creating a groove (Fig 4.7) which separates the fish from the surrounding waste wood. A narrow, deep (or U-shaped) gouge is an alternative tool for this work.

You can practise in the waste area before starting to outline with the V-tool (line in) proper. You can also use the waste to 'run in' the V-groove from a distance (this can be seen clearly in Fig 4.13). It doesn't matter how much of the waste is cut, as it will be removed in the next stage – but you must not go deeper than your background level.

You must pay attention to three aspects of the V-cut: its *depth*; *how close* you are to the drawn line; and the *direction* of cut.

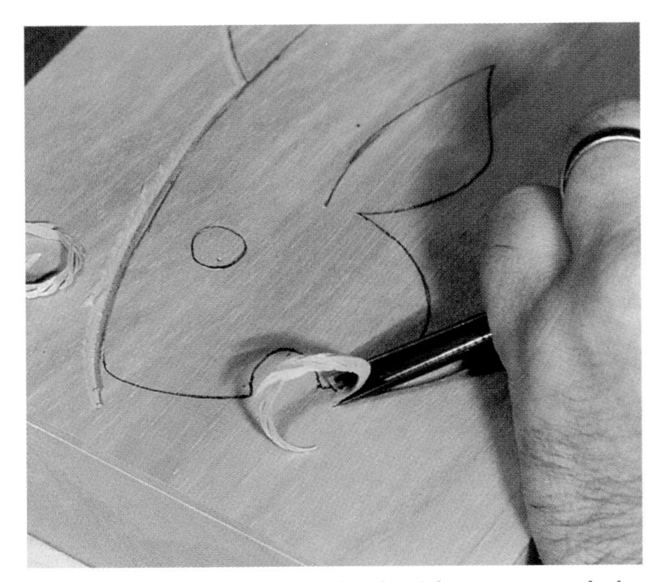

Fig 4.7 *Lining in: put the 'good' side of the V-cut towards the subject; use the waste area to make your approach if you wish.*

DEPTH

Aim to place the root of the trench just above the depth line, giving you a little waste to finish down to the background level (Figs 4.8 and 4.9).

Until you are confident, feel free to make the cut in several deepening passes.

CLOSENESS TO THE DRAWN LINE

You can come as close to the line as possible, placing the V-cut to the waste side. However, the V-tool is not so successful at negotiating tight curves, so there will be some areas you can iron out, or leave for the time being – such as the mouth. These will be dealt with in the next, setting-in, stage. At internal corners – such as where the fins meet the body – cut *inwards* from two directions, being very careful not to cut into the body of the fish.

DIRECTION OF CUT

Always try to place the 'good', clean-cutting side of the V-groove against the subject, and the 'bad' side, which tends to pull up grain, to the waste side (Fig 4.10; see also 'Grain', pages 35–8). This will mean periodically changing the direction you are cutting; and changing hands. It is also wise to work so as to have weak elements – such as the tips of fins – supported by wood. This means, for example, coming *inwards* from the tip of the tail rather than outwards and off the end (Fig 4.11).

Always react quickly to what is happening. If the grain is tearing, don't persist: reverse your direction.

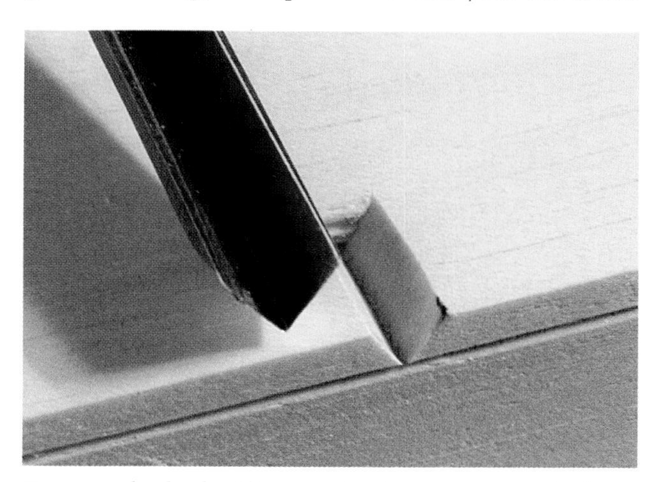

Fig 4.8 *The depth of lining in should be just above the final background level. An initial cut like this will show you the uniform width of groove to aim at.*

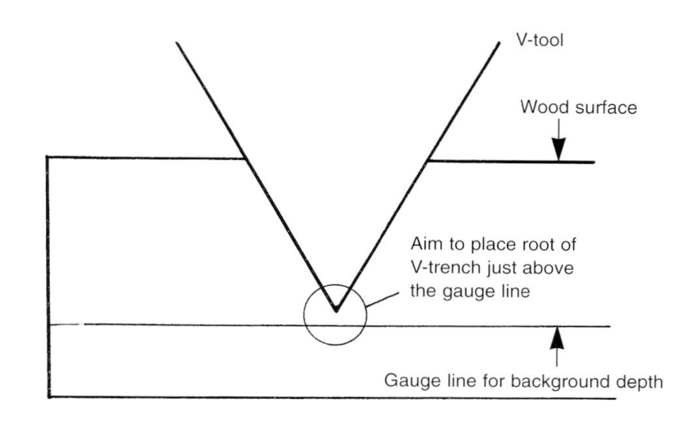

Fig 4.9 *The depth to which to line in with the V-tool. A deep or U-shaped gouge is an alternative.*

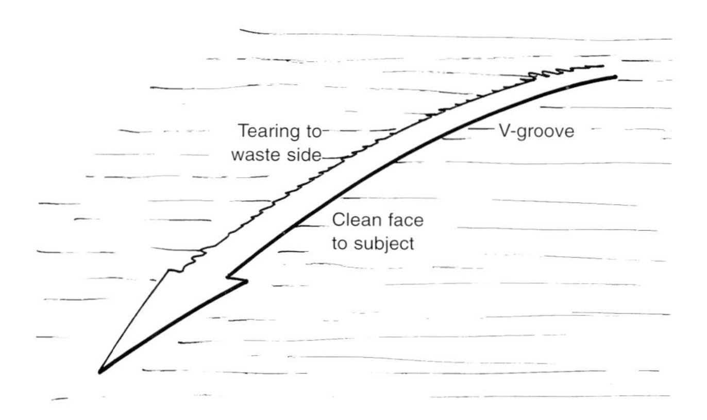

Fig 4.10 *One side of a gouge or V-tool cuts more cleanly than the other, because one side cuts with the grain, the other against.*

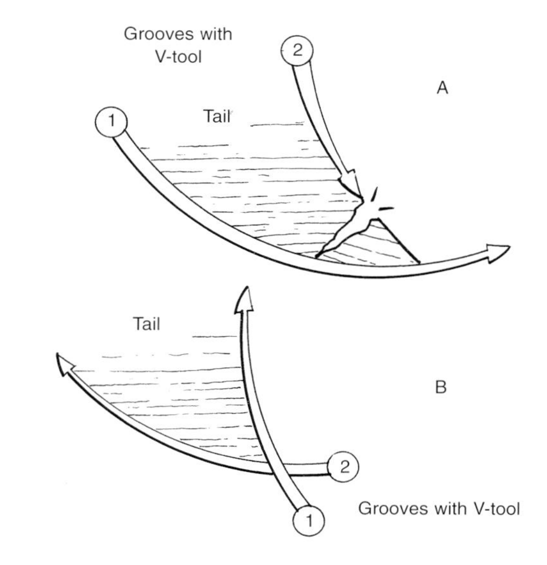

Fig 4.11 *Always work into supported wood to avoid breaking bits off.*

METHOD

V-TOOL

1 Hold the V-tool in the low-angle grip, blade hand resting on the wood.

2 Make a cut to the side of the wood to check on the depth you want to go to (Fig 4.8). *The width of the V-cut relates to its depth*, so the width of the cut is a guide to the required depth.

3 Line in the fish according to guidelines given above, switching direction as necessary. The arrows in Fig 4.12 show more or less the directions I took with the V-tool on my fish.

4 Do not pick away shavings; they should be cut free with the point of the skew chisel. Use your brush rather than wiping the carving with your hand.

Ideally the result should be something like Fig 4.13, with the V-cut even in thickness and as close to the drawn line as possible; following its simple flowing lines; going as far as possible into some recesses but leaving out awkward ones.

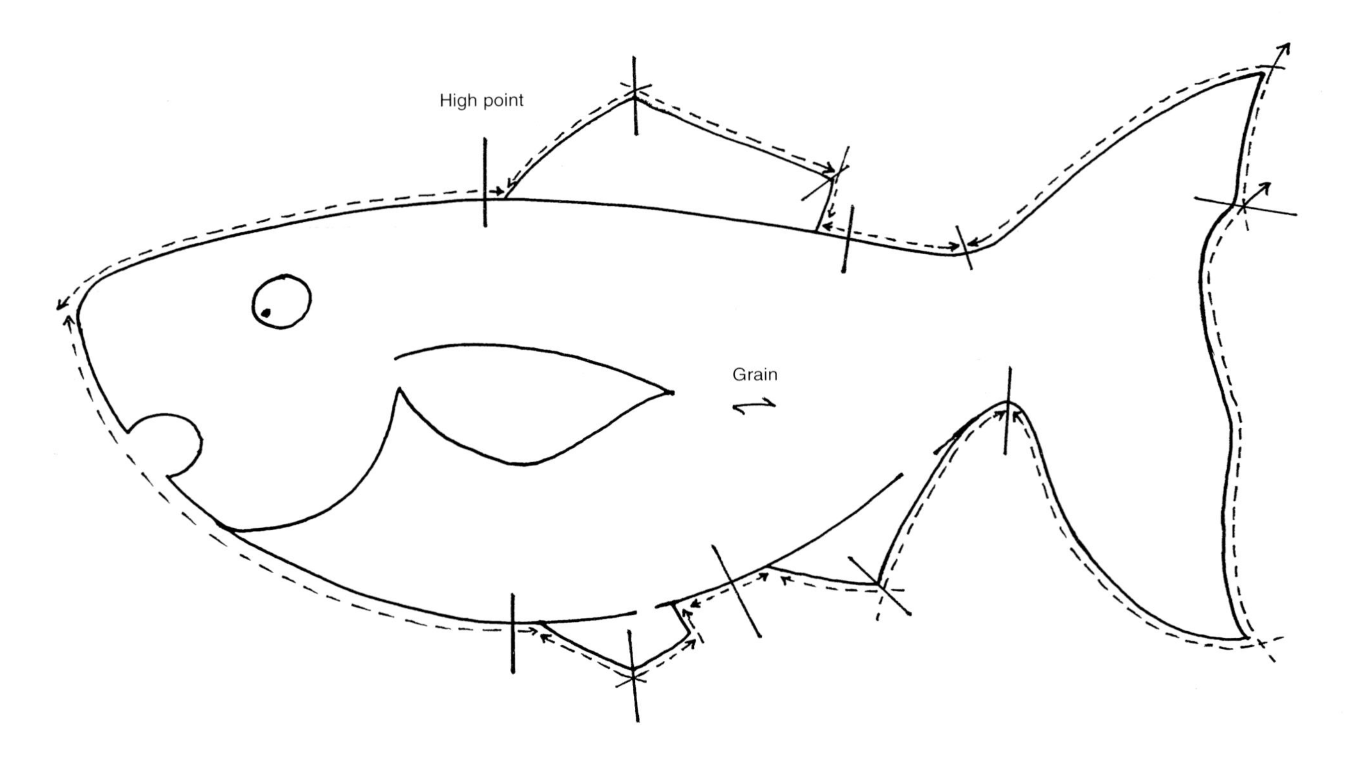

Fig 4.12 *Directions taken when lining in to make sure the 'bad' side of the cut is always placed to the waste.*

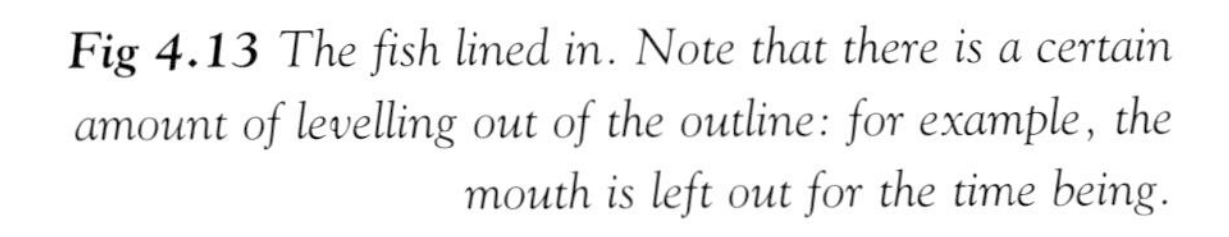

Fig 4.13 *The fish lined in. Note that there is a certain amount of levelling out of the outline: for example, the mouth is left out for the time being.*

2 GROUNDING

The background to our fish does not have to be 'engineeringly' flat, it need only *appear* or 'feel' flat. The ground must look as if it naturally comes together behind the fish, at a uniform level – as if the fish could have been cut out and stuck on.

There are two principal ways in which a background may fail to live up to this standard: the ground may *vary in depth*; or there may be an effect which I call a 'rubber ground' (Fig 4.14).

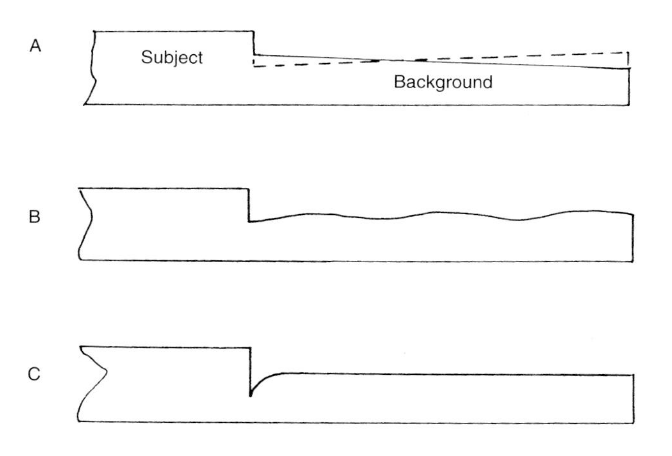

Fig 4.14 *Common problems with backgrounds.* **A**: *The ground is flat but not level from the edge, and cannot logically appear to pass behind the subject.* **B**: *Irregular ground on which the subject never looks at if it is sitting comfortably.* **C**: *Level and flat, but dipping immediately in front of the subject. This is usually a problem with setting in, and makes the subject look as if it has sunk into a soft 'rubber ground'.*

VARIATION IN DEPTH

In other words, rising or falling of the background from the edge of the wood towards the subject, our fish. A *small* variation is acceptable in handwork but it should not be readily noticeable.

'RUBBER GROUND' EFFECT

The background is mostly flat but suddenly dips immediately around the subject. This gives the impression of a background made of soft material with the heavier fish, in this case, sunk into it. This is actually a problem of setting in and is dealt with in that section.

Methodical working as described below gives the quickest and best results, and safeguards against variation in depth. The grounding stage is best considered as two distinct procedures:

1 **Lowering:** the bulk of the surrounding waste is removed quickly.

2 **Levelling:** the background is finished to the desired level.

If the relief is very shallow, the lowering and levelling can be simultaneous, and only a shallow (flat) gouge is necessary.

LOWERING THE BACKGROUND

The tool for this stage is a deep (or 'quick') gouge, chosen so that the cutting edge gains the required depth while keeping its corners clear of the wood. This is important, as wood will be torn up if the corners sink below the surface (see page 29 above).

The effect you are trying to achieve is an appearance of having ploughed even 'furrows' across the grain.

By working across the grain, any chance of cutting against the grain is avoided; and because the carving is still within the waste wood, any crumbling of the ridges between grooves will be cleaned away when the ground is levelled.

In soft wood like jelutong the gouge may be pushed by hand; harder woods may need the mallet.

Lowering is not just 'chopping away' the background as quickly as possible to get to the finishing stage. To think about it like this is to miss an important opportunity. As described here, the lowering stage lays down the basic underlying form – a flat ground – as well as just removing waste. It is worth taking trouble over this stage because, if it is done well, the final levelling and finishing off is quick and easy, simply falling into place. There are parallels in the equivalent roughing stages in three-dimensional carving.

When lowering the background with the deep gouge, pay attention to the *deepest point of its cut*: concentrate on laying this *just above the final surface depth* (Fig 4.15). As you lay down cuts alongside one another, you will be left with a series of crests or ridges; the bottoms of the troughs between them

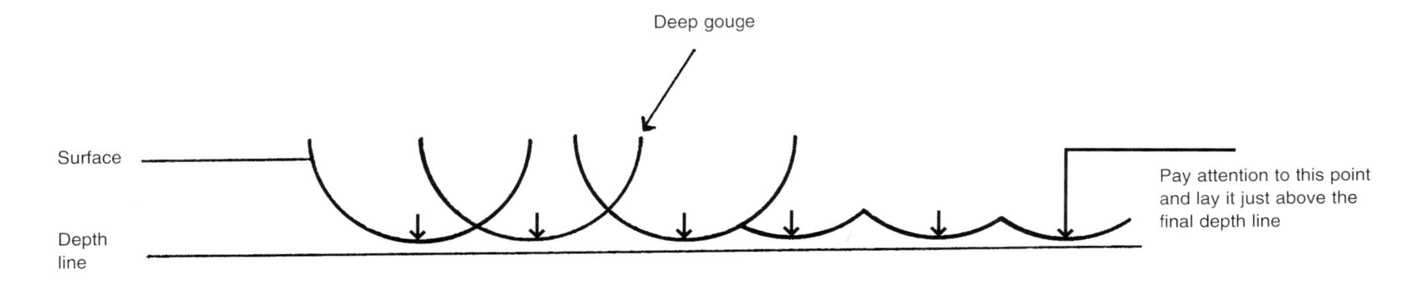

Fig 4.15 *Lowering: it is the point of maximum depth of the channels which you must always keep in mind.*

will lie just above the final surface. When these ridges are removed the clean surface will be found to be practically at the level you want it.

METHOD

No. 9 x 1/2in (13mm) DEEP GOUGE

1 Hold the gouge in the low-angle grip.

2 As with the V-tool, make a preliminary cut to the side, again fractionally above the line which marks the final ground depth (Fig 4.16). The width of this groove will give you an indication of the depth of your cut.

Fig 4.16 *As with lining in, the depth to which the background is lowered is just – but definitely – above the final level.*

3 Make your first cut at right angles from the edge of the wood inwards across the grain, to end at the V-groove before the fish. Make this furrow as uniform in width and depth as possible. As you end the cut, rock (rotate) the gouge to ease away the shaving at the V-groove. Avoid overshooting the line and cutting into the fish.

In a free design like this fish it may not be important if you cut into it – just redesign. However, it *will* matter if you are trying to make two the same. *Control* is one of the skills you are learning, so do try to end the cut precisely.

4 Place a second groove next to the first (Figs 4.17 and 4.18), matching as closely as possible. As you work along the fish, the gouge furrow will end at various angles to the V-groove. You will need to rock the gouge and turn to one side a little to come as close to the line as possible (Fig 4.18).

5 Lay down a third furrow, and so on. Remember to keep the corners of the gouge clear of the wood to avoid tearing up the grain (Fig 4.19).

6 Carry on like this, methodically working along the entire near side of the fish and over towards the far side at the ends – but always stopping short of the further edge (Fig 4.20).

It is not essential that every cut be at right angles to the edge; some change of direction is often necessary to deal with particular circumstances of the grain or the design.

7 Turn the fish around and repeat the same process from the other side (Fig 4.21), merging the grooves from the two sides where they meet.

8 Use the brush to remove waste; resist any temptation to pull away uncut shavings (Fig 4.22).

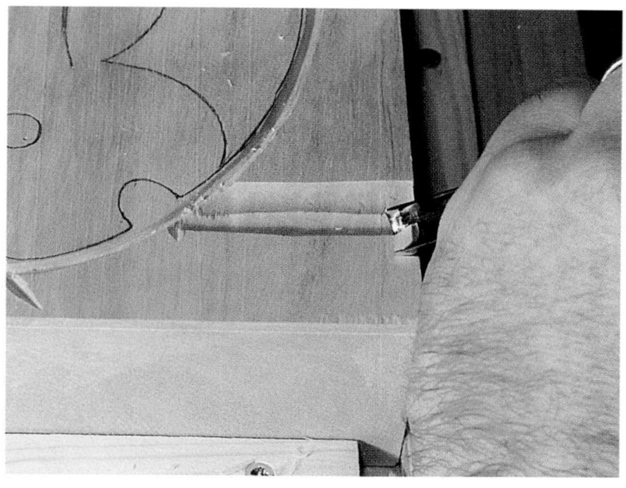

Fig 4.17 *Lowering the background. Start from the edge and carve across the grain at a consistent depth.*

Fig 4.20 *First half of the background lowered.*

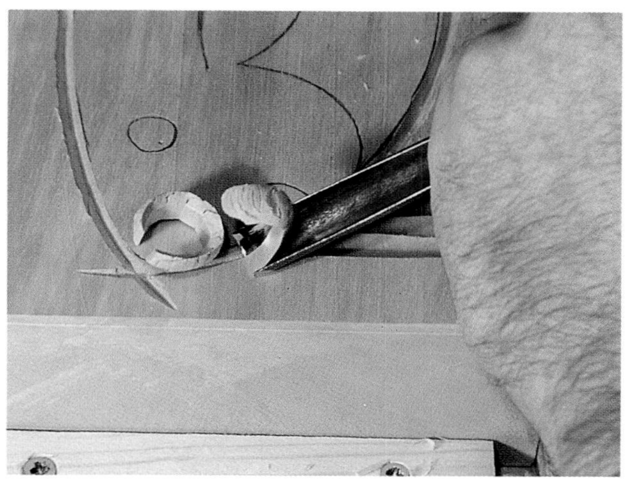

Fig 4.18 *Stop at the edge of the subject. This may involve turning the groove in sympathy with the edge of the fish, before clearing the shaving, in order to come as close as possible to the outline*

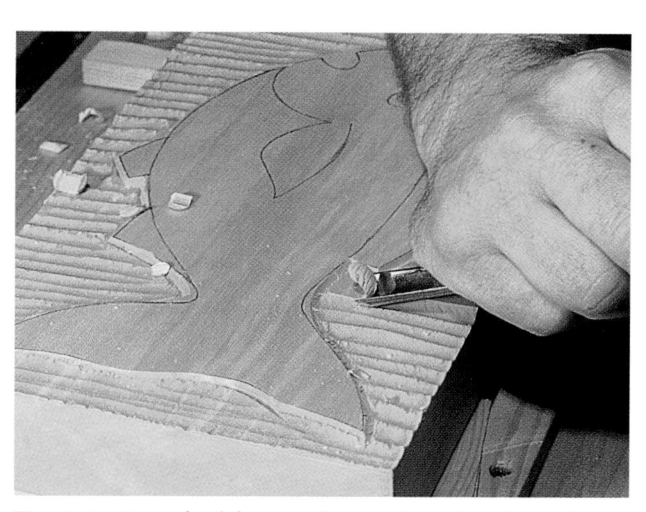

Fig 4.21 *Turn the fish around to work on the other side.*

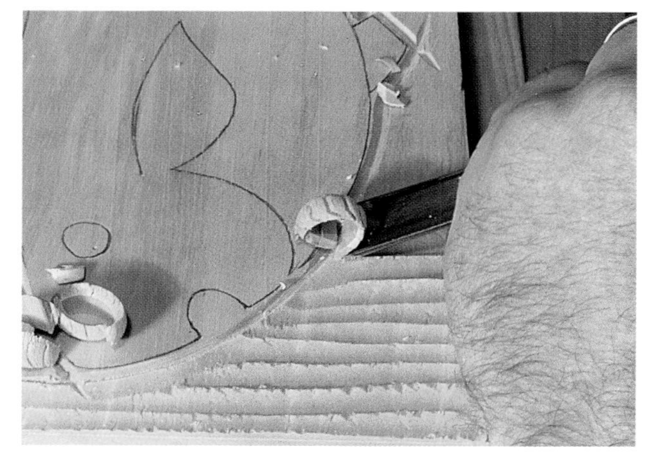

Fig 4.19 *Repeated methodical cuts at a uniform depth give a 'ploughed' look.*

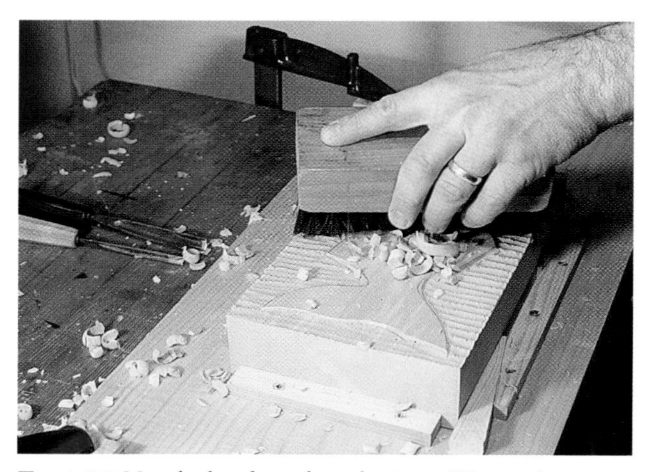

Fig 4.22 *Use the brush to clear shavings. Wiping them away with your hand or fingers will dirty the wood.*

Fig 4.23 *The background is now lowered. It is the centre of each groove, their lowest point (which lies just above the final surface), which is important, not the ridges between.*

The result should be a ground with a uniform ploughed appearance (Fig 4.23) which lies fractionally above the final ground level.

LEVELLING THE BACKGROUND

Following what was said at the beginning of the 'Lowering' section, this stage consists of removing the crests of the grooves left by the quick gouge. As these lie just above our finished depth, the result should be to arrive at a final level surface more or less straight away.

As this is the *final* surface – we will not be sanding – your tools must be immaculate, leaving no tears or snail tracks in the surface.

A particular pattern and technique of cutting is needed to smooth off a surface, as in levelling. Always use the largest gouge possible: work with the 3/4in (19mm) first, and then the narrower ones in smaller areas.

METHOD

No. 3 x 3/4, 1/2, 1/4in (19, 13, 6mm) FLAT GOUGES

1 Hold the gouge in the low-angle grip (Fig 4.24).

2 Start towards one end and work with a slicing motion, making the strokes as long or short as you feel comfortable with. Remove the crests and ridges left from the quick gouge down to the final surface.

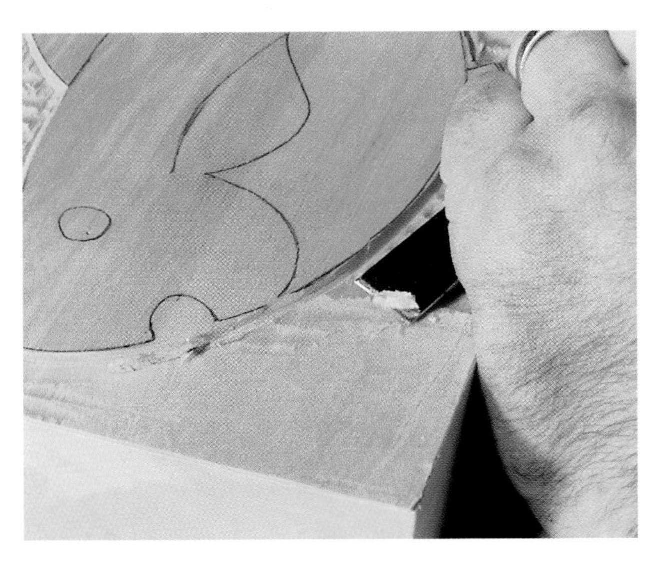

Fig 4.24 *Levelling with a flat gouge. As the ridges are skimmed off, the final, level surface appears quickly.*

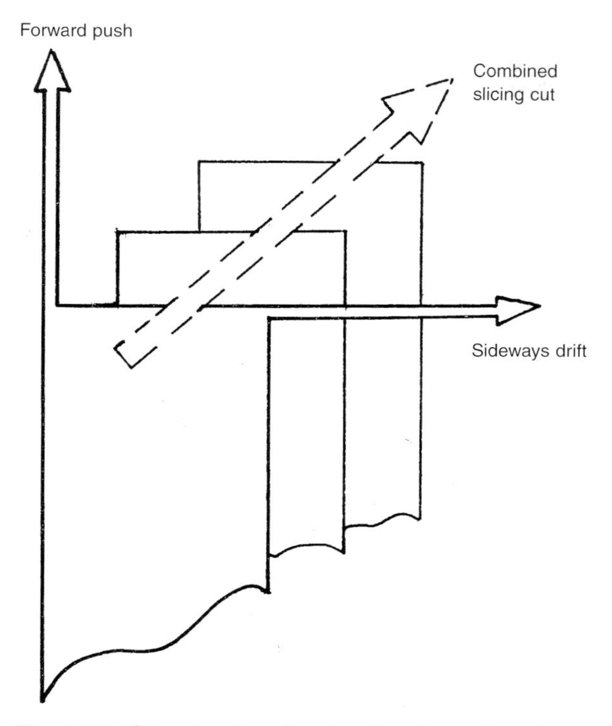

Fig 4.25 *Slicing involves drawing the edge to the side as it is pushed forwards. You can do this to the left or right, and with varying amounts of rotation of the tool, depending on its sweep.*

Fig 4.26 *Use the wall of the subject as a fence against which to run the side of the gouge.*

3 Keep the corners of the gouge clear of the wood – this means that only shallow cuts are possible with the flat gouge if you are not to tear the grain.

4 The shiniest surface comes if you cut *with* the grain; with a truly sharp gouge you can easily work across the grain. Work in this way over the ground surface.

The slicing technique is shown in Fig 4.25 (see also Chapter 3, pages 32–3). The tool moves forwards as it is made to drift sideways, paring away the shavings, sometimes in an apparently spiral or circular movement. This slicing cut is far less effort and gives a cleaner surface than if the gouge were simply pushed straight ahead.

5 Work from the gauge line at the edge – which will disappear – into the bottom of the V-cut, by the fish. To avoid running the blade into the fish, use the inside wall of the V-cut (i.e. that nearest the fish) as a fence against which to rest the *side* of the gouge (Fig 4.26). Don't let the cutting edge or corner of the gouge dig in.

If you find the grain tearing, you are working against the grain: do not persist! Instead, reverse the direction of cut – it is here that being able to reverse hands will become a valuable skill to master. If you do bury the corners, tear the grain, etc. (Fig 4.27), immediately go over the area again and clean it up. *Clean up as you go along*, policing each area before you leave it.

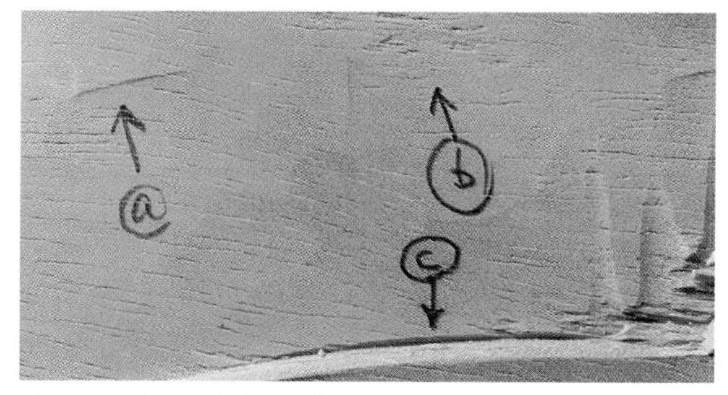

Fig 4.27 *Some faults in the levelling: (a) corner dig-in; (b) torn grain; (c) lining-in groove still present. Go over faults immediately; do not leave them until later: (b) needs to be cut in the opposite direction; (c) can be improved but could be left until the setting in.*

6 The V-trench around the fish had a depth fractionally *above* the final ground. It follows that you will be left with shavings at the edge of the fish as you finish up to it. You can leave these for the next stage or you can lightly skim them off with the V-tool (Fig 4.28).

7 Some parts of the fish may be inaccessible at this stage: the mouth, or the areas between the fins, for example. Just finish up to these as tidily as you can for the moment, and leave them to be finished off later (Fig 4.29).

8 Turn the fish around if this helps to carve the other side.

The result should be a smooth, level ground behind the fish from edge to edge of the wood (Fig 4.30). This finished surface should consist of light (very shallow), cleanly cut facets, without torn grain. Most of the fish will be well outlined, and the rest trimmed close to the outline, but with some waste still to be removed.

When you think you have finished smoothing off the background, change the direction of the cross lighting and look again. You'll probably be surprised! Tears and marks will show when the carving is oiled or waxed; *now* is the time to remove them.

3 Setting in

In this stage the outline of the subject is sharply defined with gouges. You *may* leave the edge of the fish created by the flowing V-cut in some parts, but the junction between fish and wall looks different, softer than that created by the gouges. My own preference is not to mix the two effects.

Unless you particularly want vertical walls to your outline, there are good reasons to slope them out by 5–10°: this helps with subsequent modelling – or, if the edge of a design is to be left unmodelled, sloping walls are stronger and will attractively catch a little light.

Whatever angle you choose, *do not undercut* – by leaning the handle out – at this stage (See Chapter 6, pages 122–5).

There are (at least) two distinct techniques to setting in. Which method you need, or in what order you use them, will depend on the shape of your fish and your own style of working. With practice you will happily switch between and combine the two.

These techniques are:

- **slicing** and
- **matching**.

Fig 4.28 *Because the lining in was to a depth slightly above the final ground, a drift of shavings tends to arise as the ground is levelled. These can be quickly cut off with a light repeat cut of the V-tool.*

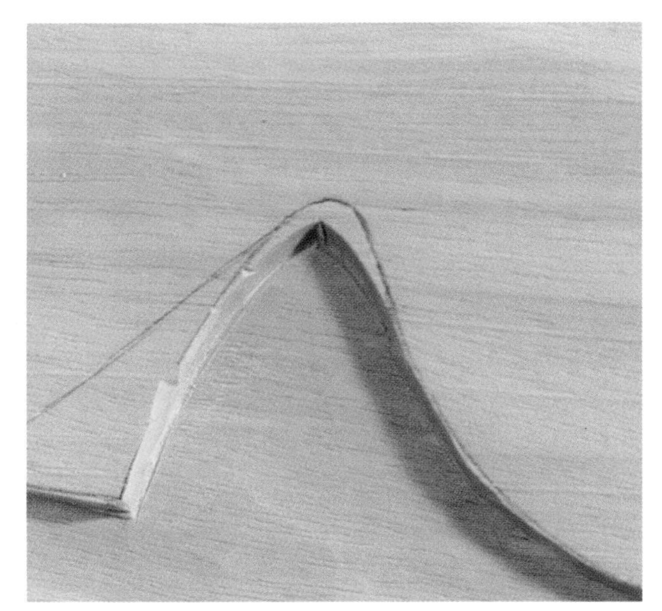

Fig 4.29 *Close-up of the lower tail stem after levelling: the V-tool cannot get in here, so areas like this are left until setting in.*

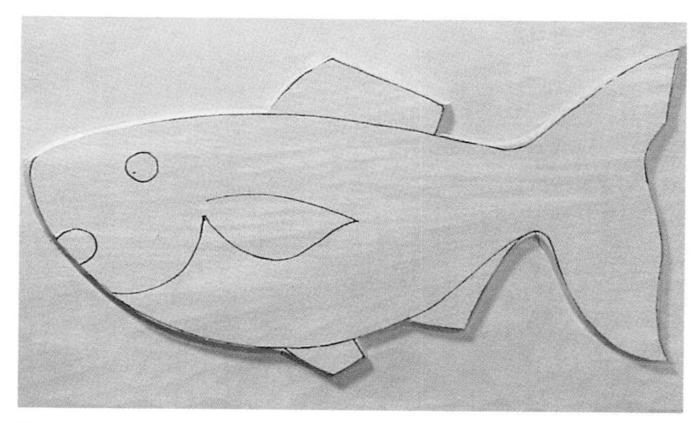

Fig 4.30 *The fish after grounding out: the background is level and smooth – in the sense of having subtle facets, rather than being 'engineeringly' flat.*

I will take different parts of the outline to show these techniques at work. You should be able to adapt them to what setting in is needed in your own design, and select an appropriate tool yourself.

As a approximate guide, Fig 4.31 notes the tools which I used at different points to set in the outline of my fish to the given size. The particular technique of setting in is described below: read through both methods before attempting them.

SETTING IN BY SLICING

Here the cutting edge of the gouge *slices along* the outline you want to set in, somewhat like a knife.

This technique is particularly useful for long, shallow curves. Any particular tool will cut a range of curves tighter than its sweep (see Chapter 3, page 33), so any one tool can be controlled to cut a variety of profiles.

Start with large flat gouges (no. 3), then move on to smaller ones. Next turn to the medium gouges (no. 6) and see what you can slice with them. The deep gouges (no. 9) are less suitable for this particular technique, but do experiment with them.

We will start on a large, slow, *rounded* curve in the outline, between mouth and lower fin.

METHOD

No. 3 x 3/4in (19mm) FLAT GOUGE

1 Hold the gouge in the pen and dagger grip for the more vertical, slicing setting-in cuts. It is the thumb in particular which both pivots and propels the tool.

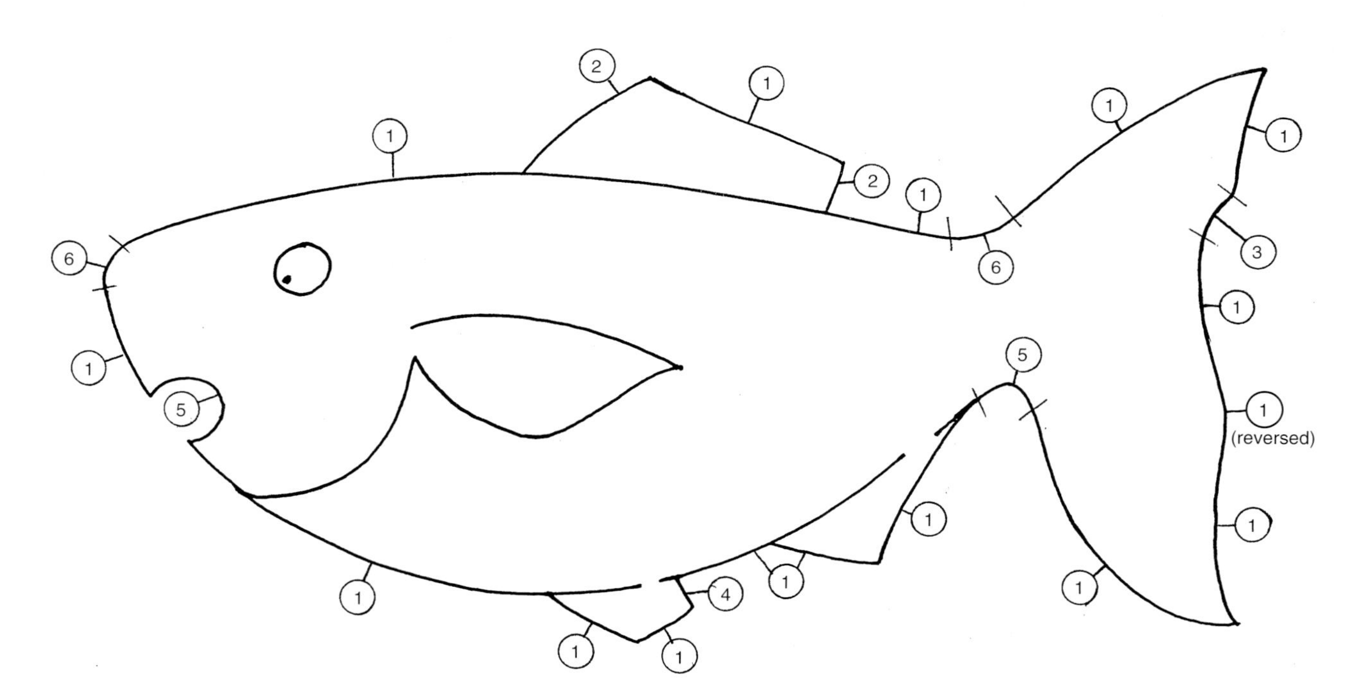

Fig 4.31 *Approximate choice of tools for setting in: (1) no. 3 x 3/4in (19mm); (2) no. 3 x 1/2in (13mm); (3) no. 3 x 1/4in (6mm); (4) no. 6 x 3/4in; (5) no. 9 x 1/2in; (6) no. 6 x 1/2in.*

2 Switch to the low-angle grip for horizontal levelling of the ground up to the walls of the fish.

3 Figure 4.32 shows the manner in which the gouge is positioned. Orientate the inside of the gouge to match the curve; lean the handle into the fish just a little; tilt the handle towards you so that the leading corner clears the wall of wood and the trailing corner is down, ready to slice.

4 Push the gouge along with your thumb behind the blade, slicing the wall with the cutting edge. Use your other hand to control the orientation of the tool at the handle.

The sweep or curve of the cutting edge will allow you to negotiate this long curve slowly, and you can imagine the blade acting like a knife, even though the handle is in a different place It is vital to control the depth of the setting in and avoid going below the ground level. You will need to estimate where the corner is, but you will soon get the feel for it. If you like, make two lighter strokes to begin with to get the finished depth.

5 Use the same flat gouge to clean up the ground to the outline of the fish (Fig 4.33), using the wall like a fence as previously described.

6 Cut all the curves you possibly can with the same tool, including tighter curves, and finish off the background in these areas before changing to a smaller flat gouge.

A note on depth

This slicing cut does need practice and, after all, this is what we are doing with the fish project.

You should aim to set in so that the corner of the gouge skates *precisely* along what will be the final ground level, and to finish the ground *precisely* up to the newly formed wall without cutting into the fish.

If you cut into the ground when setting in, not only will the cuts be seen – more so if you are going to be undercutting – but you will have to deepen the ground to disguise them. If you then only clean up the ground near the fish to remove stab marks, this abrupt change of plane will bring about the 'rubber ground' effect: the fish appears to sink into the surrounding wood (see above, page 51). It is better to lower the ground by removing wood from a wider area, so sloping the ground slowly and far less perceptibly towards the fish. The ground can still 'feel' flat, and the chances are that the sloping will not be noticed.

Next we will turn to slicing a slow, *hollow* curve – say the rear of the lower fin, before the tail. Use the same tool.

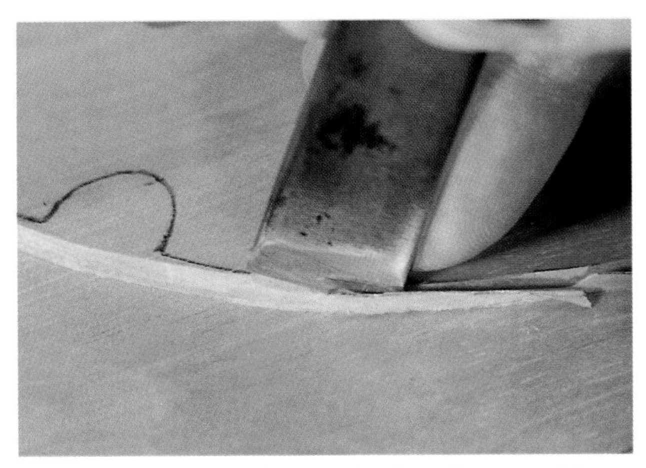

Fig 4.32 *Setting in by slicing with a large flat gouge. Note how the gouge is orientated to the curve of the subject, and that its leading corner is clear of the surface. Exact control of the depth of the trailing, cutting corner is needed.*

Fig 4.33 *Using the wall as a fence again to give the final wall/ground junction.*

METHOD

NO. 3 X 3/4IN (19MM) FLAT GOUGE

1 Hold and manipulate the tool in the same manner as just described.

2 Reverse the orientation of the gouge so that the outside bevel is against the wall to be set in. There is less need to tilt the bevel towards the fish, as the angle of the bevel itself will tend to create the slope in the wall when the blade is about vertical.

3 Slice forward in the same manner as above, controlling the depth as before. As you reach the end of the wall, the full length of the cutting edge can be brought down to finish off (Fig 4.34); this is preferable to continuing the slicing cut right to the end of the fin, which risks breaking off the unsupported fibres at the tip.

In this case the curve is tighter towards the stem of the tail, where it meets the body of the fish. Just cut as far as the large gouge can manage.

4 Finish off the ground to the outline you have set in (Fig 4.35). Using the wall as a fence is not possible when the wall is concave. A light cut is needed to avoid digging in.

5 Cut all the curves around the fish which you possibly can, including tighter ones, finishing the background before changing the tool.

The previous comments about depth, and a precise meeting of the junction between wall and ground, also apply here.

The slicing cuts with the tools in opposite orientations can be merged.

Sometimes slicing can successfully set in a *corner*, as in the tighter angles between fin and body:

METHOD

NO. 3 X 3/4IN (19MM) FLAT GOUGE

NO. 2 X 3/8IN (10MM) SKEW CHISEL

1 The cut to the sloping wall is made in the normal way, matching the orientation of the gouge with the curve of body or fin.

2 Slice along the body of the fish – being sure to cut so as to *follow the outline* of the body, which continues smoothly through the fin to the other side – allowing the cutting edge to run into the junction where the walls of body and fin meet (Fig 4.36).

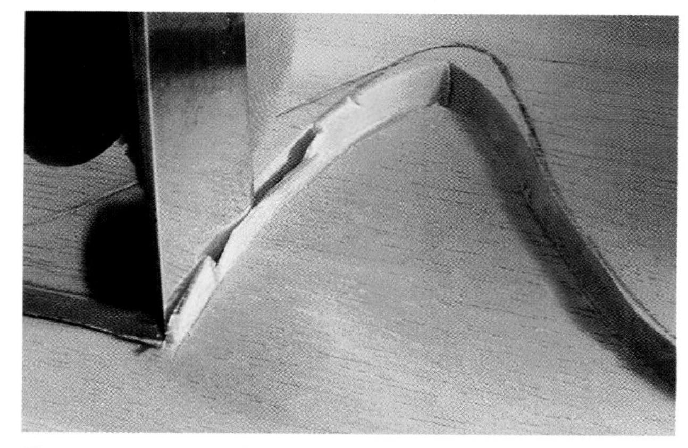

Fig 4.34 *Setting in by slicing: this time the gouge is orientated to a hollow outline. As the wall comes to an end, so the full length of the cutting edge can be used to finish off.*

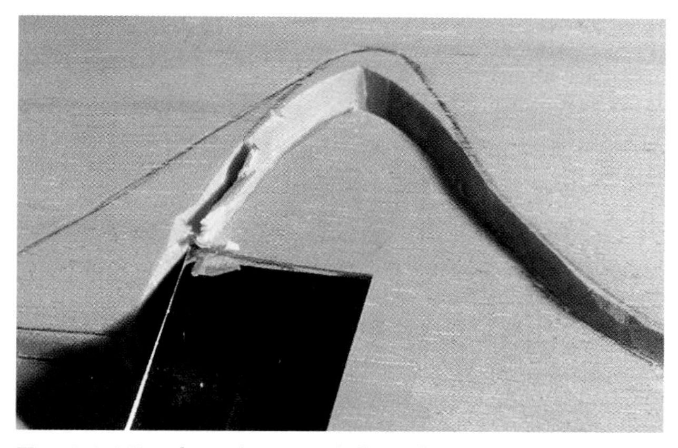

Fig 4.35 *Finishing the ground: here the concave wall cannot be used as a fence.*

Fig 4.36 *Slicing into a corner.*

3 Slice from the outside corner of the fin, so that the two cuts meet neatly in the junction.

4 If your fin is at less than a right angle to the body, a normal square-ended tool cannot reach in to clean the ground without cutting the surrounding walls. The skew chisel should now be used to nick out the corner of ground in the angle (Fig 4.37).

Fig 4.37 *The skew chisel comes into its own by reaching into an angle inaccessible to the normal square-ended gouge.*

SETTING IN BY MATCHING

Here the sweep of the carving tool is selected to equal the outline to be set in. Such matching cuts can be married together to produce extended curves.

This technique is useful for tighter hollows. The perfect curve of the cutting edge produces a perfect shape in the wood, which can be exactly repeated elsewhere.

The technique can be demonstrated in the tight recess where the tail meets the lower body. The tools have been chosen to match the drawing, and the size of my particular fish; you may need to select others according to the shape of your own fish.

METHOD

NO. 9 X 1/2IN (13MM) DEEP GOUGE
NO. 3 X 1/4IN (6MM) FLAT GOUGE

1 Start with the deep gouge and hold it in the pen and dagger grip.

2 Place the cutting edge on the drawn line. If possible, merge the cut with any previous setting in.

3 If cutting a convex surface, with the bevel side of the gouge facing away from the subject, you will need to tilt the handle a little towards the fish to give the correct slope to the walls.

4 Push down (Fig 4.38), using your shoulder to put weight behind the cut. As before, control the depth, stopping at the level of the ground. On hard wood you may need a mallet.

Fig 4.38 *Setting in the lower tail stem (see Fig 4.29) by matching the sweep of the gouge with the shape to be cut. It is quite normal in carving for a shape to be dictated by available tools.*

5 Ease the tool out by tilting the handle in the direction *along* the cutting edge. There is a danger of damage to the cutting edge while it is buried in the wood if you rock in a direction *across* it.

6 Switch to the narrow flat gouge, using the low-angle grip for the horizontal finishing of the ground.

7 Level the background into the recess (Fig 4.39), meeting the matching cut exactly at the junction of wall and ground. Control the corner of the flat gouge so as not to dig into the fish; you may only need a final delicate stroke or two to finish off (Fig 4.40).

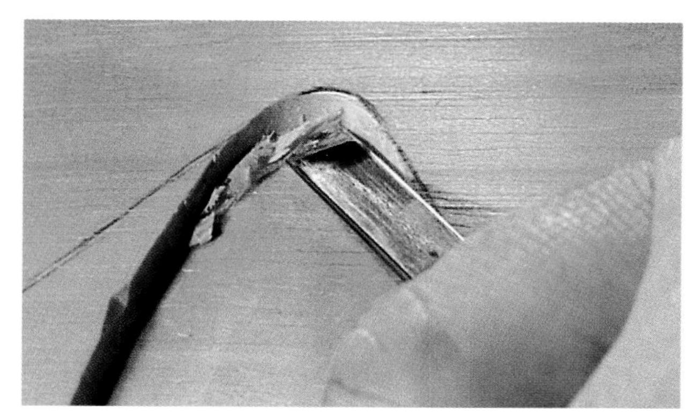

Fig 4.39 *Cleaning up in the tighter recess under the tail stem means using the corner of a narrow gouge very sensitively.*

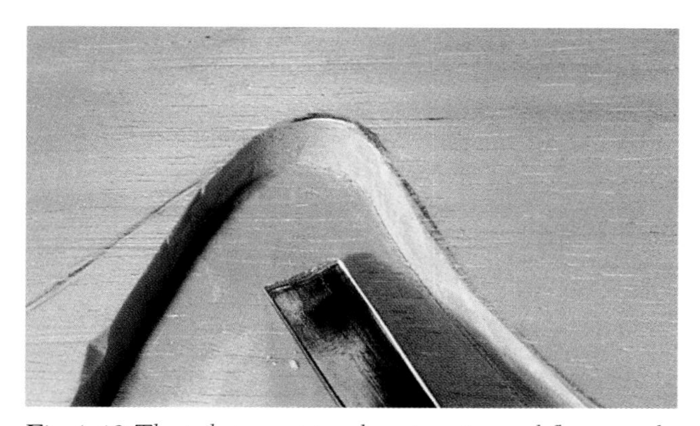

Fig 4.40 *The tail stem set in: clean junction and flat ground.*

When you are not yet confident, it may be better to set in to a little above the final ground, level as best you can, then repeat the setting in to arrive at a neat junction more carefully.

If you don't have matching shapes, then you can always modify your design to accommodate what you do have. There is nothing wrong with this, and it is common carving practice.

Setting in by matching curves can be extended to remove waste in very tight areas. The mouth of my fish is a good example of a difficult recess, and the chosen tools fit my pattern. If you are not sure of the depth to which to cut, follow this exercise to half the depth, then repeat it to finish off.

METHOD

NO. 9 X 1/2IN (13MM) DEEP GOUGE
NO. 3 X 1/4IN (6MM) FLAT GOUGE

1 Hold the deep gouge as in the last method, but make a first stab cut at the edge of the mouth. Go down to just above the background depth.

2 Repeat the stab cut while working into the recess until you arrive at the drawn outline at the back of the mouth (Fig 4.41). The waste wood inside the mouth is now cut up and easy to clean away.

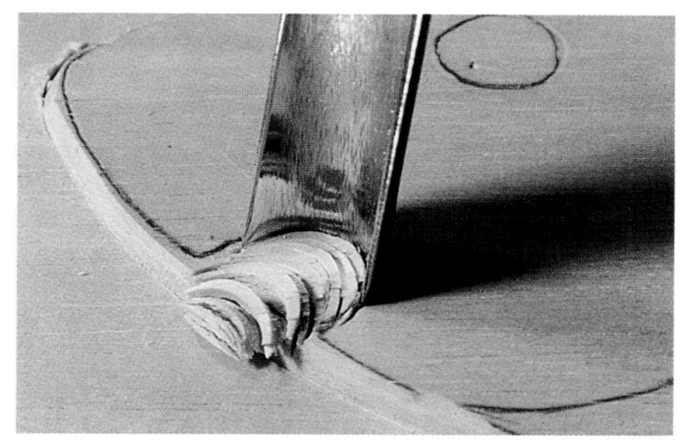

Fig 4.41 *Paring back the recess of the mouth with a matched gouge.*

3 Change to the flat gouge. This matches the shape of the sides of the mouth, as the deep gouge matched the back. Set in to the line, still sloping slightly and taking care of the depth; and merging the matching cuts (Fig 4.42).

Fig 4.42 *Matching and merging the sides of the mouth with a second gouge.*

4 Switch to the low-angle grip to clean up the area within the mouth up to the junction of the wall and ground (Figs 4.43 and 4.44).

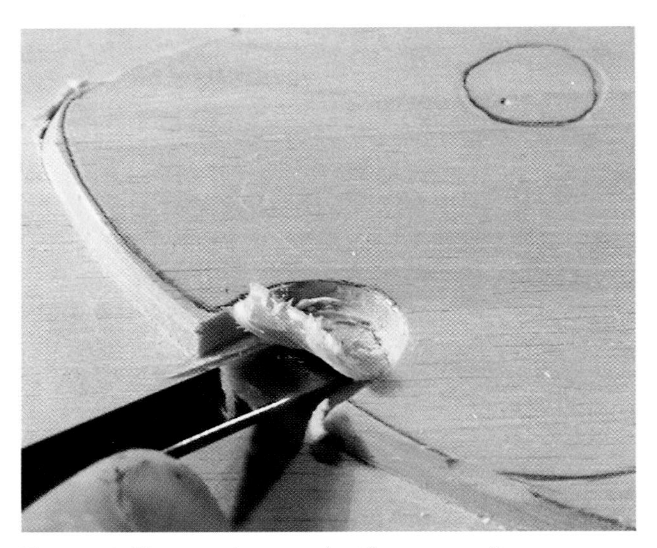

Fig 4.43 *Cleaning the ground with a narrow flat gouge.*

Fig 4.44 *The finished mouth recess, set in.*

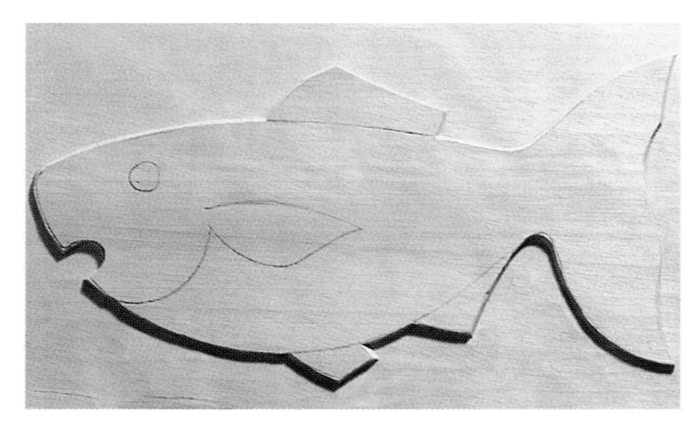

Fig 4.45 *The low relief fish after setting in.*

5 Because the wall slopes slightly, the curve at the ground is *smaller* than that on the surface of the fish, and you may need the no. 6 x 1/4in (6mm) to finish the ground edge.

Work your way around the outline of the fish, setting in using these methods. The result when the setting-in stage is finished should be a neatly outlined fish on a smooth, cleanly cut background of uniform depth (Fig 4.45). The lines of the body where they cross the fins should read true.

Ideally the tools should be controlled so that there are no stab marks around the edge of the fish and its lines are still smooth and flowing like the original drawing. There is no doubt that this takes practice, but this is what you should always be aiming at; and although it seems difficult at first, students do find it comes, and often sooner than they think.

Having set in an outline of our fish, the next stage is to give it some shape.

4 Modelling

So far we have been, literally, involved with background work. The modelling of the fish is in some ways the 'best bit' – after all, it *is* the subject. The fish, do remember, is only an exercise to learn skills: in what follows, feel free to experiment and have fun!

Bear in mind the following points:

- A low relief carving is necessarily flat. There is not much scope for playing with the third dimension – this will come in the following high relief carving. It is best to maintain this sense of flatness and keep the modelling simple.
- There is, however, scope for surface decoration, such as the fluting of the fins, or incised scales. In some ways this reflects the low relief's kinship to drawing.
- Changes of plane *within* the carving – such as the side fin standing proud of the body of the fish – can only be slight, and a good rule is always to make them less than the change of plane which is the outline. This keeps the outline strong and the nature of the subject clear (see Fig 7.6 on page 131).

Modelling normally has a preliminary rough stage and a subsequent refining stage, but here, because there is so little wood to be removed, the two are merged together.

Modelling the main shapes within the subject must come first, before adding any surface detail or decoration. This order is very important: it is a waste of time decorating the fins if you subsequently alter their shape. Leave details until last, and they will take care of themselves; you will see how this works both here in the low relief and later in the high relief carving (see the earlier account of the carving process in Chapter 3, pages 39–40).

Start by defining the fins.

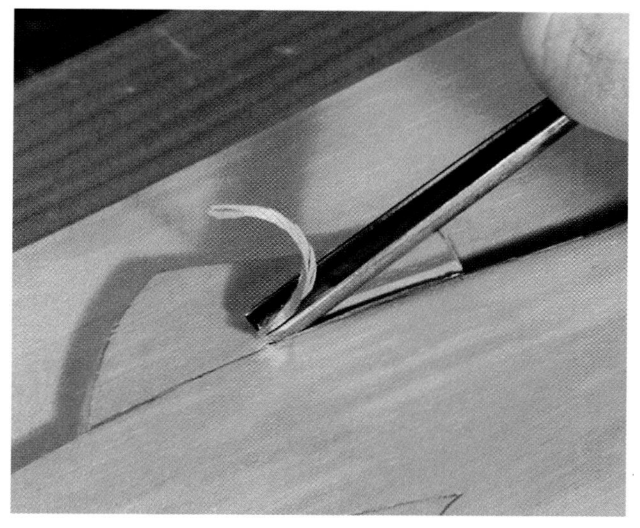

Fig 4.46 *Separating ('parting') the fin from the body.*

METHOD

V-TOOL; NO. 3 X 1/2IN (13MM) FLAT GOUGE

1 Start with any fin.

2 Use the V-tool to follow the line between fin and body (Fig 4.46). Tilt the V-tool so that the cut follows the wall angle, and cut to half the depth of wood – not down to the background. Choose the direction so as to put the clean side of the V-cut against the fish.

3 The fin itself can now be reduced to half its thickness with a flat gouge (no. 3 x 1/2in (13mm)) (Figs 4.47 and 4.48).

4 Repeat for all the outer fins.

Note that what you are doing is nothing less than lining in followed by a combined lowering and levelling. The fin is in effect a ground for the body of the fish at this point.

Fig 4.47 *Lowering the fin to half its thickness.*

The next stage is to round over the hard outline and give a sense of body to the fish:

Fig 4.48 *The lowered fin. Try and get the body line as true as possible. Note the small step to the left here: this will be removed when the edge of the fish is rounded. A larger step would be more difficult to deal with.*

METHOD

No. 6 x 1/2in (13mm) MEDIUM GOUGE
No. 3 FLAT GOUGES AS NECESSARY

1 Turn the medium gouge over so as to match the rounded edge you wish to cut, in the low-angle grip.

Inside bevels greatly increase tool control and sensitivity in these circumstances and are strongly recommended (see above, page 17). If you have not got inside bevels on your gouges, put one on and compare the cutting.

2 Cut along all the convex edges of the fish, changing direction where necessary to cut *with* the grain (Fig 4.49). *Do not round over the fins or the end of the tail, nor within the mouth.*

3 Continue along the part of the body next to the fins – but you may find the no. 3 x 1/4in (6mm) easier here.

4 Try not to dig the corners of the gouge into either the background or the fish (Fig 4.50). This is actually quite tricky to avoid and calls for relaxed control. Clean up the marks in the ground straight away with a flat gouge. Cuts within the fish will be cleaned off later – though you *can* use a flatter gouge and repeat the strokes to smooth over the edge.

Fig 4.49 *Rounding over the edge using a gouge with a sympathetic sweep. An inner bevel really helps here.*

5 In the hollows where the tail meets the body, you can come only so far with your cut before you find you are working against the grain. Go as far as you can, then stop – don't persist. Use the medium gouge to take small cuts *across* the grain, from the fish outwards, trying to keep a sense of rounding over (Fig 4.51).

6 Work your way all round the fish; finish by checking the surrounding ground for marks.

Now that the outside of the subject has been shaped, we turn to any major features and changes of plane within. In our fish this means the side fin and gill. Again the lining in and lowering creates a ground of body wood around the fin. Leave the eye for the moment.

Fig 4.50 *It is easy to dig the corners of the gouge into the subject or ground, as here.*

Fig 4.51 *Where the edge is concave, as at the tail stem, reverse the gouge and match the rounded edge as best you can.*

METHOD

V-TOOL; No. 3 GOUGES; SKEW CHISEL

1 Use the V-tool to line in the gill and side fin (Fig 4.52). As it is the body which will be lowered in this case, choose your direction so that the clean side of the V-cut is against the fin. An even depth of about one quarter that of the background is all that is required.

Fig 4.52 *Lining in the gill and side fin.*

2 Nick off any ends to the V-cut with the point of the skew chisel (Fig 4.53).

Fig 4.53 *A stop cut with the point of the skew chisel to end the V-groove.*

Your fish should look something like Fig 4.54 at this stage.

3 Use a flat gouge to lower the area around the fin and gill, so as to leave them a little proud (Fig 4.55). To avoid the 'rubber ground' effect, merge the ground gently with the body so as not to have a sudden slope before gill or fin.

4 The gouge will not be able to get into the tight corner between gill and fin (Fig 4.56); go as far as you can.

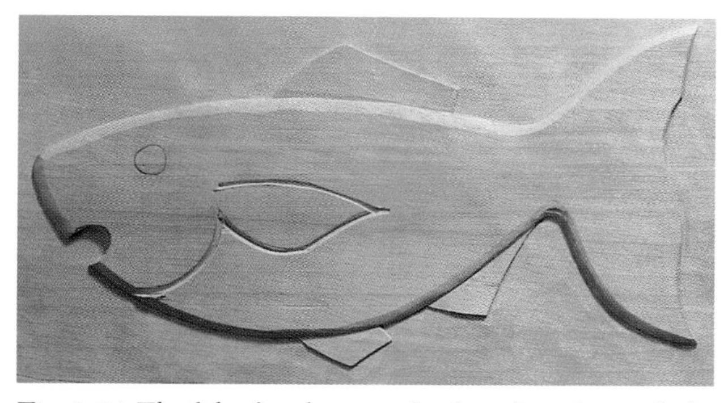

Fig 4.54 *The fish after the outer fins have been lowered, the body edges rounded over, and the gill and side fin lined in.*

Fig 4.55 *Lowering what is now the 'ground' around the fin and gill.*

Fig 4.56 *Smoothing over the body around the fin with a flat gouge. The gouge cannot get further into the angle without damaging the walls.*

5 Now set in the gill and side fin using flat gouges and the slicing technique. Run the cut into the corner between gill and fin (Fig 4.57).

6 Clean up the ground around the gill and fin with flat gouges, switching to the skew chisel (Fig 4.58) for the tight corner.

Having isolated and defined the side fin and gill, we can turn to modelling (shaping) the whole body of the fish.

This will result in final, finished surfaces: sharp tools are needed to leave fresh, clean cuts with no tears or rough snail tracks. Although the wood was originally planed, it is necessary to 'tool' the whole surface to keep a uniform appearance.

METHOD

No. 3 and No. 6 GOUGES AS NECESSARY

1 Using the largest flat gouge possible, pick up from the work done around side fin and gill and skim over the body of the fish, carving in the same way as you levelled the background (Fig 4.59). Be sensitive to the form of the fish as you shave wood away.

2 Reverse the gouge so that the rounded-over edges can be carefully merged with the main body of the fish (Fig 4.60). These edges should not look chamfered, or bevelled.

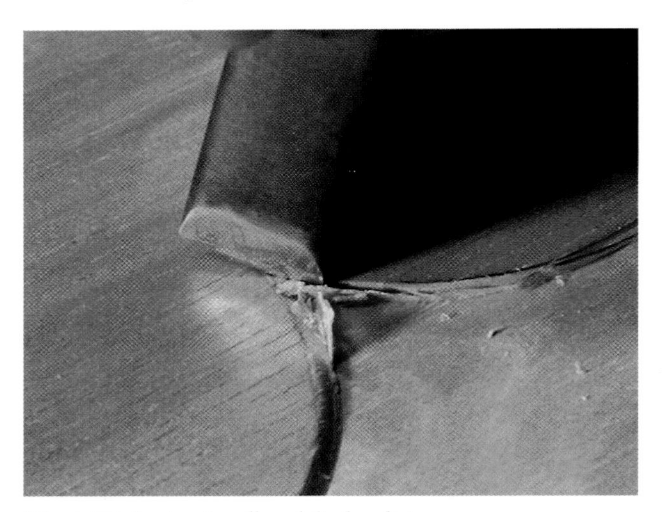

Fig 4.57 *Setting in gill and fin by slicing.*

Fig 4.59 *Marry in the ground around the fin with the rest of the body to keep a uniform appearance.*

Fig 4.58 *After cleaning up the junctions, finish off the angle with the skew chisel.*

Fig 4.60 *When you come to the rounded-over edges, reverse the gouge so that you can merge the body in, eliminating any traces of the hard chamfering which can be seen to the left of the picture.*

3 Switch to a medium gouge and hollow the gill (Fig 4.61). By 'kicking up' its edge, the gill is made lighter and the head of the fish given more character. Cut cleanly, taking the grain into account, and merge with the rest of the head, using the flat gouge inverted to match the form as necessary.

Fig 4.61 *Hollowing the gill lifts ('kicks up') the edge and adds variety by contrast with the rounded form of the body as a whole.*

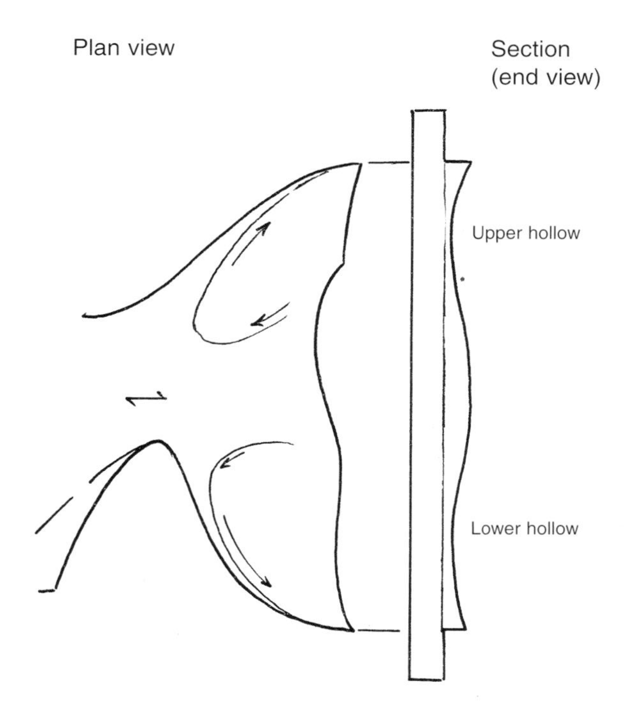

Fig 4.62 *The hollowing of the tail, seen in both plan view and end view.*

4 Your tail can be a variety of shapes; Fig 4.62 shows my design. Hollow the tail as you did with the gill (Fig 4.63), but leave the top and bottom edges strong. Create some variation by leaving the middle part of the tail unhollowed. To avoid leaving torn grain, you will need to reverse direction to merge in the two sides of the hollow where they meet at their lowest point (Fig 4.64).

5 Work your way all over the fish until all of it – body, head, gill and tail – has been modelled.

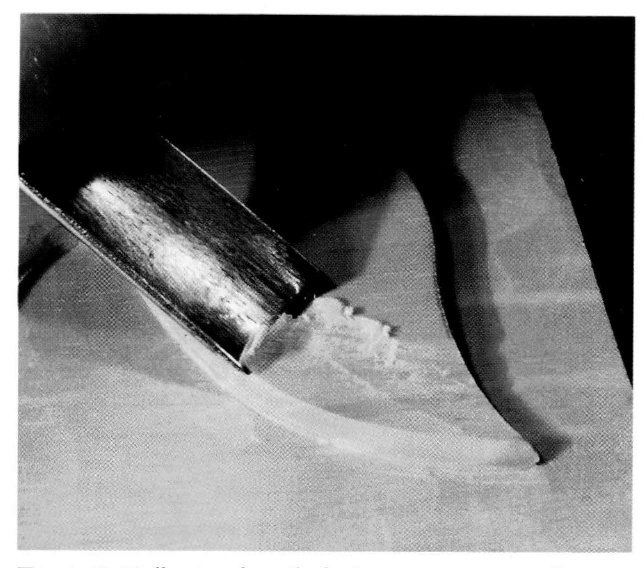

Fig 4.63 *Hollowing the tail: don't just scoop it out all over, give it a variety of form. Note how the right side of the cut in this picture shows fibres cut against the grain.*

Fig 4.64 *Now reverse the direction to work this side of the hollow with the grain.*

When this primary shaping is finished, your fish should have a similar appearance to Fig 4.65. The form of the fish is present, but it has a slightly naked look because all the decorative details are missing. The lines should be flowing and the parts distinct and logical. The carved surfaces of both fish and ground should be clean.

This standard is just normal – but good – carving. Remember that the purpose of this fish project is to learn, and to practise, so that these techniques can be applied to your own later work. Try for the best you can manage.

Fig 4.65 *The fish is beginning to take shape. Keep your cutting as clean as possible right from the beginning and there will be little need for a 'cleaning up' stage.*

5 Detailing

The next stage is to put in details, with some selective undercutting. This stage is often not distinct from the previous one, as many details could actually be said to be modelling: fluting the fins and tail, for example.

Begin with the fins.

METHOD

No. 9 x 1/4in (6mm) DEEP GOUGE
No. 3 x 1/4in FLAT GOUGE; V-TOOL

Because the grain runs in opposite directions you will need to deal with each side of the flute separately, merging these cuts at the bottom of the flute – good practice in handling grain! The sharper the tools and the more dense the wood, the cleaner the result.

1 Use the small deep gouge. You may like to draw in the flutes lightly with a pencil first.

2 Do not try to deal with the whole flute in one cut unless it is immediately obvious you have the grain lying in your favour. Take a first cut *with* the grain, and *narrower* than the final flute width, along one side of the flute (Fig 4.66). Then reverse direction and come back with the grain along the other side. You may need to coax the flute into shape if the grain is awkward.

Fig 4.66 *Adding flutes to the fins.*

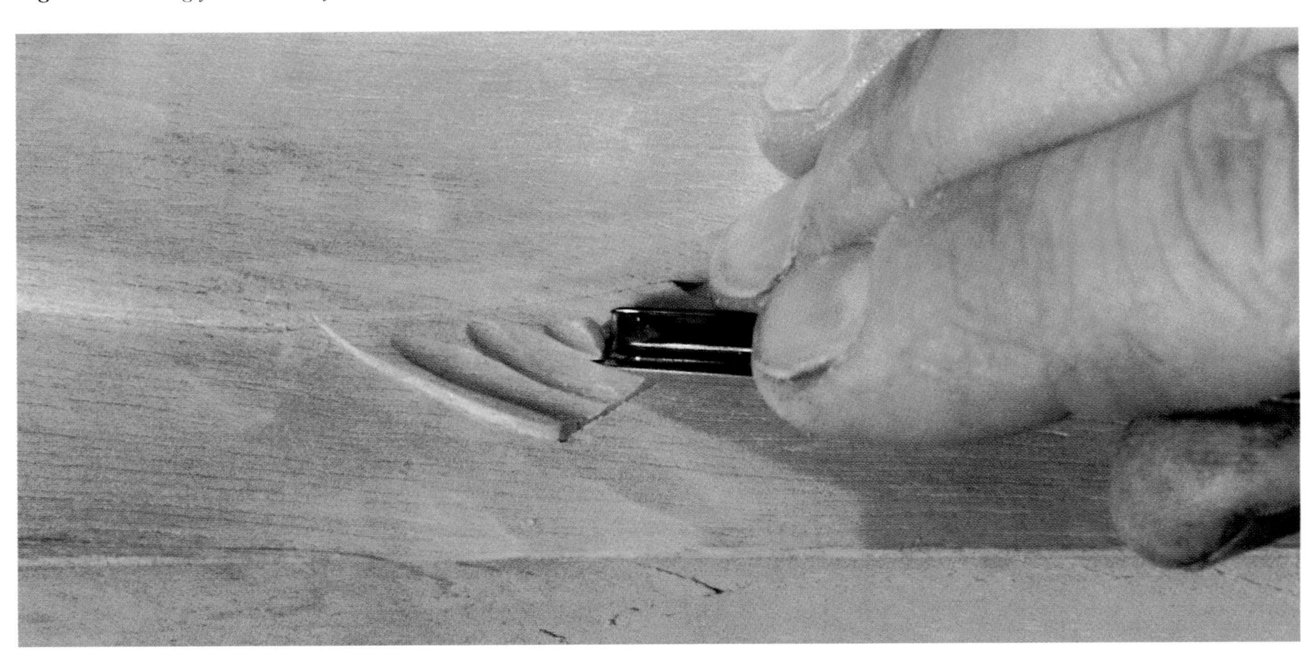

3 Create a series of flutes in this manner in one fin, then turn to flute all the other fins before moving on to the next stage.

4 Use the same gouge to set in the ends of the flutes (Fig 4.67). Bring the cut down to the background surface, but don't stab the ground more deeply than can be subsequently cleaned up.

5 Switch to a flat gouge to clean up the ground to the ends of the fins (Fig 4.68).

6 Use the V-tool on its side to undercut the sides of the fins (Fig 4.69), taking care not to make the edges too thin or lower the background in its immediate vicinity (see Chapter 6, pages 122–5).

The thinned, 'kicked-up' edge has the effect of making the fins look lighter. By contrast, the rounding over of the body edges makes the body more massive.

7 The flutes on the side fin can simply fade away as they come together. The ends of these, too, can be set in carefully.

Turn now to the tail.

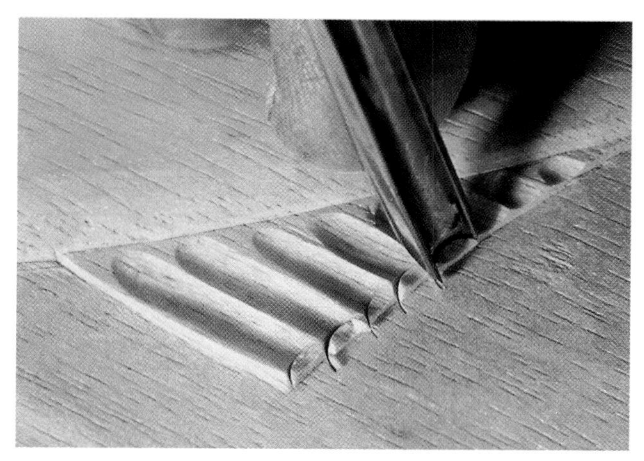

Fig 4.67 *Setting in the ends of the fin flutes. Don't stab deeper into the ground than you intend to clean up.*

Fig 4.68 *Finishing the ground around the fin.*

Fig 4.69 *A little undercutting is possible with a tilted V-tool.*

METHOD

No. 9 x 1/2in (13mm) DEEP GOUGE
No. 3 x 1/4in (6mm) FLAT GOUGE; V-TOOL

This is the same as the fluting of the fins, only writ larger. Again it is good practice at working with regard to the grain.

1 Using the deep gouge, work one side of the flute first, cutting with the grain; then the opposite side in the reversed direction (Figs 4.70 and 4.71).

   Again you can see the value of being able to switch hands.

2 You may need to make several light passes in order to finish off the flute cleanly, replacing ragged cuts with clean edges. Try for flowing lines over the tail; but to create more interest you may leave some plain areas in the middle for variation.

3 Use the same gouge to set in the ends of the flutes, taking care not to stab into the background (Fig 4.72).

4 Switch to a flat gouge to clean up the background to the ends of the tail flutes (Fig 4.73).

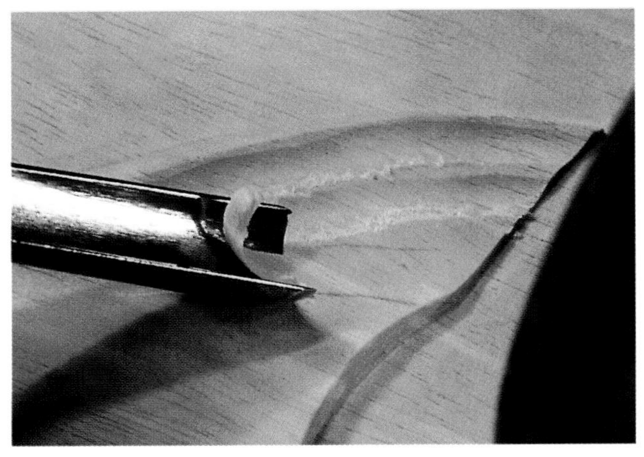

Fig 4.70 *Fluting the tail. Note the torn surface where the upper side of the gouge cuts against the grain. Don't make the initial cuts too deep, and work from the centre of each flute first.*

Fig 4.72 *Setting in the flute ends. Be careful not to stab too deep.*

Fig 4.71 *Reversing the direction of the gouge to clean the torn grain and shape the flute.*

Fig 4.73 *Cleaning the ground around the end of the tail.*

5 The V-tool can be used to undercut the unfluted part of the tail, giving the same lighter effect as with the fins (Fig 4.74).

The fins and tail are now completed and we can turn to the eye.

Fig 4.74 *Some quick undercutting of the tail is possible with a tilted V-tool.*

METHOD

NO. 9 X 1/2IN (13MM) DEEP GOUGE
NO. 6 X 1/2IN MEDIUM GOUGE
NAIL WITH FLATTENED POINT
SKEW CHISEL IF NECESSARY

Here is a simple way to carve the eye. Because low relief carving is essentially very flat, I think a flat eye best. It can be rounded over and made to appear a little more bulbous if you wish, as in the high relief carving. I suggest you practise these particular eye cuts many times on a spare piece of wood first.

1 Using the pen and dagger grip, rotate the no. 9 x 1/2in (13mm) deep gouge to make a circular cut around the eye (Fig 4.75).

   This is a sweep cut, as described in Chapter 3, page 33. The trick is to keep the leading corner clear of the wood and let this semicircular gouge dictate the direction; don't try to follow the pencil line.

2 Switch to a no. 6 x 1/2in (13mm) gouge and slice a circular cut around the eye, at an angle (Fig 4.76). Take it in careful light cuts at first. You may need to repeat both cuts in order to get a neat circular trench.

3 I used the flattened point of a nail to punch in a pupil to the eye (Fig 4.77). This sometimes fails because the fibres crush rather than punch down cleanly. Try it on spare wood first. If it is unsatisfactory, create the pupil by nicking out a triangular chip of wood with the point of the skew chisel.

Fig 4.75 *Sweeping around the eye. Let the tool do the work.*

Fig 4.76 *An angled cut to remove a shallow circular trench which defines the eye.*

Fig 4.77 *A flat-ended nail used as a punch is a simple way to form a pupil. Test on a spare piece of wood first, as with less dense grain the fibres might not crush neatly.*

The eye is now finished. The last piece of surface decoration is to put scales on the fish.

I suggest that instead of covering the whole fish with scales you apply them in discrete areas, rather as if the sunlight was dappling the body. Always in carving design we are looking for ways to introduce variation and interest. Similarly, if you have the range of tools you can create scales of differing sizes, with the smallest towards the tail and body edges.

METHOD

No. 9 x 1/4in (6mm) DEEP GOUGE

1 Use the small deep gouge in the pen and dagger grip. In hard wood you may need a mallet.

2 Angle the gouge so that the corners go in deepest and the centre of the cutting edge only lightly. The outside bevel must be approximately vertical.

3 Cut the first scale by simply stabbing in the gouge and pulling it out again.

4 Each row of scales is staggered with respect to the next (Fig 4.78). Do not rush: place your scales carefully. Try not to cut into the scale above as you push in.

5 Work irregular patches of scales wherever you think fit. Those in Fig 4.1 are a very light effect; you could stab them in more strongly.

The fish itself is now finished. Change the lighting and check one last time for torn grain or lines which could be improved – but try not to fiddle, as this will only lose the freshness of the carving. Better a few faults and a fresh look to the piece than an immaculate carving which has been overworked. Don't let this be an excuse, however!

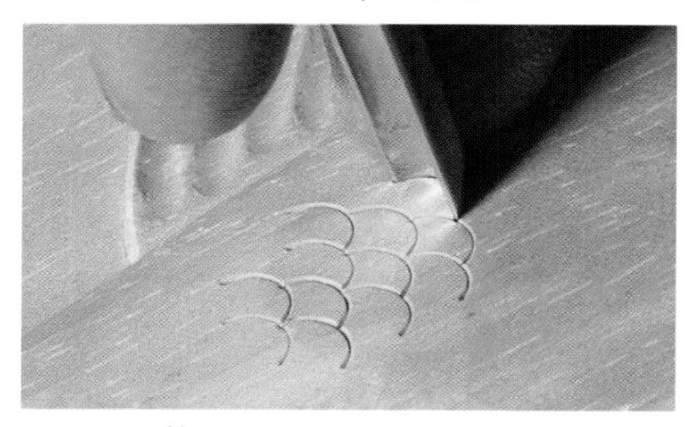

Fig 4.78 *Stabbing with a quick gouge to create scales.*

6 Background

We can now turn to final background details – if you want to put them in. Most students don't, but, in design terms, they serve to anchor the fish in space and add more interest.

METHOD

No. 9 x 1/4in (6mm) DEEP GOUGE
V-TOOL; SKEW CHISEL

1 The background is a finished surface, and drawing and erasing will only make it dirty. Lightly and simply draw in your details from the drawing. Bubbles you can place by eye.

2 Bubbles can be simply made by scoring the surface with a small no. 9 gouge, sweep-cutting in the manner in which the eye was outlined (Fig 4.79). You can change the strength of cut to vary the definition of the bubbles.

3 The lines of the reeds can be sketched in with the V-tool, nicking off the ends of the cuts with the skew chisel (Fig 4.80).

Fig 4.79 *Sweep cut stabbed into the background with a quick gouge to make bubbles.*

Fig 4.80 *Using the V-tool to 'draw' reeds into the background. Make sure they pass logically behind the fish.*

With the background, carving work is done. Congratulations! – especially if this is your first carving.

Last of all we need to 'finish' the carving, in the sense of sealing and protecting it.

7 Finishing

The simplest way to seal the carving is with clear shellac (also known as French polish or button polish). This you can usually get from hardware shops, or, failing that, one of the suppliers listed on pages 156–8. Clean brushes with methylated spirits (denatured alcohol). After the shellac, thin beeswax will enhance the surface with a sheen.

Further information on finishing can be found in my book *Woodcarving Tools, Materials & Equipment*.

METHOD

1. Shake the polish (shellac) container first and pour a little into another container for use.
2. Apply it thinly and evenly over the carving, including the sides of the wood, with a clean, soft brush (Fig 4.81). The back can be dealt with later and separately.
3. The shellac dries very quickly. In, say, 10 minutes you can give the carving a second coat.
4. When the front and sides are dry, seal the back in the same way.
5. Apply beeswax only to the front and sides of the carving. Wax on the back can leave greasy marks if you hang it on the wall, and you will not be able to write on the back. Rub on the thin beeswax with a cotton rag (Fig 4.82). A toothbrush is useful for crevices.
6. Rub off the excess beeswax and polish up with a cloth. Leave for 24 hours, then burnish with a stiff brush (Fig 4.83).

Fig 4.81 *Brushing on clear shellac.*

Fig 4.82 *Thin wax polish rubbed on …*

Fig 4.83 *… then burnished with a stiff brush.*

HANGING THE CARVING

Figure 4.84 shows a small selection of fittings, available from do-it-yourself or hardware shops, which are suitable for hanging carvings with – even much heavier ones than ours.

If, like me, you have carved this low relief from a thick block of wood and then sliced off the unused part, the resulting carving and background may be a lot thinner than you thought. So do remember that any pins or screws have to go into the thicker part of the wood – that is, the fish's body.

A very light carving may not need screws: some students have successfully used self-adhesive pads to fix hangers. Another has Velcroed hers to the wall – again with self-adhesive pads.

Two-part epoxy glue may be used instead of screws to attach fixings to a light carving such as this. Roughen the wood first and make sure the glue is *fully* cured and hard before hanging – otherwise the weight of the wood will cause the glue to 'creep' and the fixing plate to detach itself, disastrously, from the carving.

If the design of subsequent relief carvings is such that most of the thick wood is to one side, the centre of gravity will be thrown to that side too. The hanger must then be offset to compensate if the carving is to hang level. If in doubt, balance your carving on a thin edge and mark on each side of the carving the place where it balances. A line joining these two points along the back of the wood will show you where the centre line of gravity lies.

SIGNING

Yes, you should! Sign it in pen on the back and date it. There is only ever one first carving.

With this the carving is truly finished (see Fig 4.1 on page 43). Even if you are unhappy with your first attempt at woodcarving, what you have achieved is still of immense value: the most important step in any journey is the first one. As I repeat often to students, this project is not so much a carving as a means of learning carving skills. Whatever the fish looks like you will have learned something; and in this it is important to rejoice. There is nothing to stop you doing a second fish – you will find it *much* quicker as you consolidate and deepen your skills.

Fig 4.84 *Fittings for hanging relief carvings: the round escutcheon plate (left) should ideally be set flush with the wood surface. Check the available depth of wood, as well as the centre of gravity of a carving, before fixing.*

Summary

Here is a list of just *some* of the skills and techniques which you have been practising in this low relief fish project and which you will find you use again and again in future woodcarving.

- Understanding how fibres make up 'grain', and learning to work with them.
- The process of simple low relief carving: the ordering of stages and how one stage forms the basis for the next.
- The V-tool: handling it and cutting even grooves: using it in a tilted fashion for undercutting.
- Lining in, both around and within a low relief subject.
- Grounds: how they appear either as true backgrounds, or as grounds within a subject.
- Grounding out: how to lower and level a surface; the importance of methodical working.
- Setting in, in various ways: slicing and matching; how to marry cuts; how to create neat junctions; controlling the depth of cut.
- Modelling: creating form; the essential flatness of low relief; main shape before details; fluting.
- Simple undercutting and its effect when opposed to rounding over.
- Decorating a surface with tool-cuts.
- The skew chisel: stopping V-cuts; using the point to clean into recesses.
- Flat gouges: using them for setting in; slicing cuts for creating smooth, clean surfaces, straight from the cutting edge.
- Deeper gouges: handling them to remove wood quickly; sweep cuts to form circles.
- Manipulation of carving tools in general: slicing and sweeping.
- Probably nothing about fish.

CHAPTER FIVE

HIGH RELIEF CARVING PROJECT

When you have completed this project in high relief carving (Fig 5.1) you will have repeated many of the skills and techniques found in the low relief carving, and practised a number of new ones. Together, these skills will enable you to tackle a wide range of woodcarving, and to your own design.

As before, I have listed *some* of these carving skills at the end of the chapter, but again I ask you to forget about any lists for now. The fish exercise will demonstrate these basic woodcarving skills and allow you to start practising them.

Remember that the subject is not important, more a means to an end. New skills can be hard going at first: just relax and try your best. Woodcarving is potentially an extremely rewarding craft, and I hope some of the rewards come quickly.

GETTING READY TO START

The set-up, including the tools, for this high relief is the same as that for the low relief fish carving in Chapter 4. If you are using the fence and wedge system of holding – as I am here – check that the fences and wedges, or at least those on the near working side, lie *below* the depth line; this is lower than for the low relief. Otherwise the fences will get in the way of the carving tools as the background is removed.

Fig 5.1 *Completed high relief fish, using the same drawing as for the low relief.*

DRAWING THE FISH

I am using exactly the same drawing for both high and low relief carvings – this makes for a very instructive comparison and I suggest you do the same with your own design. The working drawing will be found on page 45. If you prefer to draw a fresh subject, follow the same composition guidelines as before (pages 45–6). As the ground will be cut away from beneath the fins and tail, it is even more important that you pay attention to running long grain into these elements to keep them strong.

In this carving I have not included any details in the background, such as reeds. There is a lot to think of and usually I suggest students keep the background plain in this exercise.

BACKGROUND DEPTH

The depth to which the background will be reduced in this high relief is about 3/4in (18–20mm). Score a depth line using the marking gauge as before (see page 47).

CARVING

In the previous low relief work there was little wood to remove – a few millimetres brought us to the background, and the mallet was hardly necessary. Here we have a lot more, bearing in mind that you remove a larger *cubic* volume for every linear step in depth.

You *could* use the same technique as before: lining in and lowering, repeated until the required level was reached. But this would be a time-consuming and inefficient way of carving. With so much more wood to remove, more dramatic – and some students have said 'drastic' – measures are needed.

In high relief the mallet (page 13) is practically essential for tackling preliminary rough work: it saves a lot of time, beginners find it easier on hands and wrists, and most students find it satisfyingly noisy.

As with the low relief carving, I approach the project in a step-by-step, progressive, manner. It is very helpful in the beginning to work with a set order of doing things. As your competence and confidence in carving grow you will adopt more flexible approaches, going more directly to the form you want, and more quickly. This is highly desirable and depends on practice developing your mind's eye. But for now we will work sequentially.

The stages in this high relief of our fish are:

1 **Lowering:** removing the background quickly, introducing buffer zones so that we can work both vigorously and safely.

2 **Rough setting in:** getting a rough outline of the fish.

3 **Levelling:** finishing the main part of the background and completing the grounding stage.

4 **Rough shaping:** also known as **bosting** – sketching in the main form of the fish.

5 **Setting in:** truing up the outline.

6 **Modelling:** in which secondary forms are introduced.

7 **Undercutting:** selectively 'backing off' and finishing the background where it passes beneath the edges of the fish.

8 **Detailing:** adding the final details and decorative touches.

9 **Finishing:** after the carving is completed, the fish is signed, sealed and hung.

> Please read through the instructions carefully before beginning any section, as there are usually several points to juggle with at the same time!

1 Lowering

The object is to carve away the background waste as quickly as possible.

We will reduce the waste by a certain uniform amount or level at a time. Stonecarvers sometimes refer to this lowering-by-levels as working in **lifts**. I think 'lift' is a very good term and I shall borrow it here; it points to a certain relativeness: when the background is lowered by a level, so the subject is apparently raised or 'lifted'.

Working by regular lifts is unashamedly systematic. There are other ways of working, of course, but in my experience this one reduces a deep ground quickest. Although it may seem formal, it is a very professional approach and one with which beginners feel comfortable.

So we begin with the first level or lift:

METHOD

No. 9 x 3/4in (19mm)
DEEP GOUGE and MALLET

Lift 1

We will be cutting away wood quite vigorously in this early stage and there is a danger of chopping straight into the fish. To avoid this, we draw in a 'buffer zone'; you needn't draw it if you can imagine it.

Deal with one half of the carving, then the other, turning the fish round.

1 Start by drawing the buffer zone as a prominent line 1/8in (3mm) *outside* the outline of the fish, using something like a red crayon. Make the line simple and clearly visible, ironing out recesses where the gouge is too large to enter (Figs 5.2 and 5.3).

2 Hold the gouge as described for mallet work (Chapter 3, page 25). Work *across* the grain: the orientation of the gouge to the wood is the same as in the lowering stage of low relief (page 51).

Fig 5.3 *Starting the first lowering cut, working in from the edge. The red line defines the 'buffer zone' at which the cut will stop.*

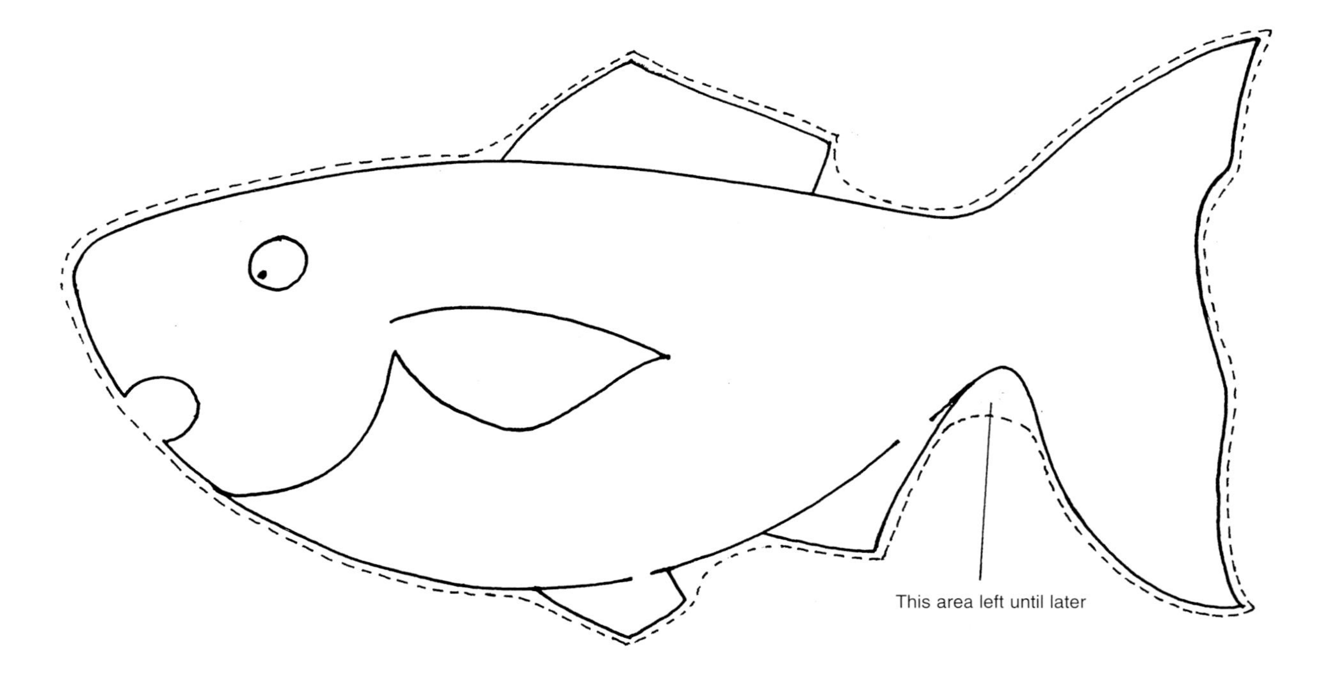

Fig 5.2 *The 'buffer zone' can be drawn or imagined; it evens out the profile and protects the fish from vigorous gouge work.*

3 Place the cutting edge of the gouge on the side of the wood, with its corners clear of the surface.

Keeping the corners clear limits the depth of cut and prevents uncontrolled tearing of the wood. For a deeper cut a larger tool is desirable (Fig 5.4).

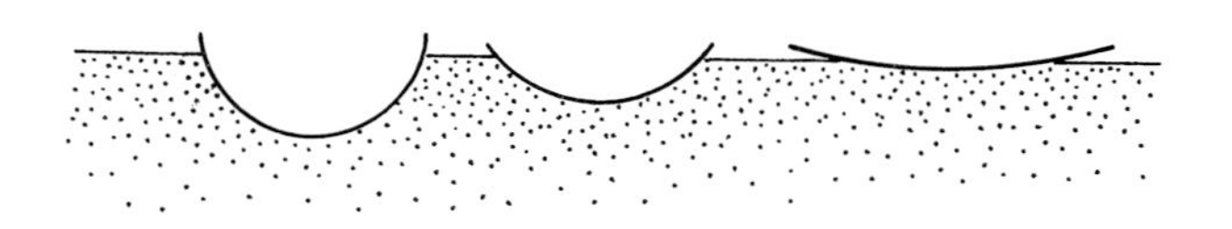

Fig 5.4 *Keeping the corners clear is a good rule for clean carving; deeper cuts need deeper, or 'quicker', gouges.*

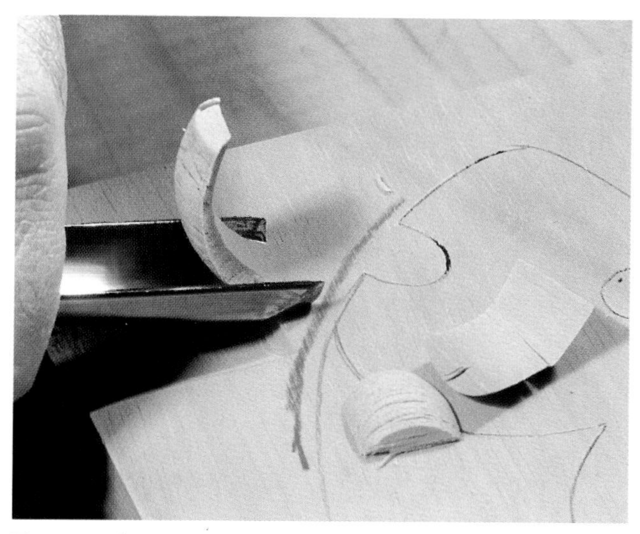

Fig 5.5 *The cut continues at a uniform depth straight across the grain, corners clear.*

4 Using the mallet, run in a first groove parallel to the surface, up to the red-line buffer zone; then stop and remove the gouge (Fig 5.5).

5 Run a second groove alongside the first and parallel to it, running it up to the red line and stopping.

6 Lay down deep parallel furrows of equal depth, always stopping short of the fish, and working from one end of the carving to the other. Think 'level'. At either end of the wood you can run your cut towards the far side (Fig 5.6), but stop short a quarter of the way from the far edge, to avoid breaking out (see page 29).

7 When you have been along the whole of the near side of the fish you will have completed the first lift on this side.

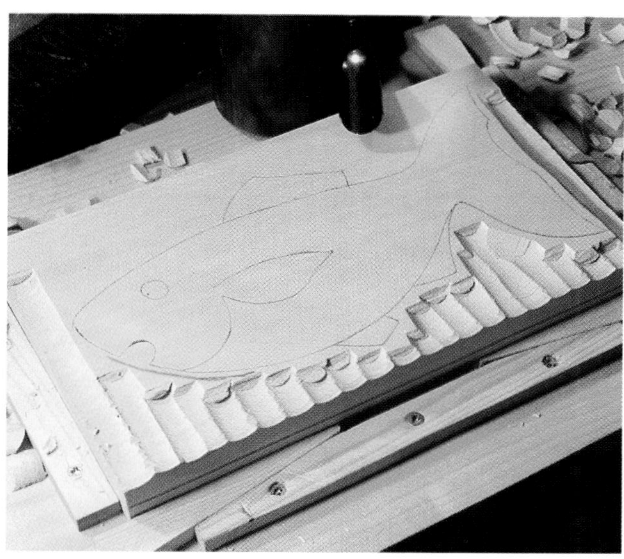

Fig 5.6 *Cut as far as possible, but always stopping short of the far side at each end. Note the depth of the first 'lift', and how the grooves stop short of the buffer zone.*

Figure 5.7 shows the result after the first lift is finished on one half of the fish. The same 'ploughed' effect was seen in the lowering of the low relief background.

As before, consistent depth of cut is evident from the uniform width of cut. I repeat: it is important to work methodically even at this early stage.

The furrows stop short of the fish. Because you are deliberately working *across* the grain the shavings break away easily and you needn't worry about grain direction.

Fig 5.7 *First lift completed on first half of the fish: uniform, methodical cutting.*

METHOD

TOOLS AS BEFORE

Lift 2

1 Start in the same way with mallet and gouge. This time place the cutting edge of the gouge *between the troughs of the first lift*, so as to remove the crests of the first set of cuts with the second (Fig 5.8).

2 Using the mallet, cut across evenly – keeping the corners clear of the wood – and stop when you reach the buffer zone.

3 Place the gouge for the next cut and create a second furrow in the same way.

4 Repeat along the wood, from end to end, leaving an even series of furrows (Fig 5.9) and a more prominent untouched area immediately around the fish.

This completes the second lift on this half of the fish.

The reduced ground should still be parallel to the original surface, and must always appear so. As with the low relief, the lowering stage is the groundwork for the subsequent levelling.

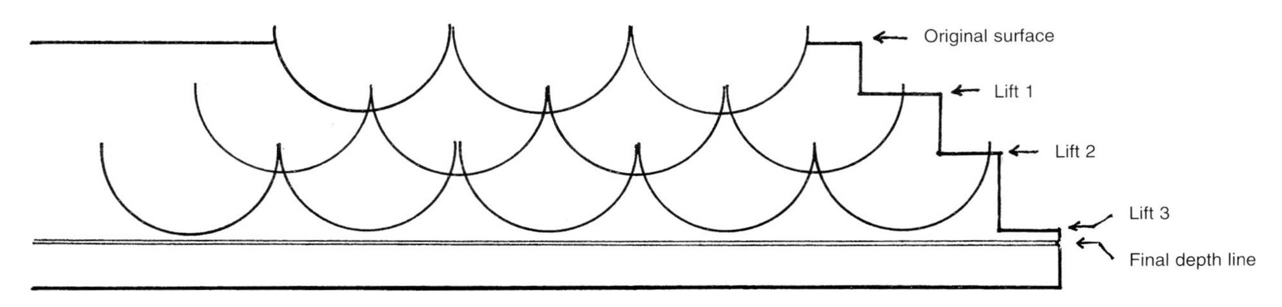

Fig 5.8 *Reducing a ground by levels or 'lifts': stagger each lift with respect to the previous one for quickest waste removal.*

Fig 5.9 *Cut the second lift in the same manner as the first, staggering the cuts with the first lift and having a sense of 'ploughing up' the ground.*

METHOD

TOOLS AS BEFORE

Lift 3

1 Cut the next lift, again by positioning the grooves halfway over those of the previous level, and stop each cut before the fish.

It is not necessary to follow the red line of the buffer zone exactly – use it as a guide.

2 It is best to finish one complete lift at a time, ploughing from one end of the wood to the other. You will see the ground reducing quickly and uniformly. Stop at what you estimate to be about half a lift above the depth line (Figs 5.10 and 5.11).

Stopping short of the final depth gives us a second buffer zone, protecting the final background surface.

3 Turn the fish around and repeat the process on the other side, again stopping half a lift above the depth line. It should become obvious why deep gouges are sometimes called 'quick'.

Figure 5.12 shows the sort of result you should have after this lowering stage: vigorous, even ploughing, stopping safely short of the subject. The ends of the furrows will look square and broken off. The lowering stops short of the depth for now, allowing us to outline the fish roughly without fear of damaging the background.

2 Rough setting in

Here we trim back as much of the buffer zone around the fish as we can; the object is to outline the subject roughly, easing us into the next stages.

Notice that the first tool we use is the same as that used in the previous stage. It would be more usual to finish the rough setting in on one half of the fish – while using the same tool – *before* turning the work around. Turning the fish around is 'down time' for tools: no actual carving is undertaken. As a rule, work to reduce down time as much as possible. However, for this exercise, the process of working is more easily seen if we work all round the fish.

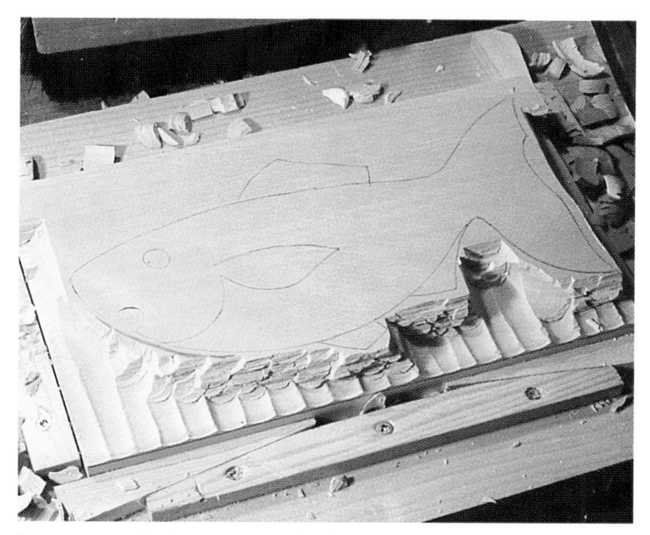

Fig 5.10 *The lowering of this half of the fish is now finished.*

Fig 5.11 *Side view showing the uniformity of cut, stopping just above the depth line marked with the gauge.*

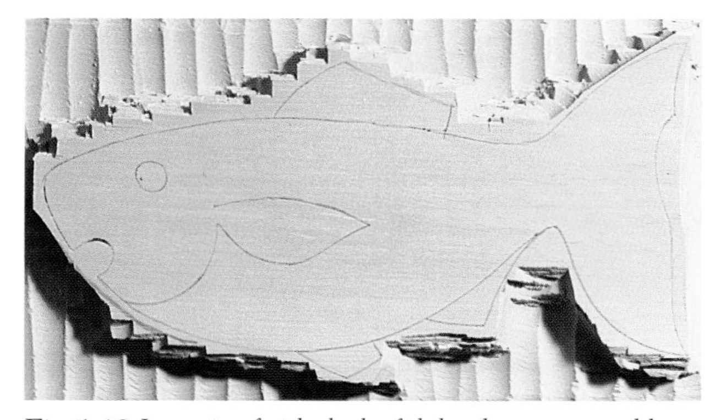

Fig 5.12 *Lowering finished: the fish has been protected by the zone of waste wood.*

Before beginning, let me remind you to refrain from three poor ways of carving:

- Don't pull off bits of wood – this tears the grain in an uncontrolled way and the fingering makes the wood dirty. Cut away chips cleanly and use your bench brush regularly to clear away waste.
- Don't scrape wood with the edge of the tool – this blunts the tools and tears the grain.
- Don't lever off bits of wood – this damages cutting edges and splits grain uncontrollably.

METHOD

TOOLS AS BEFORE

1 Offer the gouge upright to the surface of the fish, placing the cutting edge in the waste wood of the buffer zone with the corners clear. Note that the bevel tends to push the gouge forwards as it descends: this means that to come down truly vertically you have to lean the gouge outwards a little (Fig 5.13). It is the *bevel* which needs to be vertical.

2 Use the mallet to chop a vertical wall down to the waste at the ground (Fig 5.14).

3 Repeat the cut, using the gouge in the same way. You can stab into the ground a little because we deliberately left some waste wood – but do bear in mind where the ground will be, and err on the cautious side.

4 Work your way along the fish, including the tail, but leaving the mouth. Cut back the buffer zone but stop shy of the true and final outline of the fish.

5 Work into recesses as best you can; at the end you can switch to the no. 9 x 1/2in (13mm) to get in closer between the body and tail if you wish. Be careful working around weak parts such as the tips of the tail – 'nibble' rather than chop.

6 At the bottom of the vertical cuts – at the junction between wall and rough background – you will be left with a drift of waste wood (Fig 5.15). As a final action, and *without lowering the ground further*, clean away any bulky parts of this waste with a few horizontal ploughing cuts of the same tool. Don't bother with small corners of waste at the junction – they will be removed shortly.

7 Turn the fish round and repeat on the other side.

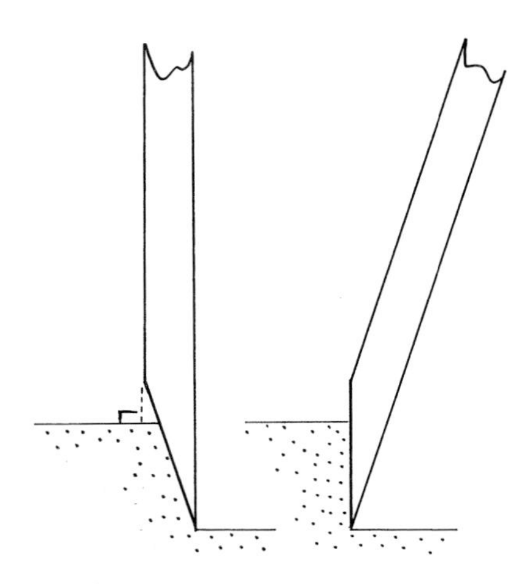

Fig 5.13 *The tool must be tilted outwards to set in vertically when the bevel is against the subject.* ***(A)*** *blade vertical, bevel cuts outwards;* ***(B)*** *bevel vertical, so wall will be vertical.*

Fig 5.14 *Trimming back some of the waste wood of the buffer zone.*

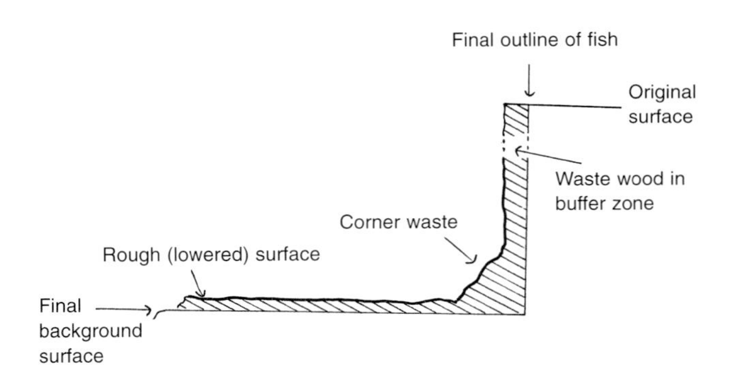

Fig 5.15 *Hold back the rough vertical and horizontal cuts to avoid stabbing into the ground or subject. The corner waste can simply be left for the time being.*

The result (Fig 5.16) will begin to reveal the fish in very rough outline with vertical walls, surrounded by coarse but disciplined furrows.

This stage is completed by quickly tidying up the outline and defining the fish a little more:

METHOD

NO. 3 x 3/4IN (19MM) FLAT GOUGE

1 Use the pen and dagger grip. You can use the mallet, but by putting your shoulder and weight behind the gouge you will find you can pare the soft wood away easily.

2 Orientate the gouge to match roughly the contour of the edge of the fish: either the inside of the gouge or the bevel will be vertical, as before.

3 Pare straight down into the ground waste (Fig 5.17).

4 Repeat the cut, merging it with its predecessor. Work along the fish, tidying the rough outline to something nearer the drawing of the fish. Bear in mind the following:

- Where there are points with weak grain – such as the tips of the fins – work from the point, *into* the mass of wood. If you work outwards the unsupported grain towards the tip will fracture and the point crumble.
- Where the outline forms an inner angle, use the corner of the gouge to cut and slice into it (Fig 5.18).
- Most importantly, take care not to cut beneath what will be the final background level.

5 When you have completed one side, turn the work around and clean up the wall of the fish on the opposite side.

The result will be an even clearer sense of the fish with the background unchanged (Fig 5.19). The high relief carving is now roughly set in and the background lowered.

It may be that you did cut into the outline, or broke the tip of the fin off. Don't worry, just alter the outline of the fish. It *would* matter if you were making two the same; in this case control over events is important!

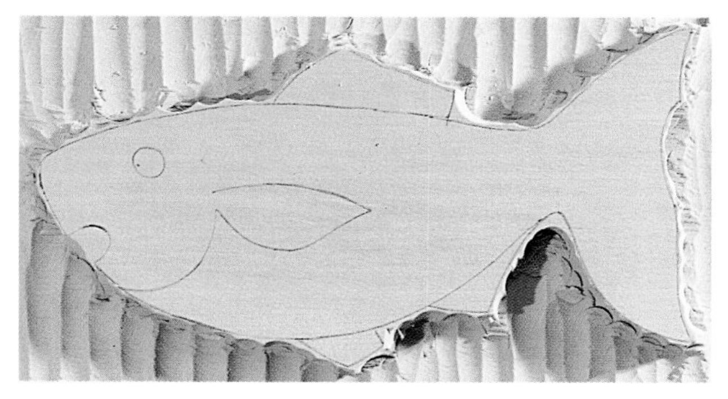

Fig 5.16 *The waste buffer zone has been trimmed back. It is not necessary to clean up the corner of waste left at the junction of fish and background at this stage.*

Fig 5.18 *... including the fins. Note how the short grain at the end of the fin tends to crumble; care is needed here.*

Fig 5.17 *Roughly setting in – trimming the outline of the fish to an appropriate working shape, ...*

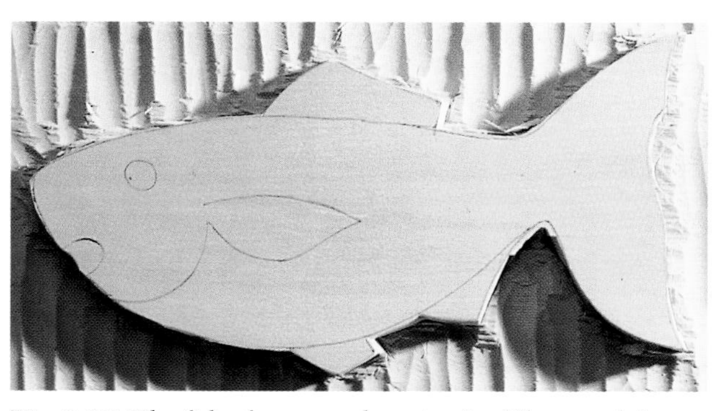

Fig 5.19 *The fish after a rough setting in. The mouth is untouched and stem of the tail only approximately outlined.*

3 Levelling

Turn now to cleaning up the background, leaving it smooth, lightly tooled and level over most of its surface as in the low relief carving. The wood immediately around the fish will remain a little rough until more accurate setting in later. The tool for this stage is the last one you used. Seeking efficiency (less down time), the background could have been levelled at the same time as the walls of the fish were pared to the rough outline.

The work here is more or less the same as in the low relief levelling, and indeed you should see this as another opportunity to practise this extremely important skill: finishing a smooth surface 'straight from the chisel'.

One difference from the low relief carving is that there is more waste to remove. We left wood to a depth of half a lift above the final surface level to protect it. You should not find this a problem, however – just keep working over the ground. If you think you have left it a bit too thick, you can save time by lowering the surface a bit more using the deep (or medium, no. 6) gouge again, without the mallet. End, as with the low relief, a shade above the depth line.

Additionally, we are not working up to a V-groove this time, and will need a small amount of vertical cutting to release shavings from immediately around the fish.

Use the large flat gouge where you can, and other gouges, as will be described, wherever necessary to match outline curves a little better.

METHOD

No. 3 x 3/4in (19mm)
also No. 9 x 3/4in and 1/2in (13mm)
No. 6 x 3/4in; No. 3 x 1/4in (6mm)

1 Start towards one end and work with slicing cuts (see Fig 4.14 on page 51), removing first the crests or the rough furrows in the background.

2 Return to where you started and work from the gauge line at the edge – which will disappear. Lower the background to its final depth as you level over the surface (Fig 5.20).

As the background is levelled, some waste will remain like so much flotsam washed up against the walls of the fish.

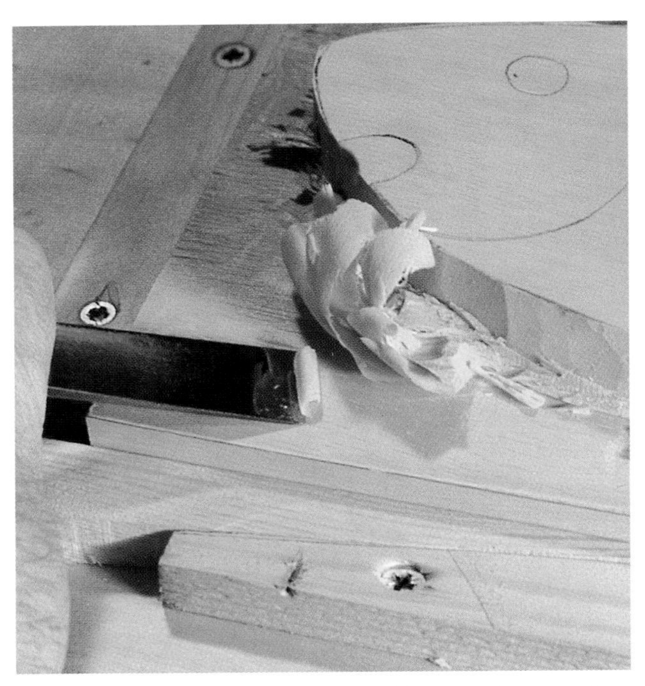

Fig 5.20 *Levelling the background. The waste is 'pushed' towards the fish, ...*

Because you took the trouble to keep the background flat as you lowered it, you should find it relatively easy to maintain a sense of flatness. Bear in mind the following advice:

- Work methodically.
- Don't bury the gouge corners in the wood.
- Be aware of the lie of the wood fibres – the grain – and change direction straight away if your cut tears.
- Clean up as you go along, policing what are now areas of finished carving.
- As you pare away the wood, have a sense of 'pushing' the waste in front of you towards the fish (Fig 5.20).

3 Trim vertically down these walls, as you did for the rough setting in, to release these shavings (Fig 5.21). Leave the mouth for now. Try to meet the horizontal surface neatly. This may mean repeating the levelling cut carefully.

4 As you work the vertical cuts around the walls of the fish you can change tools so as to get a little nearer the outline in the tighter curves – around the stem of the tail in my case.

Fig 5.21 *... where it is trimmed off. Take care not to stab the background.*

5 Don't worry if the exact junction is not too neat; the corner itself will disappear wherever the fish is undercut. Above all, *try not to stab into the background*. If you do, then you will have to clean up to avoid the cut being seen; this may well mean lowering the ground further and spoiling the sense of flatness (see 'Rubber ground effect' on page 51).

The result (Fig 5.22) is the fish appearing to be cut out as the smooth background continues evenly from one side to the other. The outline of the fish is neat and its flowing lines preserved. This is still only an approximate setting in, but worth doing neatly as it gives us a better sense of the fish for the next stages.

Fig 5.22 *The fish when the grounding out stage is completed. The smoothly carved background is finished – no more work will be needed.*

This takes us to the end of the grounding out stage in the relief carving.

Describing the process by which we arrived at this point (ready to move on to the fish itself) seems to have taken a rather long time. Once you have grasped the process it is actually quite quick, especially with soft wood like jelutong. It is worth just summarizing the process before moving on.

Summary

- Cut straight into the background with a deep gouge, without lining in.
- Leave a buffer zone around the subject to protect it.
- Lower the background in lifts (consistent levels).
- Stop short of the background depth, leaving another protecting buffer zone.
- Use the deep gouge to trim back the first buffer zone to the subject.
- Switch to a flat gouge and tidy the subject outline.
- Level and finish the background with the flat gouge, up to the subject.
- Tidy the junction between ground and subject, taking care not to stab the ground.

Now we have the silhouette of our subject grounded out, we can begin to give the fish some form.

4 Rough shaping

In this rough shaping stage the main masses and planes will be established, laying the foundation for later more refined shapes and details.

Our fish is a simple high relief project: one subject, plain background. It will benefit from a simple treatment. Without being too technical about fish anatomy, one of the reasons I like the fish as a subject for these exercises is that one end is thick and the other thin. This gives us the chance to work with two basic sculptural forms: rounded (the lump of the body) and hollow (the edge of the tail).

The first thing I do before beginning the roughing stage of any carving is to stand back and think. I try to visualize what the main shapes of the carving will be like, sometimes imitating the form with my hands in the air over the subject. Do this. (If you have company you can make the effect even more weird by mumbling.) Most importantly, get a sense of:

- **High spots**: these are masses where little or no wood will be removed, and from which everything will flow 'downhill' into the subject. For example, in my fish (Fig 5.1) the high parts are along the centre of the body (from the gill to just beyond the end of the side fin); also the tips and centre of the tail.
- **Flow**: how one part actually runs and continues into another. For flow in my fish, look particularly at how the tail lifts up at its end; how the underside of the tail merges with the body; and how the body itself rolls gently away all around.
- **Planes**: which parts are separated, and at what levels. The gill and side fins in my fish are internal changes of plane; the other fins are set back on the outside; the eye bulges.

This stage of 'thinking' is very important. It is not true that 'you cannot carve wood back on again'; however, doing this is more advanced work than we are doing here, so get some idea of what you want your fish to look like before removing wood. Keep the fish simple.

We begin practical work, using my fish again as the model, by marking what I call the 'form horizon' – the point where the wood of a rounded subject turns away out of view like a hill before being undercut (see Chapter 6, pages 122–5).

This line is the outermost point of the relief carving – its outline three-dimensionally, as seen from a normal straight-on viewing position. All the vertical walls you have just roughly set in will be cleaned up and refined as the fish is modelled – hence our not bothering to make them too exact. The form line will eventually be removed.

METHOD

PENCIL

The concept of form horizon is illustrated in Fig 5.23.

1 Use your finger as a guide to the pencil.

2 Run a line along the edge of the fish about one third up from the background (Fig 5.24).

3 As you reach the tail, bring the line up to its tip (Fig 5.25). The fins will lie on this line (see Chapter 3, pages 41–2), and we turn to them next.

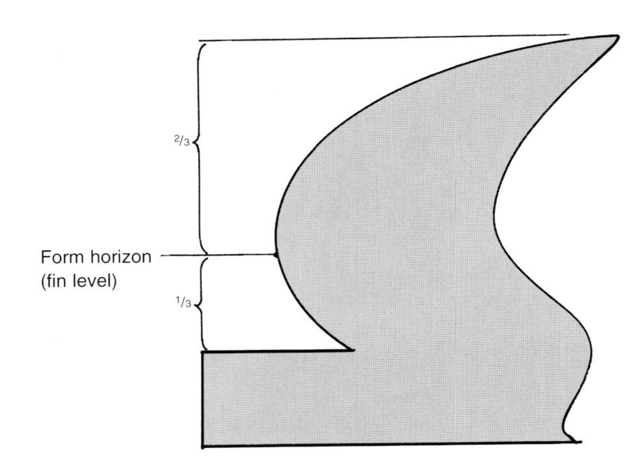

Fig 5.23 *The form horizon is a point over which a rounded form disappears – rather like a hill. Beneath it the wood will be undercut, somewhat sharper than the 'natural' line of the hill so as to give a stronger appearance of three dimensions.*

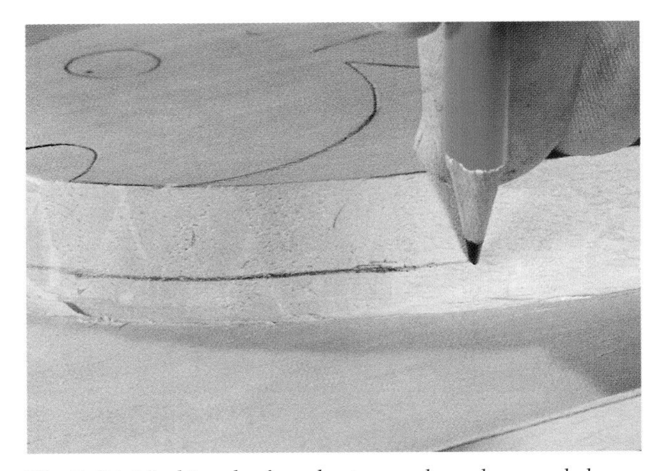

Fig 5.24 *Marking the form horizon, where the rounded body will disappear from view. Below this level the fish will be cut back to create more of a sense of three dimensions.*

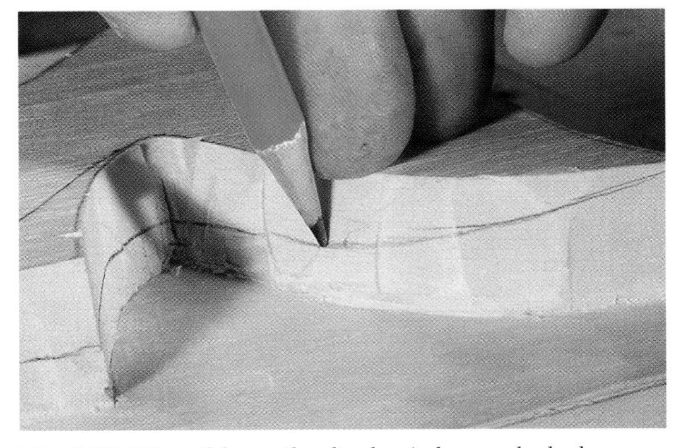

Fig 5.25 *The tail has a 'hard' edge (whereas the body is 'soft'), which rises up to the tip.*

OUTER FINS

METHOD

V-TOOL; No. 3 x 3/4in (19mm) FLAT GOUGE

The fin is lined in and lowered, as for low relief carving. This makes the fin waste wood until its level is reached.

1 Hold the V-tool in the low-angle grip.

2 Cut a V-groove on the fish surface on the fin side of the body line (Fig 5.26); tilt the V-tool away from the fish to leave a vertical wall at the body.

3 Repeat the cut until the root of the V lies at the depth line.

4 Use the flat gouge to reduce the fin to the correct depth (Fig 5.27). The V-tool groove will disappear.

An alternative approach to steps 3 and 4 is to line in with the V-tool, remove waste with the flat gouge, then line in again, repeating both steps until the required depth is reached.

5 Use the gouge vertically to dress the body line around the fish and tidy up the junction (Fig 5.28).

6 Reduce all the outside fins in the same way.

Figure 5.29 shows the result: the planes of the fins are now distinct from that of the body; the line of the body at top and bottom remains continuous.

Next we tackle the main shaping work, starting by rounding over the body towards the edges to give it some initial form.

Fig 5.26 *Parting the fin from the body with a V-tool.*

Fig 5.27 *Reducing the fin with a flat gouge.*

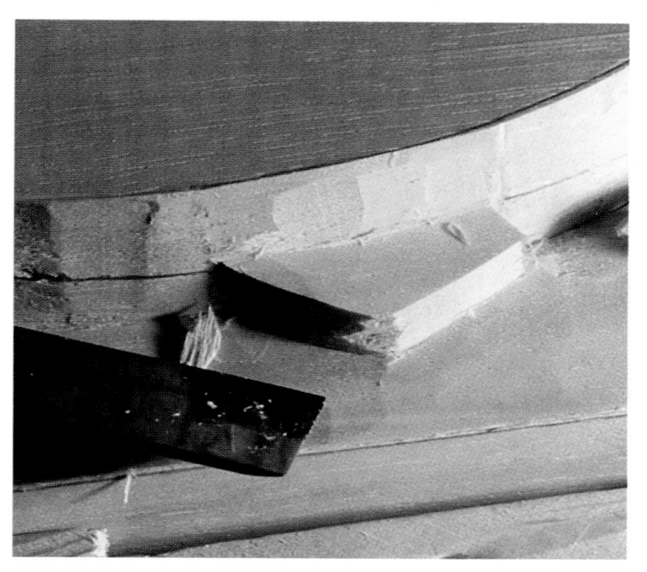

Fig 5.28 *The fin lowered to the line marked around the fish.*

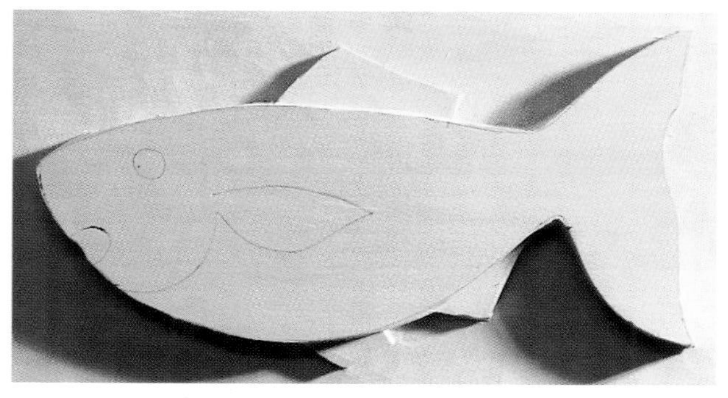

Fig 5.29 *Fish with fins cut back – although they are still not accurately set in at this stage.*

BODY

METHOD

No. 3 x 3/4in (19mm) FLAT GOUGE

1 Hold the gouge in the low-angle grip, 'upside down' so that the sweep or inner curve is orientated to the shape we wish to make – in this case, rounding over the edges.

2 Begin taking wood from the edges of the fish (Fig 5.30), working *with* the grain. If you have any doubts, this is essentially the direction taken by the V-tool in Fig 4.12 (page 50).

3 Work both sides of the fish body, towards the front, and back to the stem of the tail (Figs 5.31 and 5.32).

4 More wood is removed towards the base of the tail to give a more interesting shape. As the beginning of the tail is the narrowest part, so the body will lose most of its flatness in this area.

5 The rounding over should include the body next to the fins, finishing the body line and the junction with the fins smoothly and tidily.

6 Although you may start with large cuts which take off the main corners, have a feeling for the wood you will leave behind: the form of the fish beneath. Take the corners off the large cuts in turn, overlaying cuts to round the surface (Fig 5.33). Use different gouges to match the form of the body. A completely smooth surface can be had if you are able to match the curve of the gouge exactly to the shape you want to produce.

Fig 5.31 *The gouge is orientated in sympathy with the form that is required. Quite bold cuts can be taken.*

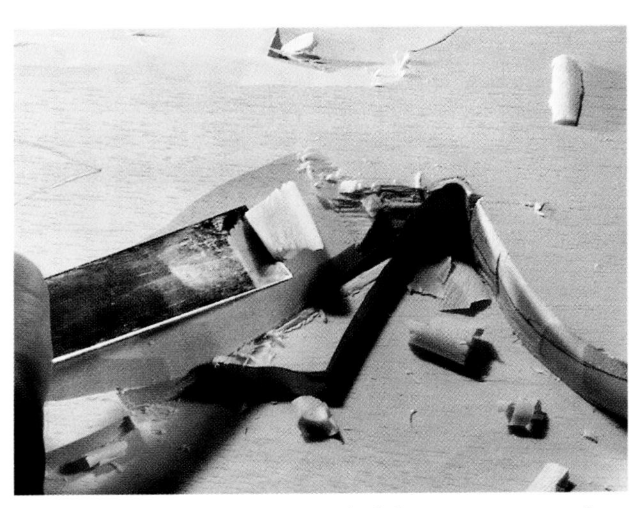

Fig 5.32 *As the tail stem is reached the gouge is reversed so as to take more away from the main mass and give this area some variety of form.*

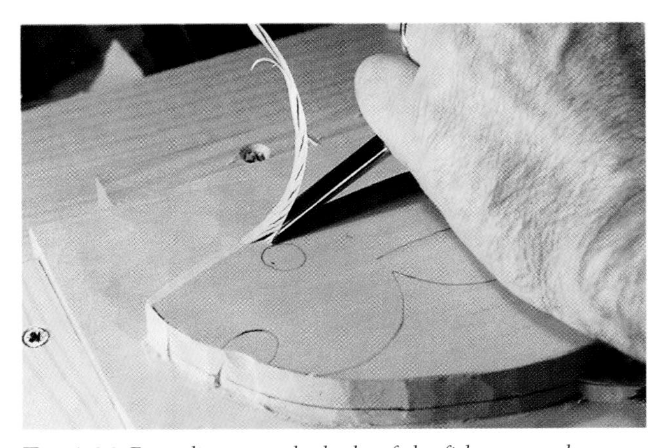

Fig 5.30 *Rounding over the body of the fish – enough to startle anyone!*

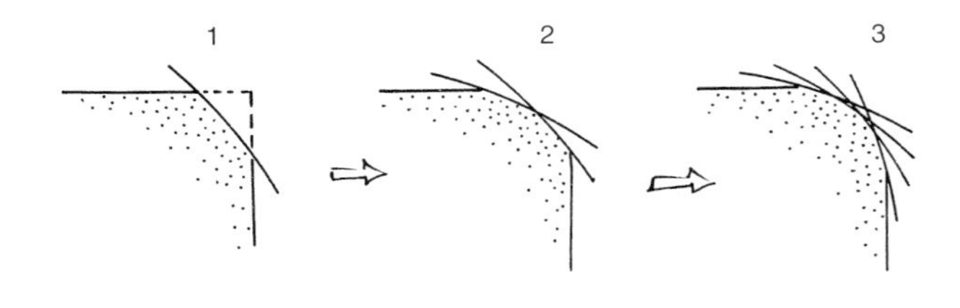

Fig 5.33 *A curve can be created by multiple flat cuts. It is best to pick a gouge which will do the work in as few cuts as possible, but overcarving is often necessary and may be the simplest way.*

7 Instead of making the fish symmetrical across its section, it is more interesting to make it a little more pear-shaped (Fig 5.34). To give the fish more of a 'belly', remove more wood from the top than the bottom.

8 Do *not* remove wood from where the eye will be, and leave the tail for the moment.

9 Do *not* round over the edge *below* the pencil line. Rather, come down to the line and pay a little attention to getting the outline of the fish smoother, even removing the pencil line if necessary.

The result (Fig 5.35) is that the body of the fish is rounded over and fuller, looking solid. Strong but flat tool facets are apparent on the wood surface, flowing along the form.

Just after this photograph was taken I took some more wood from the upper part of the fish to make it more potbellied.

You will need to carve away a substantial amount of wood to arrive at this look – the amount surprises many beginners. Try to remove the waste in confident, simple strokes of the gouge rather than picking away or fussing. Always keep in mind the form beneath.

From the body itself we can now turn to rough-shaping the tail. The rounded form of the body is relatively easy to handle. The tail, however, is hollow: the lie of the wood fibres presents a particular situation which is frequently met in woodcarving and causes students problems to begin with. Here we have a chance to tackle it.

Give some thought to the shape of the end of the tail before you carve (Fig 5.36).

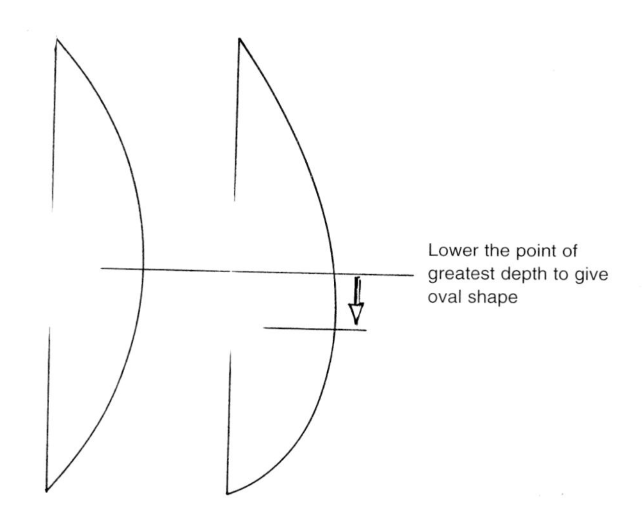

Fig 5.34 *Left: a fish symmetrical in section; right: a more interesting section with a bit of a 'belly'.*

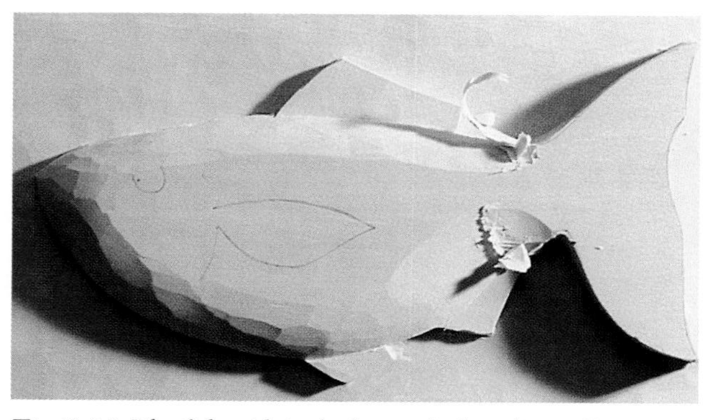

Fig 5.35 *The fish with its body roughed to shape. Removing wood around the tail stem also gives more of a belly.*

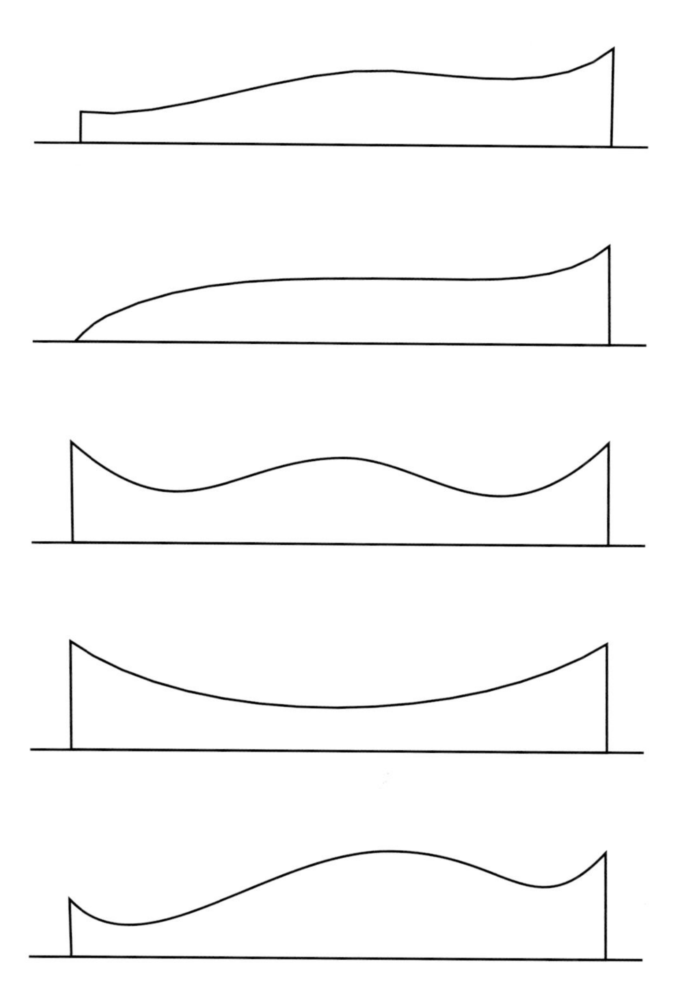

Fig 5.36 *Some tail options, seen end-on.*

TAIL

METHOD

No. 3 or No. 6 x 3/4in (19mm)

Begin with the top half of the tail:

1 I mostly used the flat gouge for the upper part of my fish's tail and the medium one for the lower, switching wherever the shape I wanted demanded it. Hold the gouge in the low-angle grip. Start your cut at the tip of the tail, leaving it quite high, and direct it towards the narrower stem of the tail – where the tail meets the body (Fig 5.37).

2 Repeat the cut. As the tail begins to take shape, you will cut more and more into the stem.

   In this direction you are carving 'downhill', *with* the grain, and making long clean shavings.

3 At some point you will find that you have reached the bottom of the hollow of the stem, where the form rises 'uphill' into the body. At this point *you must stop* and not persist against the grain (Fig 5.38).

4 To shape the hollow of the tail stem you must reverse the direction and carve from the body side, so once again working downhill. (Fig 5.39).

   Carving with the grain like this will hopefully seem obvious to you, from work we have done before. But this isn't the problem – that comes next!

5 Carry on shaping the body and tail into the stem, orientating the gouge upside down for the body if its form requires it. Try to bring the downhill cuts from each side to meet neatly in the middle.

6 You will find it very difficult, if not impossible, to join the tool cuts from each direction neatly in the middle of the hollow (Fig 5.40).

   Two things usually happen:

   - Firstly, you find you are digging deeper – cutting from one side then the other in an effort to clean up. Panic sets in when you find yourself digging below the level at which you wished to stop.

Fig 5.37 *Beginning to shape the tail. Don't round over the end!*

Fig 5.38 *Stop cutting from the tail direction as soon as the grain changes to 'uphill' ...*

Fig 5.39 *... and switch to cutting 'downhill' from the body side.*

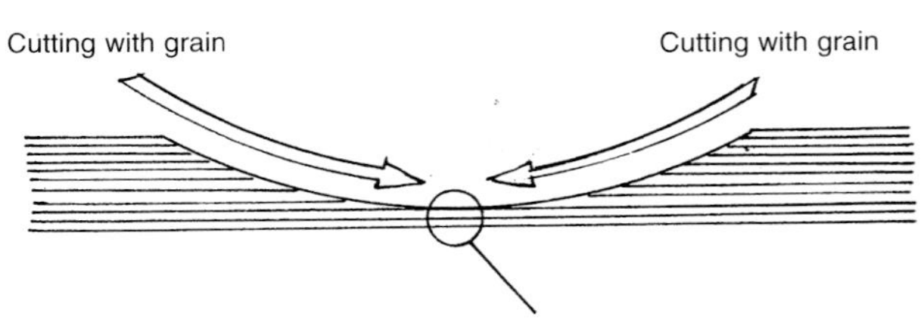
Cutting with grain
Cutting with grain
This area is as far as each cut can go before it goes against the grain

Fig 5.40 *It is difficult, when cutting 'downhill' from one side, to meet cuts coming downhill from the opposite side exactly; there is a risk of cutting uphill – against the grain – at the end of each downhill cut, and deepening the recess more than you intended.*

- Secondly, in paying attention to merging the cuts, the smoothness of the hollow which you were trying to carve is lost: the shape becomes more angular, almost V-like, where the opposing cuts meet.

The trick is to remove the waste *across* the grain at this merging point (Fig 5.41). To do this:

- choose a gouge having a sweep matching, or close to, the hollow you want – a narrower no. 3 often answers;
- make sure the cutting edge is as sharp as possible;
- use a slicing cut which in part works with the grain as the gouge travels across it, and so gives a finer surface to the cut;
- the lightest of strokes may be needed to finish off.

7 Cutting down the body, down the tail and across the area where these slopes meet, continue to shape the top part of the tail.

If you *have* created an angle rather than a smooth slope, then you must take more wood from the sides of the slope and hardly any from the bottom angle in order to restore a smooth curve (Fig 5.42).

Fig 5.41 *A slicing cross cut is needed to clean up the grain at the joining area.*

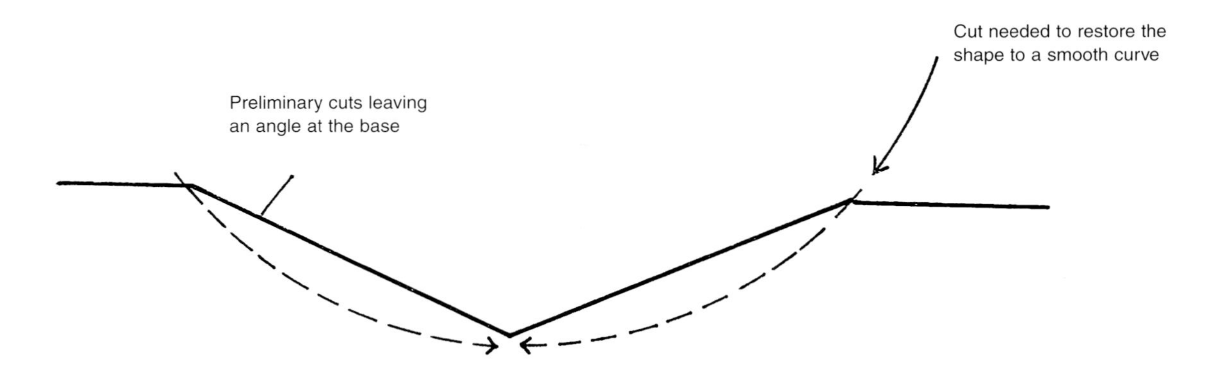

Fig 5.42 *If you have created an angled recess you need to take firm, decisive cuts beneath the flat faces to get back to a curve; avoid cutting further into the deep centre.*

Turn now to the lower half of the tail.

METHOD

TOOLS AS BEFORE

1 Work in the same way as you did with the top half of the tail (Figs 5.43–5.45). Quite a lot of wood must be removed to get an elegant tail and stem. It really helps if you can interchange hands.

2 Finish shaping the tail by carving more wood from the centre: the body of the fish is taken lower at the stem (Fig 5.45), rising up at the tail.

The result (Fig 5.46) is that the overall, rough shape of the fish (rough in the sense of surface finish) – its body, tail and fins – has been established. The forms flow into one another and the cuts are clean, with little tearing of the grain.

Next we need to turn to truing up some of the fish's outline.

Fig 5.43 *Shaping the lower half of the tail: sweep round into the tail stem, bearing in mind the pencilled edge line.*

Fig 5.44 *Come in from the body side.*

Fig 5.45 *Clean up by slicing across the grain as before. Reducing the tail stem a little lifts the tail more and gives a bigger sense of volume to the body of the fish.*

Fig 5.46 *The fish after vigorous roughing out of body and tail, leaving wood around the high points – eye, gill and tail – untouched.*

5 Setting in

The fish has two types of outline:

- **Hard**: the sharp edges of thinner parts such as tail and fins – the 'edge' proper.
- **Soft**: where the outermost part of the fish rounds over and out of sight (like a hill) and the part is more of a mass – the 'form horizon'.

The soft outlines are approximately in the right positions and will only be defined a little more before they are undercut; leave these until the later undercutting stage. It is the *hard* outlines (in particular the tail) which we need to set in accurately in preparation for eventual undercutting.

In the previous stage we carved the tail in three dimensions; in other words it now exists where we want it in space. (If you are not sure that this is so, then return and finish shaping it.) This means that the *edges* of the tail are correctly placed in terms of their changing depth. We will true up the very outline of these edges next, from below which the wood will eventually be undercut.

Although both hard and soft parts of the outline will eventually be undercut, *resist the temptation to undercut anywhere yet!*

METHOD

No. 3 x 1/2in (13mm) FLAT GOUGE
No. 6 x 1/4in (6mm) MEDIUM GOUGE

1. Start with the bottom half of the tail, at the tip, and work towards the body of the fish. This is an example of working *into* the mass of wood: by keeping the wood fibres supported there is less risk of the tip breaking off.
2. Hold the no. 3 gouge in the pen and dagger grip, orientated to the curve of the tail edge.
3. Use a slicing cut to shape the edge of the tail into a flowing line (Fig 5.47). You need only dress the top 1/8in (3mm) of the wall, as the wood beneath will be removed with the undercutting. Nevertheless, keep all walls vertical.
4. As you approach the tail stem the curve gets tighter, and you will need to switch to a tighter sweep of tool and reverse its orientation to negotiate the corner (Fig 5.48).
5. Returning to the flat gouge, merge the tail stem into the rear fin (Fig 5.49). Again it is not necessary to trim as far down as the background; concentrate on the edge of the fin itself.

Fig 5.47 *Setting in the tail by slicing. The sharp corner along the edge is its final place in space. Below this line wood will be removed by undercutting, so it is not necessary to slice down to the background.*

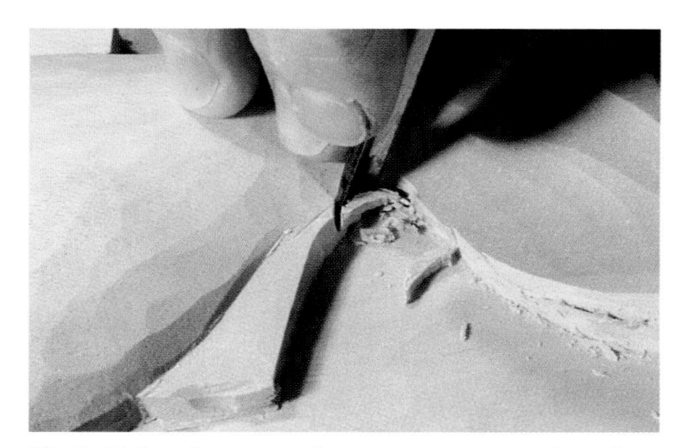

Fig 5.48 *Switching to another gouge to continue the outline, merging carefully.*

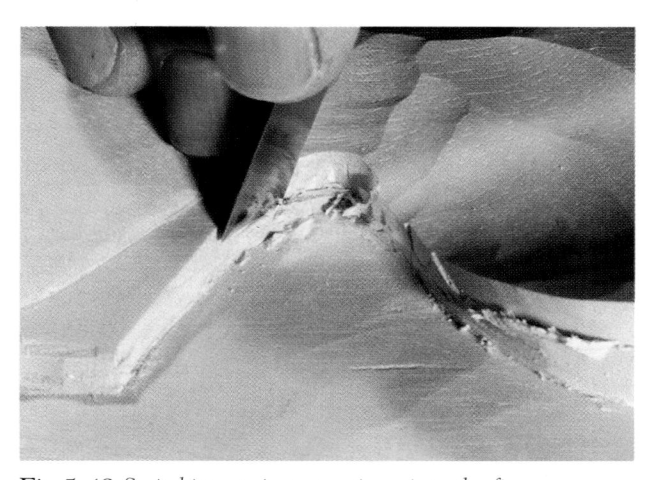

Fig 5.49 *Switching again to continue into the fin.*

6 You may find that this lower back fin has somewhat merged into the body during the rough shaping. As you set it in, you can make a point of defining the fin again by the usual method of lining in and lowering (Figs 5.50 and 5.51).

7 Also give a crisp edge to the end of the tail.

8 When the tail is complete, set in the fins, either by slicing or matching (see pages 57–62), along with their junctions to the body (Fig 5.52).

This setting-in stage is quite short compared with that in the low relief carving, because here we are only dealing with selected parts – the hard edges – and even these we are not taking down to a background, with a junction which must be cleaned up. We will have to do this work, but it has been moved to the undercutting stage.

When the hard edges are cleanly and smoothly outlined, with curves flowing into the body, we can return to the body of the fish.

Fig 5.50 *Parting off the fin; follow the body line.*

6 Modelling

The rough shaping stage left the fish with a general form containing a lot of 'modelling'. There are, within this general shape, some secondary planes – the fin and gill – definite areas where distinct changes of level occur. These are dealt with first. The general shape can also be refined, with body and tail consolidated.

In doing this, you must leave enough wood for a bulging eye. The eye itself, with the mouth and other details, will come later, maintaining the principle of creating the main forms or shapes first.

So, two parts to deal with: the side fin with the gill; and the surface form.

Fig 5.51 *Lowering and levelling the fin at the same time with a flat gouge.*

Fig 5.52 *Setting in by matching the shape of the gouge to the required outline will give a perfect line.*

SIDE FIN

METHOD

V-TOOL; No. 3 GOUGES; SKEW CHISEL

This should be familiar ground, as it is more or less the same as in the low relief except that, having more wood to play with, a stronger appearance to the fin is possible.

1 Line in the fin with the V-tool (Fig 5.53). Remember to direct the cut so the 'good' side of the V-cut defines the fin.

2 Use the point of the skew chisel to stop the end of the V-cut on the top edge of the fin (Fig 5.54).

3 Lower the wood around the fin with a flat gouge (Fig 5.55), using the fin as a fence to steer the blade (see above, page 55).

4 Merge the ground you have now created around the fin with the rest of the fish.

5 Use the skew chisel to clean the corner between fin and gill.

6 With a fin having gentle curves – as here – a little undercutting is possible as the edges are set in. Tilt the V-tool away from the fin and run it around to remove a little wood from beneath the edge (Fig 5.56). A more efficient, and certainly more professional, way would be to undercut and clean the edge of the fin *at the same time* as lining in.

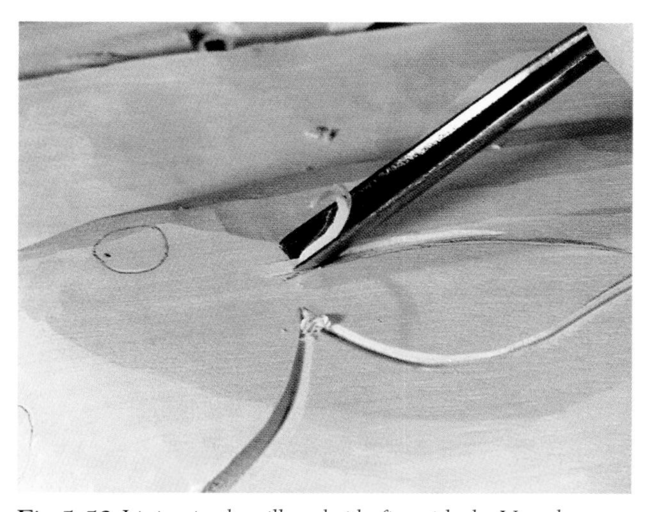

Fig 5.53 *Lining in the gill and side fin with the V-tool.*

If your fin is a complicated shape and needs to be set in with gouges, I suggest you leave the setting in until the following undercutting stage.

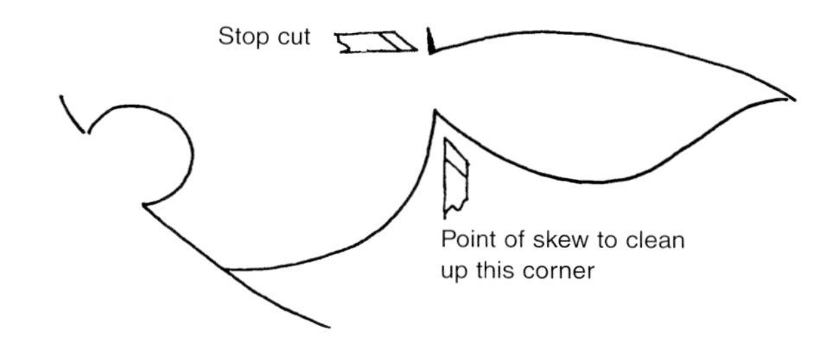

Fig 5.54 *Using the skew chisel to stop the end of the V-groove and to clean up the acute angle.*

Fig 5.55 *Lowering the ground around the fin.*

Fig 5.56 *Slightly undercutting the fin with the V-tool, at the same time as cleaning up the edge.*

SURFACE MODELLING

METHOD

No. 3 GOUGES

Enjoy this stage! Here the fish really starts to come together and gets its definitive form.

1 Work over the surface of the fish removing crests from previous cuts. Leave a hill of wood for the eye and work over the area where the mouth will be. This removes the pencil lines, but don't worry – these can be redrawn.

Remember to

- orientate the gouge to match the surface (Fig 5.57);
- reverse hands to reverse directions;
- react quickly to changes of grain;
- work lightly across the grain where hollows make grain-merging difficult;
- clean up as you go along.

This is no different from the way we levelled and smoothed over the flat background, except that the surface is three-dimensional.

2 The gill can be hollowed (Fig 5.58) to add more interest to the head.

The result (Fig 5.59) should be an emerging fish character – I feel that at this point the fish is 'caught'.

The surface should be cleanly cut and lightly faceted, the edge lines still 'sweet'; the tail is strong, and strongly different in character from the body; the gill has some form; the side fin is clear; there is wood left for the eye.

The next stage is to define the fish even further by undercutting, before moving on to a final stage of adding details.

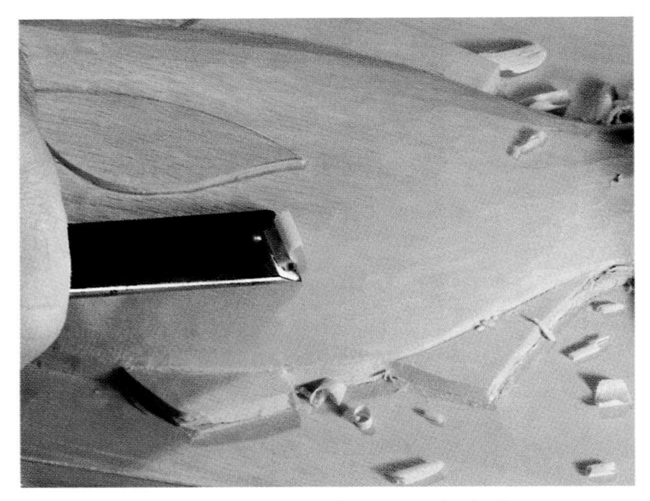

Fig 5.57 *Modelling and smoothing over the body.*

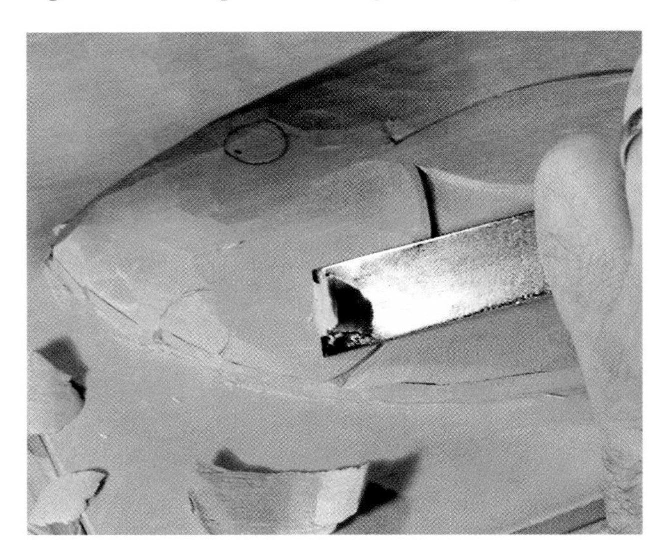

Fig 5.58 *Hollowing the gill, which gives a more interesting shape to the head.*

Fig 5.59 *The fish has a strong form even though it is not undercut yet. Note the small mound where the eye will be.*

7 Undercutting

You may find it useful to read the discussion of the principles of undercutting in Chapter 6, pages 122–5, and the notes about edges and form horizons in Chapter 3, pages 41–2. Here we are putting the 'theory' into practice.

Undercutting always involves finishing the junction between subject and background.

It is important to consider where the form horizons lie – in other words, where the form softly disappears from view like a hill. We will treat these differently from sharp edges. We drew the form horizon around the body of the fish and into the hard edge of the tail. This line now lies along what I called the 'soft' outline, which arose as we rounded over the fish body. Some of this line may have been skimmed away as the body was rounded over; if you can visualize this line, there is no need to redraw it. The 'hard' outline edges of tail and fins we have already set in.

These two outlines (hard and soft) must merge so that the undercutting, whatever the amount in any particular area, will be *continuous* around the fish.

Different tools and different techniques are needed for undercutting different parts of the outline, by differing amounts and with the grain running in different directions.

I shall demonstrate four important techniques in my fish, taking them one at a time. Sometimes it is a combination which is needed. These techniques can be adapted to your own design. Figure 5.60 gives an idea of where I used different methods in the demonstration fish.

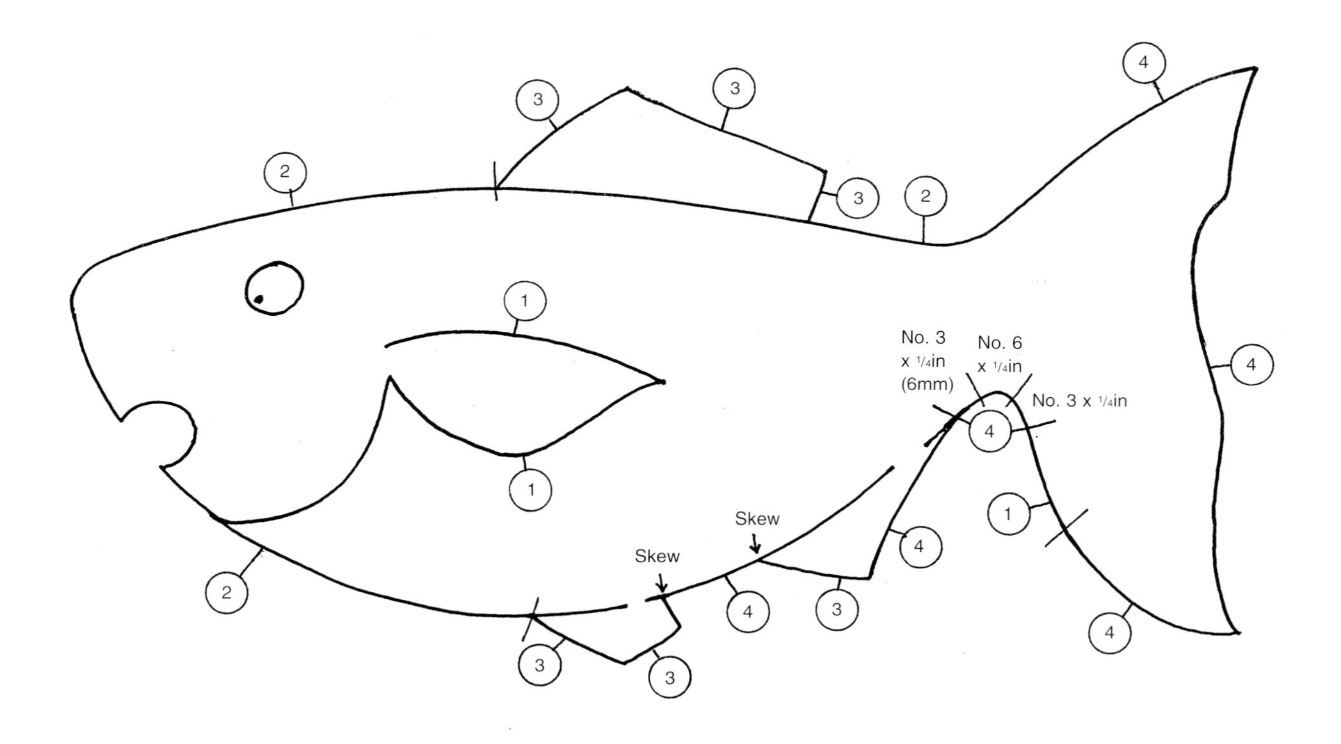

Fig 5.60 *Undercutting methods: numbers refer to the four separate methods described in the text.*

METHOD 1: V-TOOL ONLY

V-TOOL

Sometimes the V-tool on its own may be sufficient. We have already met this simple approach above, with the side fin. It is useful where only a small amount of undercutting is needed, although with a larger V-tool, of course, substantially more wood may be cut away.

1 Begin with the lower back fin.

2 Hold the V-tool in the low-angle grip.

3 Offer the tool to the wall of wood at the side of the fin, paying attention to the direction of the grain.

4 Tilt the V-tool so that its lower corner is above (clear of) the background.

   It is important not to dig the lower corner of the V-tool into the background, nor to cut below the background with the apex of the V-tool (Fig 5.61). The upper corner of the V must clear the surface edge of the wood, if it is to avoid digging into it, tearing the grain and possibly detaching the fin.

5 Start with a light cut and repeat it to deepen the undercutting (Fig 5.62). As the V-tool cuts, the angle at which the upper side of the tool is offered to the wall gives the wall-to-ground angle.

   A wall-to-ground angle of about 20–30° away from the vertical is all that is needed here to give the necessary effect.

6 When you are finished you will be left with a small corner of ground waste beneath the fin (Fig 5.61). This will need levelling into the main background. However, leave it until you have changed to a flat gouge for finishing or cutting elsewhere, since you will be continuing with the V-tool in the next method.

7 Cut a V-groove beneath the edges of the top fin, two lower ones, and anywhere else that has a low, hard edge. On my fish, for example, I made the lowermost part of the gill/body outline a hard edge.

Although the V-tool on its own may be sufficient, I return to the fins in Method 3 to clean up and set in a surface edge more precisely (with a matching gouge). Also, the V-tool creates a soft junction because its apex is actually rounded. A hard, sharp junction line is formed elsewhere around the fish, with gouges. My own preference is not to mix these two effects, or at least not noticeably, so setting in the edges unifies the effect at the junction.

So, although I start with the V-tool I will finish off the fins with gouges.

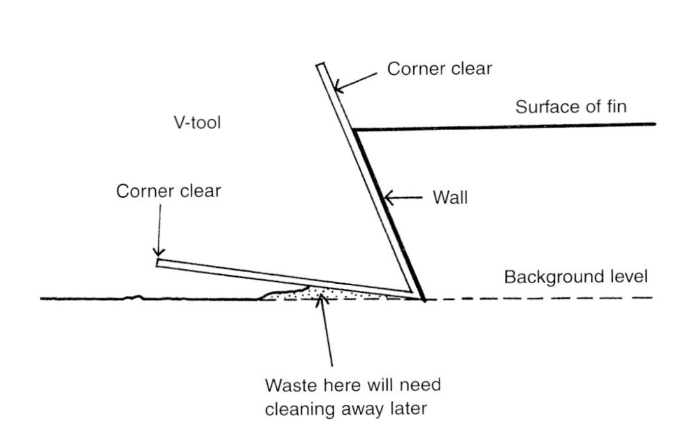

Fig 5.61 *Using the V-tool to undercut: keep corners clear of surface edge and background.*

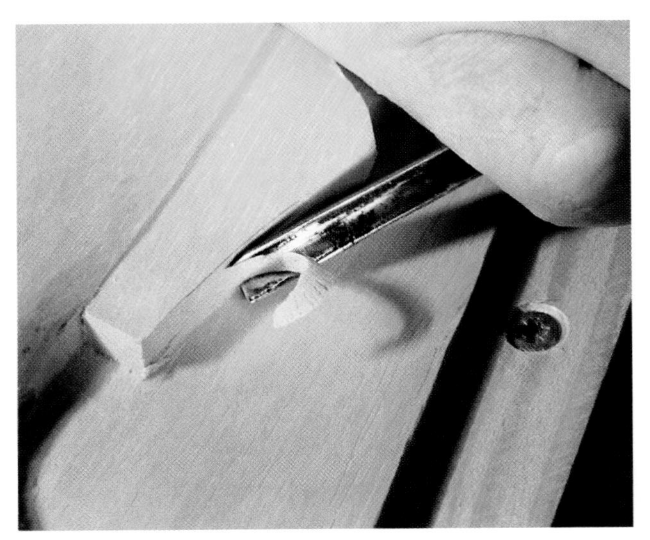

Fig 5.62 *Undercutting the fins with the V-tool.*

METHOD 2: SOFT EDGE

V-TOOL; MEDIUM GOUGES

This technique is suitable for full, soft (rounded) edges, which includes most of the body of the fish.

1 Run the V-tool around these areas in the same manner as above, taking care with the grain direction and not digging into or lowering the ground (Fig 5.63). Keep below the form horizon line (Fig 5.64) to give clearance for the corners of the gouge which follows. Only a small amount of undercutting is needed. If you are uncertain, err on the shallow side.

Fig 5.63 *Removing waste from around the body with the V-tool.*

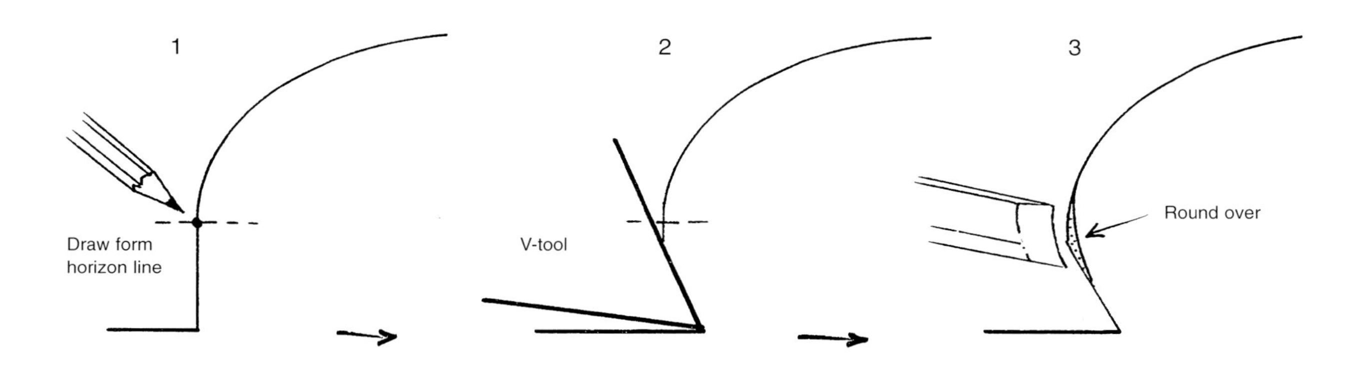

Fig 5.64 *Remove waste below the form horizon with a V-tool, then round over and undercut with a suitable gouge.*

2 Switch to a medium gouge, the sweep of which fits the rounded edge of the fish, and round it over into the V-groove (Fig 5.65). Control the lower corner of the gouge to avoid digging into the background.

3 Continue as far as you can, stopping at the fin or any other change of plane. Leave the junction with the ground at these points until the next 'method'.

4 Try and create a flowing outline to the fish as you remove the form horizon line.

5 Swap hands when you change tool direction. You may still need to turn the fish around.

Fig 5.65 *Rounding over the soft edge into the undercut.*

METHOD 3: MATCHING

GOUGES AS REQUIRED; SKEW CHISEL

The areas where this technique is appropriate are the same as in Method 1: a hard edge near the background, such as around the fins, where some preliminary work may still be done with the V-tool. The pure sweep of the gouge will make certain that the edge profile is immaculate.

1 The wider flat gouges (no. 3) fitted the fin edges of my fish. Orientate them to match the profile of the edge, and tilt them at an angle of about 20–30°.

2 Push down to undercut the fin, without stabbing the background (Fig 5.66).

Where the fin has already been undercut with the V-tool, the main job is to clean the surface and bring the wall to an exact junction with the background. Where some of the edge has not been V-tooled, you can pare back to the appropriate wall angle a little at a time.

3 Finish off the background to the undercut wall of the fish wherever you can (Fig 5.67).

4 You are now left with the junctions between the fins and the soft edge of the rounded fish body. For this the skew chisel is indispensable. Use the long corner of the skew to pare down the undercut walls into any junctions (Fig 5.68) and in from the ground.

Do not pull or tear wood away; always *cut* it cleanly. Use the brush to clear waste and see what you are doing.

5 Finish the ground up to the fish with flat gouges.

This is also a place where fishtail gouges are an asset; like the skew chisel, they get nicely into recesses.

When this stage has been completed you will have undercut all round the body, including the fins, and will be left with the tail of the fish. I deliberately separated these two ends: the body is a rounded form and the fins low relief, and the methods we have used so far deal with these situations where only a small amount of wood needs to be removed.

The tail, however, rises up and needs to be undercut substantially more. It also presents cross grain at the ends, and some of the work may well be done *against* the grain. It is here that the extremely important slicing technique can best be seen in action.

Fig 5.66 *Undercutting by matching. Although some work has been done with the V-tool, precise cutting with the gouges will always give a better edge at the surface and a sharper wall-to-ground junction.*

Fig 5.67 *Cleaning up the ground beneath the undercut. Sometimes the merest touch is needed to remove a final shaving.*

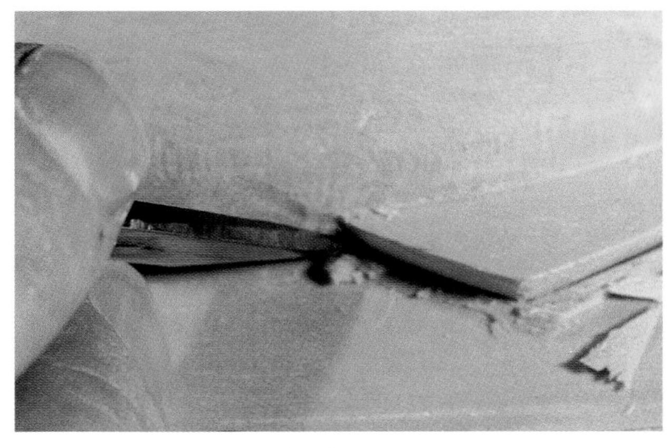

Fig 5.68 *The skew chisel will clean up a recess like this where square-ended tools can't reach.*

METHOD 4: SLICING

V-TOOL; No. 3 x 1/4IN (6MM), 3/4IN (19MM)
No. 6 x 1/4IN (6MM)

The undercutting is in two parts:

- first, as much waste wood as possible is removed;
- then the roughly undercut wall is cleaned up and properly shaped.

Start with the lower side of the tail and begin by removing waste:

1 Think for a moment about the amount of wood you intend to remove, and from where.

2 Begin by using the V-tool to cut away wood from beneath the tail (Fig 5.69), carving in from the tip.

Where a lot of wood needs to come away, the V-grooves can overlap. Towards the tail stem, where the undercutting is lighter, converge the V-grooves. It is the *bottoms* of the V-cuts that you need to bear in mind – rather like the bottoms of the furrows when you levelled the background. Lay these slightly shallower than where you reckon the undercut wall will end up. Don't cut into the background. A deep (or U) gouge would be an alternative to the V-tool.

3 Take away as much wood as you can before moving on. Either lean over the fish to do the far side, or turn it round; or finish off one side of the tail completely at a time.

4 When the bulk of the waste wood is removed, the slicing cuts to finish the undercutting can begin. The cut is essentially the same as when we set in the low relief fish outline, but here there is more wood to remove and the undercut varies in amount and depth.

Use the largest flat gouge, orientated to the curved edge of the tail. Hold it in the pen and dagger grip.

The gouge is chosen for a width that will keep the corner clear of the surface edge. It can be made to cut a tighter curve than its sweep, so by manipulating the gouge it can be made to negotiate smoothly the curve of the undercut.

5 Begin the cut at the tip of the tail, leaning the gouge out to the correct angle (20–30°). Push the gouge along with your thumb, paying attention to where the lower corner is. Feel the gouge slicing along and down (Fig 5.70). Don't try to take the cut to full depth in one go. Cuts need to be confident.

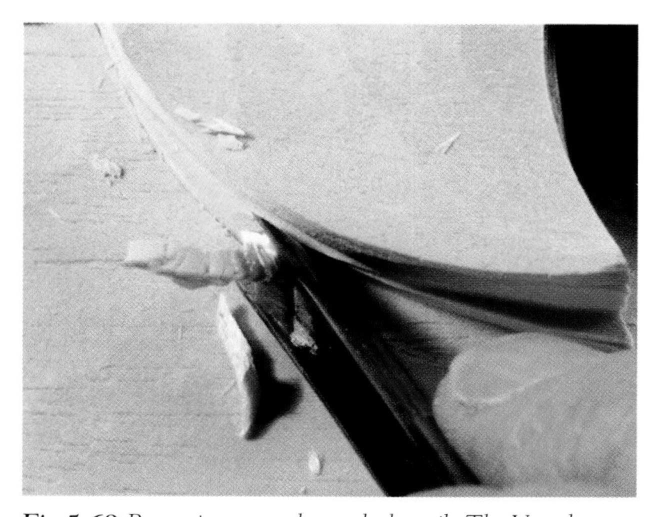

Fig 5.69 *Removing waste beneath the tail. The V-tool grooves can converge into the tail stem. A deep or U-shaped gouge is an alternative, but cannot run so far into the stem.*

Fig 5.70 *Slicing the undercut along the lower part of the tail. Note the angle at which the blade is offered to the wall. The cutting edge must be wide enough to clear the surface. The gouge can be controlled so as to slice the increasingly tight curve into the tail stem.*

Stop at the tail stem, where it hollows into the body and the curve is too tight to negotiate. Go the full depth of the undercut but don't cut into the background.

When using the slicing technique, you will see that you have to pay attention to three factors:

- where the *lower corner* is in relation to the background;
- how the cutting edge of the gouge is contouring the *surface edge* of the tail;
- the angle at which the tool is held as it cuts back the wall between these two points.

It sounds complicated, but really it is a matter of 'feel'. Essentially, this is a juggling act you are engaged in. Students find that to begin with they tend to pay attention to one of these factors to the detriment of the others – for example, they concentrate on the surface edge and find they have cut into the background. By breaking it down in this way, if you are having a problem, you may be able to see which way the answer lies.

Take it easily, without removing too much wood at a time, and you should be able to keep a flowing edge beneath which is a (more or less) flat inward-sloping wall down to a line where the junction will be. If anything, cut a little shy of the background depth.

6 Use the same flat gouge to level the background underneath the tail to the junction (Fig 5.71).

Fig 5.71 *Cleaning up the ground beneath the tail. Cuts to the wall may have to be repeated so as to arrive at the ground junction precisely.*

7 Switch back to the slicing cut from above to get the junction neat. Remember, if you *have* cut into the background, to remove wood from a wide area to eradicate the marks, so as not to get a 'rubber ground' effect (see page 51).

8 Switch to the no. 6 gouge to slice round under the tail stem (Fig 5.72), both undercutting and setting in.

9 The smaller flat gouge is needed to clean up the background in this tighter space (Fig 5.73).

I suggest you deal with both sides of the tail before turning to the end.

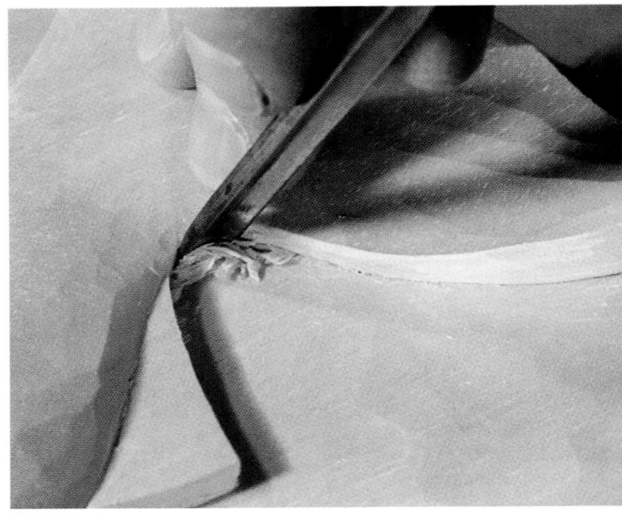

Fig 5.72 *Slicing under the tail stem with a smaller gouge, merging with the wall beneath the tail. Note the finished ground junction beneath the tail.*

Fig 5.73 *Finishing the ground beneath the tail stem with a narrow flat gouge.*

Undercutting the end of the tail causes students the worst problems. Visualize cutting down from the surface edge inwards to the junction with the ground: you must be cutting *against* the grain. Students think you can never cut against the grain. You can – with very sharp tools and light slicing cuts. It is here that the slicing cut really shows its capabilities. You need to use the edge of the gouge somewhat like a knife and slice across the grain at the same time as you slice against it. The secret lies in your thumb.

10 Use the V-tool to cut away wood from beneath the end of the tail, as before (Fig 5.74). You could use a deep gouge here. Don't make the angle of undercutting too deep by excavating more wood than you need to: 20–30° is the correct angle we want. And, as always, pay careful attention to the level of the background: avoid going beneath it.

A note on holding

As a general point, since the fish carving starts flat on the workbench, students often feel that this is the *only* way it must be placed. If you have trouble seeing what is going on beneath the tail – and you probably have been finding yourself bending down or over – you can change to holding the carving upright in a vice (Fig 5.75). In this position you can get at deeper undercutting more easily.

Wood must be positioned so that the carver can get at the work easily. As the carver, always feel free to adjust your work any way you like.

11 When the bulk of the waste is gone from under the tail, begin slicing cuts across the grain, maintaining the angle of the undercut. This slicing is discussed in more detail in the panel on page 102.

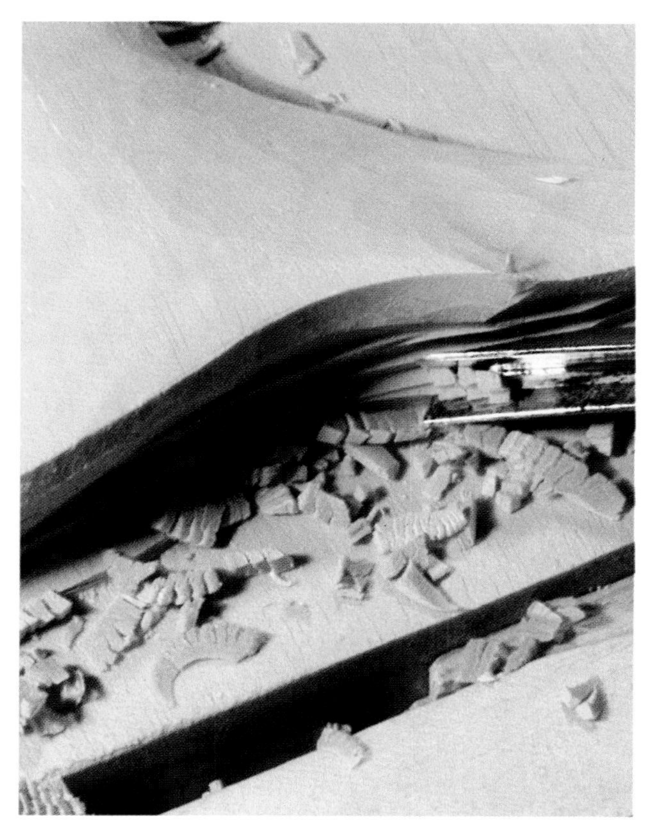

Fig 5.74 *Using the V-tool to remove waste wood beneath the end of the tail. A deep gouge would be an alternative. In both cases, come in from the outer edges to avoid splitting out the grain.*

Fig 5.75 *Holding the work vertical allows you to slice beneath the tail more comfortably.*

The hand position for the slicing cut is shown in Figs 5.76 and 5.77. This is not a fixed – not the only – position: feel free to experiment and find a comfortable way of working.

Note, however, the fingers of the blade hand resting on the wood, and in particular the *thumb* of this hand. The fingers resting on the wood lock the thumb into a stable position. The thumb is on the trailing edge of the blade.

It is the thumb which is at the core of this technique: the thumb is used as a *pivot*. Two principal movements of the blade are possible:

- the lower corner and the adjacent cutting edge can swing, using the thumb as a fulcrum; or
- the blade can be pushed forwards by the thumb from behind.

Combine these two movements and the cutting edge will slice smoothly across at the same time as it is pushed forward. With a sharp edge you can remove wood against the grain.

As you clean and improve the undercut surface by slicing in this way:

- start by paring away *thin* shavings;
- control the lower corner of the cutting edge – which must end up running along the line of the background junction, without actually cutting into the background;
- resist the temptation to make the angle of undercutting more acute – this will only make for difficulties in cutting with the grain, without gaining anything visually;
- don't lever up the handle as you slice, especially around the tips of the tail, as the short grain here is liable to break off easily;
- use the brush to clear shavings – don't pick with your fingers.

12 Finish the ground beneath the tail up to the junction, which should be neat and tidy. You may find switching to a small flat gouge useful for the final few strokes that are sometimes needed to finish off (Fig 5.78).

13 Check around all the junctions between background and fish, as well as the ground itself, before moving on to the final detailing stages.

Fig 5.76 *The thumb in the pen and dagger grip is extremely important: the blade pivots on this as the corner slices forward.*

Fig 5.77 *A view from the other side of the finger position in Fig 5.76. The fingers rest on the wood for better control.*

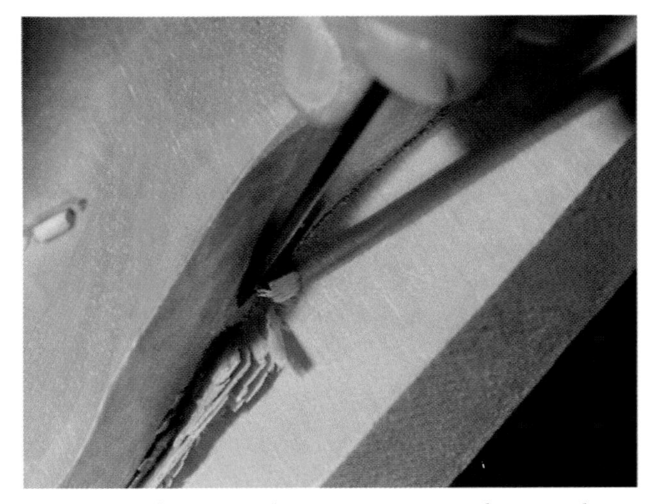

Fig 5.78 *Delicate use of a narrower gouge, almost stroking with the sharp corner, cleans up the final junction.*

Fig 5.79 *The fish after modelling and undercutting. At this stage the surface of the fish is still a bit faceted and needs smoothing over a little more before details are put in.*

The result (Fig 5.79) will be a quite strongly developed fish, standing out from the background as the undercutting creates stronger shadows and a sense of thinner edges. The outlines of the fish should be true and flowing – as in the original drawing. Surfaces, both of subject and background, should be cleanly cut. A small mound has been left for the eye. The background should all appear as one unit, merging all round and beneath the fish. You should aim at having no stab marks or traces from the previous stage.

8 Detailing

Some of these final 'details' could certainly not be called merely decorative – the eye or mouth, for instance – but the term 'detailing' implies that the principal masses or forms do not need further work: they are established correctly in space and contain the material for the details. The test is that if this were not so, details would be cut away when the form was refined further. So some fine modelling might still be needed: the surface of the side fin or gill, for example – which must be done before any fluting.

In my fish there are four areas to detail or finish off: the mouth, the eye, the tail and fins, and the scales. These I will describe in turn.

MOUTH

To make the exercise a bit more challenging we will create a back to the mouth, so making full use of the depth. This is an important principle in relief carving: *make full use of the available depth*.

Most students cut down to the background and omit any back to the mouth (see Gallery); do this if you prefer.

METHOD

No. 9 x 1/2in (13mm)
No. 3 and No. 6 x 1/4in (6mm)

1 Before the mouth itself can be carved, the wood into which the mouth will be cut must have been given its final overall shape. If you haven't done this yet, shape it now before going on to the next step.

2 Lightly draw in the mouth.

Fig 5.80 *Cutting back the mouth, keeping above what will be the further edge of the mouth.*

Fig 5.81 *Slicing in the back of the mouth and junction.*

3 Cut back into the mouth from the edge, as we did with the low relief fish (pages 61–2), but stop 1/16in (2mm) above the background (Fig 5.80). The wood in the mouth will crumble away, leaving a rough 'floor' for now – we must leave a little depth to form the further edge of the mouth, which is carved in low relief.

4 Switch to the no. 6 gouge. Use this narrow medium gouge to undercut slightly the hollow of the mouth down to the floor level – still 1/16in (2mm) above the background (Fig 5.81). It should make a neat sweeping cut at the bottom as you slice it round.

5 Finish off the inside of the mouth. Match this junction cut with the corner of the narrow flat gouge (Fig 5.82).

6 Draw in the back of the mouth.

7 Use the no. 6 x 1/4in (6mm), or another suitable gouge, to set in the far edge of the mouth (Fig 5.83).

This is our normal low relief setting in; you may need a mixture of gouges, or a slicing cut, to create the shape you want.

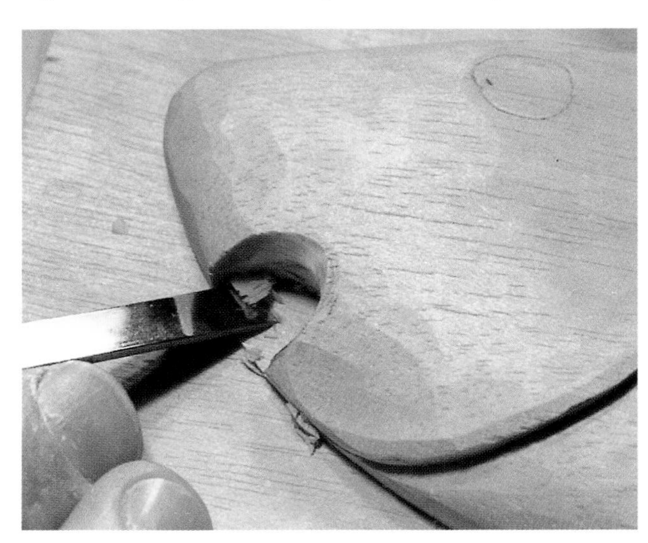

Fig 5.82 *Levelling the floor of the mouth.*

Fig 5.83 *Setting in the edge of the back of the mouth.*

Fig 5.84 *Finishing the ground up to the back edge of the mouth.*

8 Finish off the background up to this edge with the small no. 3 (Fig 5.84).

EYE

Here is an example of matching the form to the tools available. The eye is the same size as for the low relief (page 71); the difference lies in its being fuller, carved from the small mound left especially for it.

This is a tricky bit of carving for beginners; I suggest you practise on a spare piece of wood first.

METHOD

NO. 9 X 1/2IN (13MM)
NO. 3 AND NO. 6 X 1/4IN (6MM)
NAIL WITH FLATTENED POINT

1 Roughly draw in the eye where you want it.

2 Sweep round a circular stab cut with the no. 9 gouge to set in the outline of the eye (Fig 5.85).

3 Remove the ground around the eye (Fig 5.86) with the flat gouge. Merge this area with the rest of the fish's body.

4 Round over the eye with the no. 6 x 1/4in (6mm) used 'upside down' (Fig 5.87). You can also use the no. 9 itself. Be careful here not to dig away wood around the junction of eye and body.

Fig 5.85 *Sweeping cut to set in around the eye. Allow the tool to do the work.*

Fig 5.86 *Clearing away wood around the eye.*

Fig 5.87 *Rounding over the eye.*

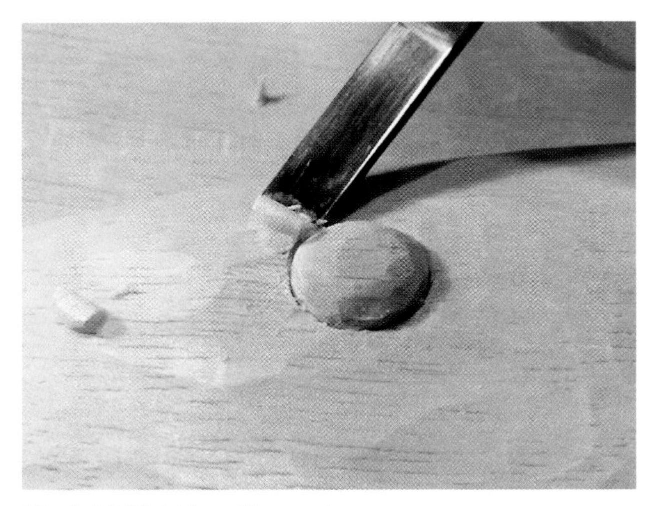

Fig 5.88 *Finishing off up to the eye.*

Fig 5.89 *Punching in a pupil with a flattened nail. In this direction the end grain of the eye is depressed; nearer the centre of the eye, the fibres would tend to crush.*

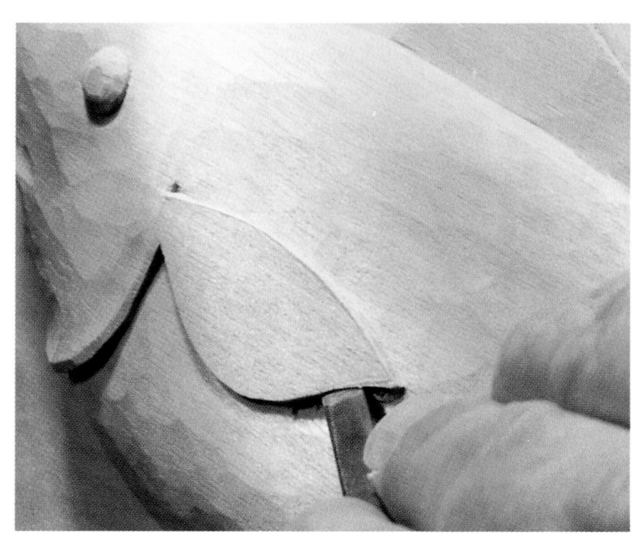

Fig 5.90 *Undercutting the side fin.*

5 Clean up the ground again up to the eye (Fig 5.88).

You need a delicate, controlled touch to shape the dome of the eye (and in particular the edge) neatly. It is controlling the corners of the gouge which gives most trouble and which needs most practice. You may need the narrow no. 3 gouge to take off a touch here or a whisker there to get the form.

6 I used a flattened nail to punch a pupil into the eye (Fig 5.89). This can only be successfully done into *end grain*; the side grain near the centre of the eye would tend to crumble. Tap the punch straight in and pull it out without levering to the side. To punch across the grain you need to create a little 'eye' first by rotating a very small no. 9 gouge until a pip of wood jumps out; then punch this hole deeper.

TAIL AND FINS

Before fluting the tail and fins you need to be satisfied with their underlying forms, finishing them off and undercutting if necessary (Fig 5.90).

The fluting is essentially the same as that undertaken in the low relief. The difference is that the flutes are carved into an undulating ground, rather than in the flat, and that they can be deeper because there is more wood.

METHOD

No. 9 x 1/2in and 1/4in (13 and 6mm)
No. 6 x 1/4in

1 Start at the tail with the larger deep gouge – or the no. 6 gouge, if only light fluting is required. I suggest you lightly draw in the direction of the flutes to guide your carving.

2 Cut from the high points – the tips – and work downhill, which is with the grain (Fig 5.91).

3 As with the low relief flutes (pages 68–71), you will need to switch directions with the changing grain, taking off smaller cuts to the 'good' side of the flute first, finishing off in the hollow middle.

4 You will find that pivoting on the heel of the blade hand in the low-angle grip will let you smoothly swing the cutting edge as you push the tool forward (Fig 5.92).

Fig 5.91 *Fluting the top part of the tail.*

Fig 5.92 *Try to get smooth-running flutes by pivoting on the heel of the blade hand.*

See this as yet another chance to practise tool control. Aim for flowing lines rather than mechanical symmetry or equality of flute size. This is handwork, and the natural inequalities which arise from this give any carving a lot of feeling and personal character.

5 Flute the fins using the smaller deep gouge (Fig 5.93). Cut the two sides of the flute separately, as before, so as to work with the grain as far as possible, and take shallow cuts rather than deep ones.

Fluting is a little trickier here than on the tail: the body of the fish can get in the way of the direction from which you wish to present the gouge. A shortbent gouge would clear the body more easily, but you should be able to manage it with the straight tools here.

6 When you have fluted the fins, shape the ends with the small no. 6 gouge (Fig 5.94), which is the right width for the ends of the flutes. Angle the gouge away from the fish a little to undercut more sharply just the top 1/32in (1mm) or so.

There are many ways to treat the fins and tail besides fluting (see Gallery). I think fluting is a challenge to working with the grain, and therefore I favour it in the context of the fish as an exercise.

Fig 5.93 *Fin flutes: the direction of cut will need reversing to deal with the torn grain on the 'bad' side of the flute.*

Fig 5.94 *Setting in the ends of the flutes. Since the fins are already undercut, the cuts need only be made to just beneath the edge.*

SCALES

The scales are treated as in the low relief carving (see page 72). The only difference is that this time they are stabbed into a rounded form and must pass round and over the edge.

METHOD

No. 9 x 1/4in (6mm)

1 Tilt the gouge so the *bevel* is vertical. The corners of the tool go into the wood the deepest.

2 Stagger the scales, trying not to cut into previous ones.

3 Continue around the edge (Fig 5.95).

4 Do not lever the tool to one side, or undercut the scales – in both cases they will tend to come away, leaving you with the option either of gluing them back on or resurfacing the area.

I have still chosen to cut mine lightly, and arranged them in selected areas to give a dappled effect. To make the scales stronger you can cut deeper, but there is then more danger of scales breaking away.

5 Another way to strengthen the appearance of the scales is to use the point of the skew chisel to remove a small triangle of wood from between each pair of scales (Fig 5.96). This, although tedious and needing precision, creates more shadow and so a stronger effect.

And finally ...

Check the fish and background over once again for blemishes. I always suggest changing the lighting; it can be a nasty shock.

The result (Fig 5.97) is your completed high relief fish carving, ready for the final (finishing) stage. The fish should show clean, fresh, flowing lines; a lightly tooled surface; a strong sense of relief; and, above all, character!

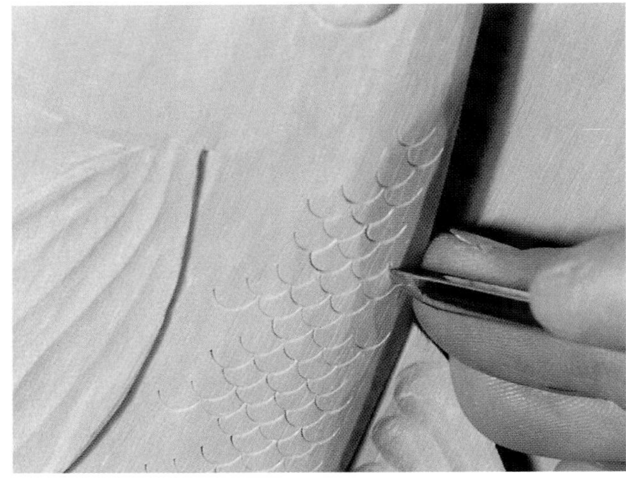

Fig 5.95 *The scales, formed as in the low relief fish, continue around the soft edge of the body.*

Fig 5.96 *If you remove wood here, either with a skew chisel or the corner of a fishtail gouge, a shadow is created which gives a stronger appearance of scales.*

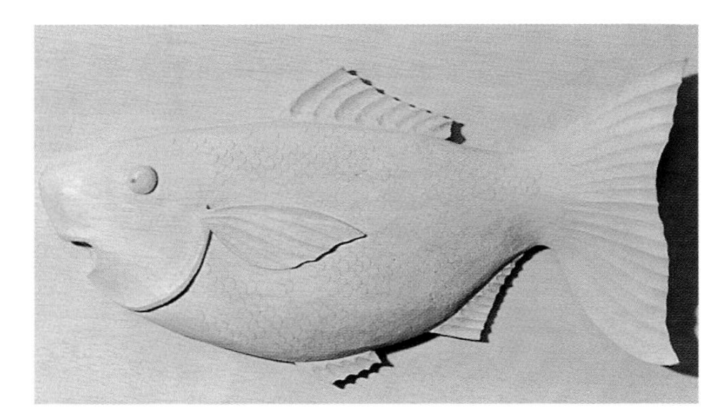

Fig 5.97 *The finished carving before sealing and waxing. Change the lighting and inspect for torn grain before moving to the final stage.*

Fig 5.98 *Brushing on clear shellac with a soft brush, to be followed by waxing and burnishing with a stiff brush as before.*

9 FINISHING

In this stage I include: finishing, in the sense of sealing and polishing; signing; and hanging (the carving, not the carver).

The finishing method I used is the same as that for low relief (see page 73). Remember not to wax the reverse side (Fig 5.98).

SIGNING

I urged this for the low relief carving and I would urge it again. Many students don't wish to sign their first carving, because they don't like it: either the design, or the workmanship. *They* are embarrassed, whereas *I* think it an occasion for rejoicing in the student's merits. There will never be a more difficult carving than the first one on the learning curve.

Sign the carving – on the back, in pen, if you wish. Another way is to stab in on the front with carving tools to compose the letter shapes, after trying the shapes on spare wood first. You will need to support the carving around the edge to avoid damaging it; and press lightly, not too hard!

HANGING

Finally, hang the carving as described in the previous chapter (page 74).

SUMMARY

Congratulations again: I hope you are satisfied with your fish!

If not, I hope at least that you feel you have learned a lot about the process of carving in relief, and the many techniques which are demonstrated in this book. I hope you have also learned the value and desirability of really sharp carving tools.

Here is a further list of some of the things you have learned:

- Understanding more about handling wood; when and how it is desirable to work across and against the grain.
- The process of simple high relief carving: a sequence of working and how one stage underpins the next.
- How low relief carving is found within high relief.
- Working with (shaping and modelling) a more three-dimensional form.
- Repeat practice in handling carving tools in general: lining in, grounding out; smoothing surfaces and finishing straight from the chisel; creating neat junctions; controlling the depth of cut; fluting; surface decoration.
- Grounding out quickly; methodical working.
- Setting in to deeper levels and in various ways: using the V-tool, slicing, and matching; merging cuts.
- Undercutting in a variety of ways in various situations to exploit the effect of light and shadow as the form gets deeper.
- Tackling 'hard' edges and 'soft' form horizons.
- Not much more about fish.

These low and high relief skills are a foundation on which to begin woodcarving, and like all foundations remain present no matter how high the subsequent structure. I use them continually; they appear both in carving in the round and even in lettering.

The crucially important next step is for you to practise what you have just learned – and regularly. There are two things you can do:

Repeat the fish exercises

My experience shows that a student completes a second fish in something like a third to a half of the time taken to carve the first; a third fish is even quicker. It is an excellent learning exercise and nothing but benefit comes from repeating it, especially with a different design.

Go on to your own relief carving (see Chapter 7)

For this you need to think about the design, and get a larger piece of wood. You may also need to extend the range of your carving tools. The Gallery of Students' Work (Chapter 8) shows a fraction of the subject matter available to you.

CHAPTER SIX

FURTHER TECHNIQUES

The low and high relief fish projects were deliberately designed with simplicity in mind: a single subject, not too large or deep, and so on. The idea was to learn some basic carving skills, with challenges but not too many problems.

When these exercise projects have been completed you will want to put newly learnt skills into practice. Suggestions on how to proceed in designing a next relief carving, and what tools you may need in the future, are the subject of the next chapter.

In this chapter, however, I want to add a little more to the skills you have practised by looking at three things:

- how to remove background waste more quickly than we have been;
- how to deal with enclosed grounds *within* a relief carving;
- and undercutting, in a little more detail.

Together this further information will help you tackle larger and more involved relief carvings.

REMOVING BACKGROUND WASTE MORE QUICKLY

In both relief carving projects I ask students to proceed methodically, 'ploughing' regular furrows across the grain and lowering the ground by lifts. As the wood fibres are cut short in this direction the waste falls away and the level drops quite quickly.

Removing the background of larger carvings can take a long time; it can also be hard work, not to say tedious. There are ways in which we can up the speed of waste removal; not quite 'tricks', but ways of cutting that get the wood to co-operate in its own destruction. We could, of course, put some electrical power to our elbow, but let us start with ways of using the ordinary carving tools more efficiently.

FASTER WOOD REMOVAL BY HAND

LARGER TOOLS

This is the obvious place to start. Larger deep gouges will cut away bigger bites of wood in the lowering stage (Fig 6.1). Students naturally buy larger tools fairly quickly once their carvings, in relief or in the round, increase in size (see pages 135–6: 'Additional tools').

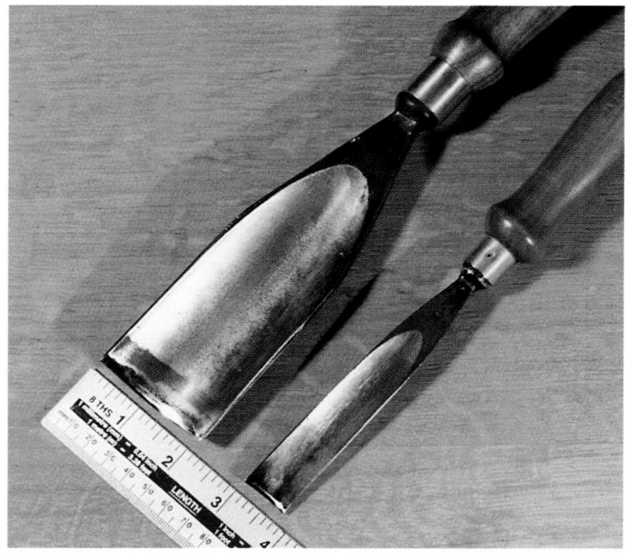

Fig 6.1 *Students often find, as I do, that large gouges (such as this 2in (51mm) version, shown to the left of the largest one recommended for the projects) require an uncomfortable amount of effort to use and are hard on the joints.*

Large carving tools can have drawbacks, however. It is often forgotten that a larger blade is effectively a bigger wedge of metal and more force is needed to drive the bevel and cutting edge into the wood. Above a certain size of gouge and mallet the work can be unpleasantly hard and stressful on the joints. Students who have bought the most enormous tools available soon realize that they are more suitable for gorillas. There is a balance to be struck for any individual between the effort and the results; I suggest you increase gouge and mallet size a little at a time, rather than in big leaps.

SAWING

Where there is a free edge or corner to the waste wood, there is always the possibility of sawing a piece away. In the high relief fish carving, for example, both corners at the head and some material behind the tail could have been cut away right at the beginning with a handsaw (Fig 6.2). Make the first cut safely above the horizontal background level so that the vertical cut removes the waste and there is less danger of cutting into the ground.

There are some who see sawing as somehow 'cheating'. It isn't: it is common sense and common carving practice among professionals.

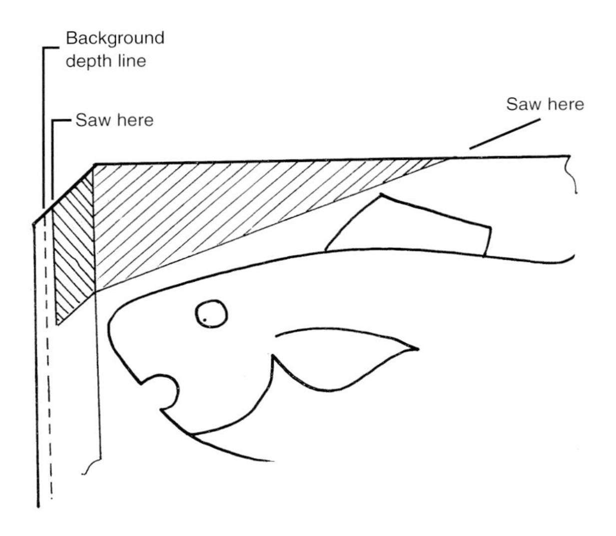

Fig 6.2 *Quite a useful amount of wood can simply be sawn off before carving starts – this is not 'cheating'!*

Besides increasing gouge size there are two ways of using the deep gouges you already have which will greatly increase the speed of waste removal. For these you must deliberately work with – that is, with regard to – the wood grain. Try them on a piece of practice wood first.

BURSTING OUT

A basic principle of cutting with carving tools (as we saw on page 29) is to keep the corners of a gouge clear of the wood. This is an excellent habit to adopt from the start, preventing wood splitting out to the side in an uncontrolled way. There are times, however, when you can turn this principle around, deliberately sinking one corner so that it acts like a wedge and bursts out short grain.

METHOD

No. 6 or 9 x 3/4in (19mm) GOUGE

1 For this technique the groove must run *across* the grain. Start to one side of the wood, say the right, and near the edge if it is available.

2 Make the first deep groove in the same way as your first lowering cut (pages 78–9), stopping short of the subject and running parallel to the surface. However, this time lower the right corner of the gouge until it sinks below the wood surface (Fig 6.3). As you cut now you will find that the right corner acts as a wedge and pushes up the unsupported grain to the edge of the wood.

Fig 6.3 *Drop the corner of the gouge below the surface and cut across the grain to burst out extra waste wood.*

3 Take a second cut to the left of the first (Fig 6.4). By sinking the same corner, the bevel will prise out a substantial shaving of what would have been the ridge between the two grooves.

To make the grain burst out you need fibres which are unsupported (as are those at the edge of the wood) or short (between ridges). Repeat the pattern of ploughing with a sunk corner, working to the left.

4 Try making a deeper groove before bursting to the side. Try with both medium and deep gouges, both with and without the mallet.

You do need to be continually alert to the lie of the grain, and to practise so that you know what is possible with this technique.

Carving in this way does have an element of risk; but whenever there is a safe opportunity, bursting away waste wood can considerably increase the rate of roughing out.

Fig 6.4 *Side view of the same operation. This technique needs an unsupported edge into which the waste can crumble.*

TRENCHING

METHOD

NO. 9 X 3/4IN (19MM)
NO. 3 X 3/4IN; MALLET

1 For this technique the groove must run *across* the grain.

2 I am using a block of practice wood. If it were an actual carving, you would start at one side of the wood, cutting in with the deep gouge as for your first lowering cut, stopping short of the subject. However, instead of working along, 'ploughing' the surface, deepen the groove and, widening it only as much as is necessary to get good access, create a trench that descends to just above the background level (Fig 6.5).

3 Leave a gap of untouched wood – with jelutong, say about 1 1/2–2in (30–50mm) – and run a second trench across the grain in the same manner.

Fig 6.5 *Use a deep gouge to cut channels (trenches)* across *the grain.*

Fig 6.6 *Split off chunks of waste from between trenches with a wide flat gouge or chisel.*

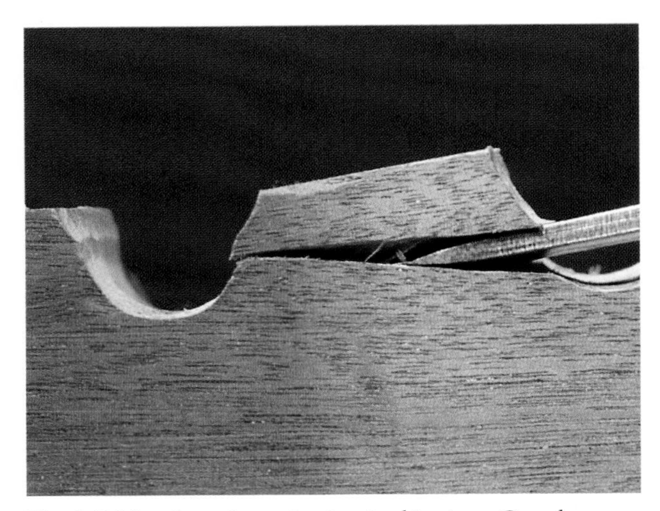

Fig 6.7 *Note how the grain rises in this piece. Care has to be taken with the direction of the cut so that you do not inadvertently split into areas you wish to keep.*

4 Work your way along from end to end of the piece of wood.

5 Switch to the flat gouge. The wider the flat gouge the better; and better even than a flat gouge would be a wider carving *chisel*, which acts as nothing less than a straight wedge. I am using a carving chisel in the demonstration. If you have one – or a carpentry chisel – try it and compare the results.

6 Place the cutting edge within one of the trenches but aiming along the grain. By striking the gouge or chisel with a mallet you should be able to split off a sizeable piece of short-grained wood between trenches (Fig 6.6).

7 When the first chunk of wood has gone, you are free to move on to the next (Fig 6.7).

8 Remove as much short-grained waste as possible before reverting to final 'ploughing' which finishes in the usual way a fraction above the final level.

Don't try to split off too much in one go, especially to begin with, and pay careful attention to the way in which the wood is splitting (Fig 6.7). You may need to reverse direction to avoid the split descending below, or too rapidly towards, the background level. How near you can go to the final level depends on how the fibres respond to splitting.

This technique deliberately takes advantage of the weakness inherent in short wood fibres. First we create short fibres, then we knock them off. Quite large chunks of wood can safely be cleared.

The procedure works best with straight-grained timber. Jelutong, lime, oak, and many carving woods can be treated this way provided the grain runs true. Some woods, such as yew or mahogany, and woods with twisted, interlocked or otherwise irregular grain, are less predictable.

You need to know your material and not be too dashing! The more predictable the grain, the wider the trenches and the more boldly you can split off waste. The more unpredictable, the closer you must play it. It is not always possible to control events and in some cases this method may be too risky. When it works it is satisfyingly dramatic and saves a lot of time.

Mechanical methods of removing wood

For relief carving there are two machines which can remove the waste quickly: the electrical router, and the power drill.

ROUTERS

Unless you are into woodworking in a more general way, it is unlikely that you will have a router (Figs 6.8 and 6.9). If you are, then the chances are you know all about it!

Fig 6.8 A typical router preparing for work on a panel. This one is fitted with an extractor to catch dust and wood chips which would otherwise fly out.

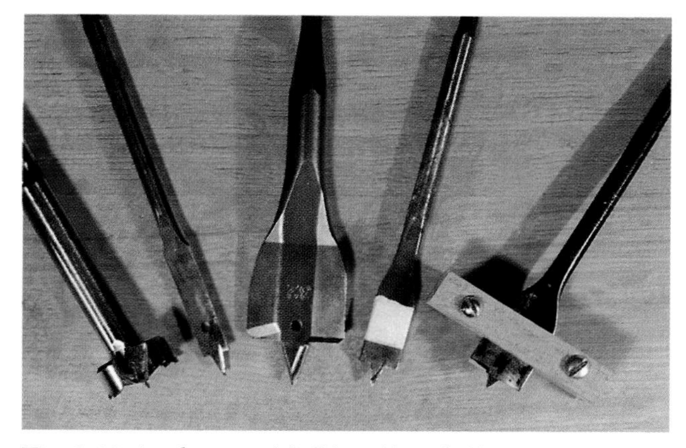

Fig 6.10 A selection of drill bits (from left): Forstner bit; narrow and wide flat bits; flat bits with rough depth mark of masking tape; flat bit with reduced point and wooden depth gauge.

Fig 6.9 The router will waste away wood quickly and cleanly. On the walls two 'lifts' of cut can be seen to get to the required depth. A smaller cutter would have worked the recesses even deeper.

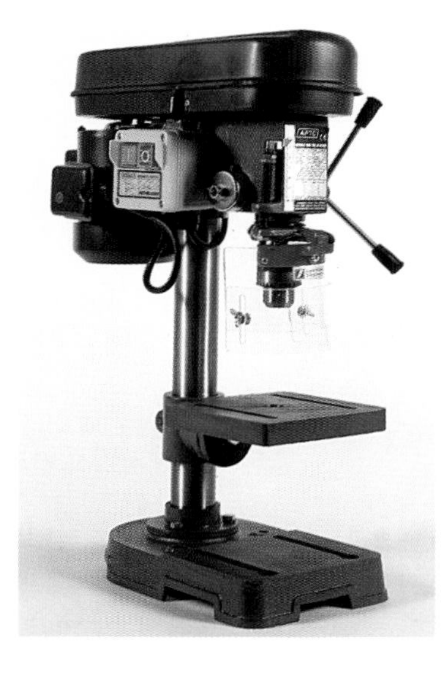

Fig 6.11 The APTC CH6 1/2in Hobby Drill: a lightweight drilling machine (press) for occasional use. (Photograph courtesy of Axminster Power Tools)

The router is a noisy, dusty, expensive machine which is nonetheless versatile, time-saving, and soon pays for itself in the hands of a professional carver. For the beginner, and at the level to which we are working in this book, I would not advise buying one, although I would advise knowing about them and filing details in your notebook.

DRILLS

Power drills are very common in households today and, unlike the router, can hardly be said to be specialist tools.

Different bits (the actual hole-makers) are produced for different purposes (Fig 6.10). Wide bits are needed to remove waste quickly, and the cheapest and simplest type, which fits drills of smaller chuck sizes, is the **flat bit**. It is these we will look at here.

As a general principle, the wider the bit, the more powerful the drill needs to be. The wider bits can be quite difficult to control in a portable drill if you are not used to them.

We can use the drill with a wide bit not only to remove background waste quickly, but to set a uniform depth. In my workshop I have a **drill press** (Fig 6.11). This is a permanently mounted drill which is raised or lowered for boring by a wheel. The work is fixed to a table beneath, and very accurate repeat holes can be made: a safe way of proceeding with very wide bits, but limited by the reach of the drill from its stand.

Again, a proper drill press is inappropriate to most carving students who are not also general woodworkers. However, the manufacturers of many portable drills also produce presses or stands into which these drills can be mounted. This is certainly something to think about. The depth of hole can be fixed accurately and boring is straight in and out without the possibility of wobbling to the side. The limitation is in the distance from the drill bit to the mounting, but even so these stands will deal with a useful size of relief carving.

Without any stand, the drill must be used freehand. Buy flat bits in a range of sizes (say 1/4in or around 6mm increments) so that you can get into recesses. Read the instructions on how to sharpen them – you will need a small triangular file – and keep them sharp.

More than anything, you will need to limit the *depth* to which you bore. Your drill may have a depth stop. If not, then here are two suggestions:

- Wrap masking or electrical tape around the flat bit at the level you want to stop at. This is fine for short runs, but there is a tendency for the tape to be pushed up by the edge of the hole when it is drilled, so the holes get a little deeper each time.
- Make a wooden stop (Fig 6.10, far right) which grips the bit and limits the depth. Make sure it is fitted tightly or it will creep up like the tape.

Remember that these flat bits have a protruding centre point. This leaves a small hole in the centre of the cut when the drill bit is withdrawn – *it is the bottom of this point hole which is the depth to which you must measure*, not the flat recess around and above it. Some of these bits are made with a long point, which can usefully be ground shorter. Place the point hole just above the background level. If your depth stop is true, you will end up with an array of points from which to finish to a uniform depth with the carving tools (Fig 6.12).

Holes can be overlapped, but always allow plenty of wood for the bit to cut into. There is a tendency for the flat side to snag unpleasantly against the wall of a first hole as the second one overlaps and cuts into it.

You don't have to bore every bit of waste away. Remember that you can split short grain by placing the holes judiciously.

Fig 6.12 *Boring away the background waste can save a lot of time with deep or large reliefs; and uniform boring gives a level ground to start from. It is the depth of the central point that matters. Note how there is a danger of the grain splitting out at the unsupported edge.*

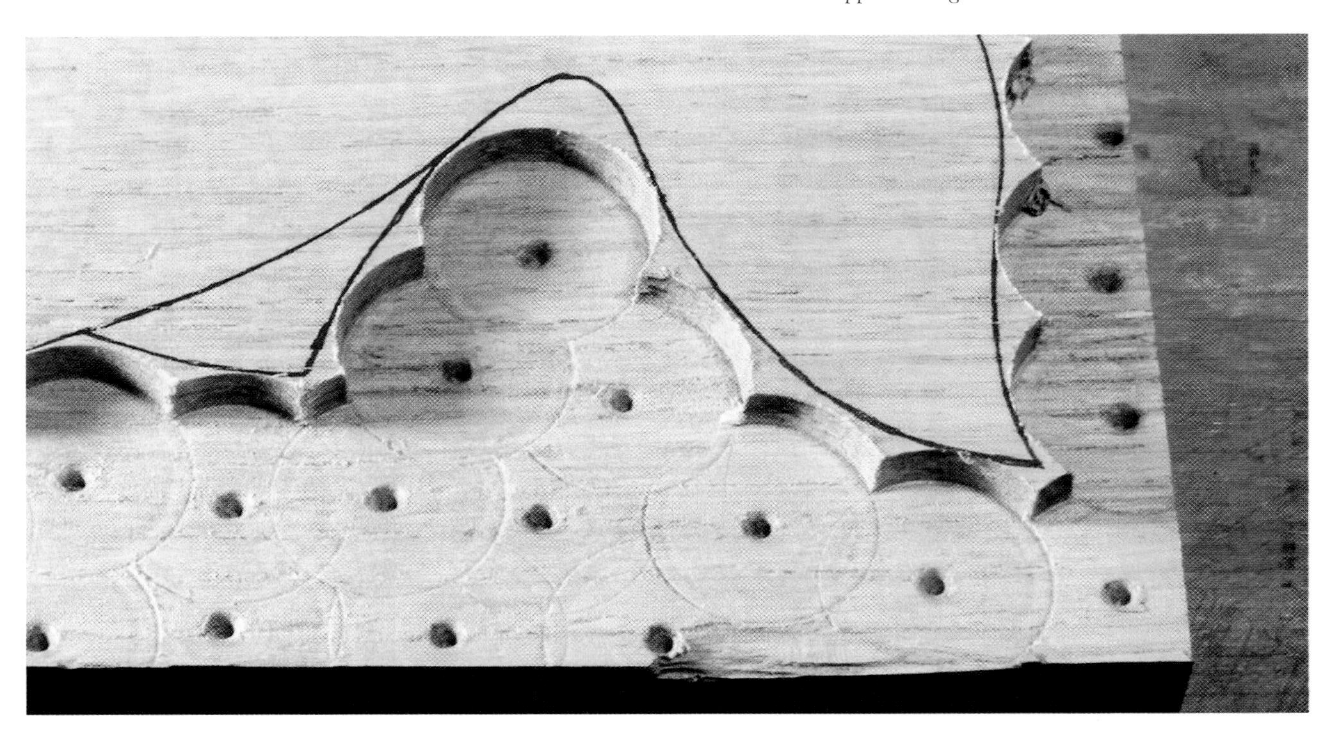

DEALING WITH ENCLOSED GROUNDS

To turn our fish drawing into a relief carving we removed the surrounding wood, so creating a background. We cut in from the edge of the original block, on which we had marked the depth from which to work; and within the fish itself we 'raised' the fin by removing wood from around it.

In both cases we could get at the waste wood and set in the shape easily. This is fine for a simple subject, but many times a relief carving will be more complicated – the wood we want to remove may be completely surrounded by wood we wish to leave. There is a variety of ways of tackling this situation, although the actual method will depend on circumstances. What follows are a few thoughts and options.

Tools which are very useful for getting into recesses for levelling the ground (whether this is part of another subject or actual background) are shortbent flat gouges (Fig 6.13) and skew chisels (Fig 6.14). The bent skews are available facing either left or right, and should be bought as a pair; a width of 1/8in (3mm) is useful.

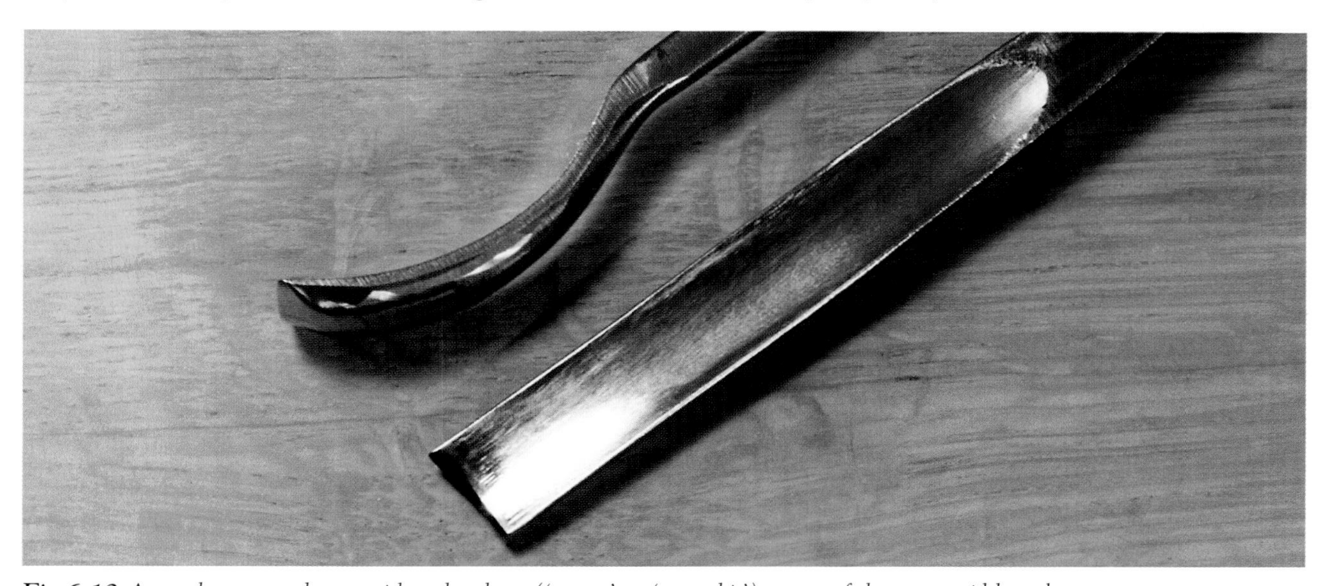

Fig 6.13 *A regular gouge shown with a shortbent ('spoon' or 'spoonbit') gouge of the same width and sweep.*

Fig 6.14 *1/8in (3mm) shortbent skew chisels, left and right cutting; always buy them in pairs.*

SHALLOW GROUND

The approach is the same as for the side fin in the fish:

1 line in the area to the waste side;

2 lower the waste;

3 level the ground;

4 set in;

5 finish off.

You may of course vary this; setting in after the lowering stage, for example. Another common (and perhaps better) method is to:

1 lower the waste;

2 line in or set in;

3 level and finish off the ground.

By removing the waste up to the subject first, the wood at the edge of the subject falls away easily as it is set in, effectively dispensing with the need to line in.

DEEP GROUND

There is not too much problem with removing wood when you have a reasonably large area to work in: removing waste, setting in and so on as before. You may need shortbent gouges (Fig 6.15); you may even find you can bore out some of the wood first, as discussed earlier. It is really another aspect of working with deep enclosed grounds that needs to be looked at, which causes deep problems for students.

In our high relief carving we roughly set in the fish, and then rounded the body over. Students, if they are carving, for example, leaves, tend to repeat this pattern, setting in the whole outline of the leaves first, exactly down to the ground (Fig 6.16). Two things happen:

1 The walls of the leaves are neatly set in at the full depth everywhere – even though *only a fraction of the outline may finally be at this full depth*. Sometimes none of it may be: the highest point in the carving might be in the middle and the edges considerably lower.

Fig 6.15 *For the shortbent gouge to cut into a hollow it must be* moving forwards; *otherwise it is levering the fibres rather than cutting them.*

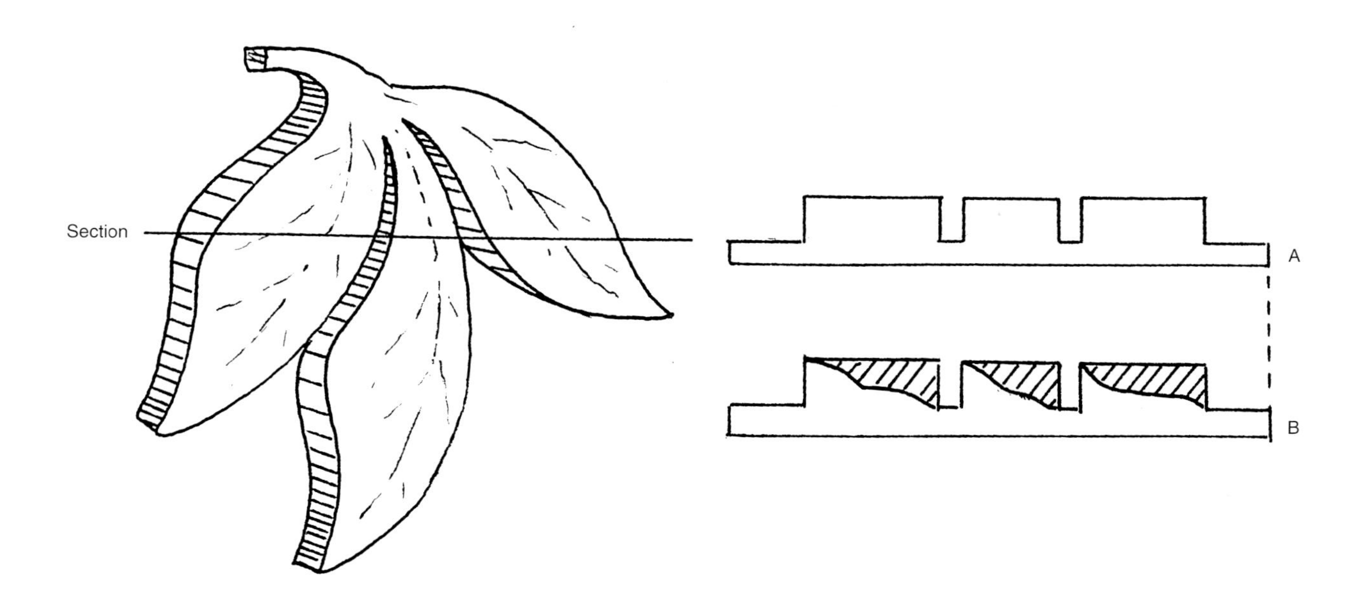

Fig 6.16 *If the ground around this leaf were lowered as in* **A**, *not only would difficult channels be laboriously created, but also vulnerable edges and cross grain. Far better is to cut the leaves to rough shape (removing the hatched areas in* **B**), *redraw, and then lower: this is far less work and potential trouble, but does take confidence.*

2 Narrow, deep channels may be created between leaves or stalks. The bottom of these channels is difficult to get at because of the high enclosing walls; even the sides themselves may be awkward to set in.

To begin with, the student is doing work which will be undone. In the high relief fish we only set in roughly before starting to shape. We actually only really needed to take care of the form horizon – the maximum extension of the form, above and below which wood is removed (by rounding or undercutting).

Walls enclosing channels may eventually be reduced to near ground level as the edges of the leaves are reduced, so extra work is done. The case is worse, however, because not only does it take longer to excavate these narrow channels, but the walls – some of which may be short grain – are more vulnerable. It is easy to break them by levering with the blade.

In both cases the carving is not only inefficient but potentially risky. Students work this way because they are following the initial pattern rather fixedly (even stoically), without much thought, but feeling more confident than the alternative method which I suggest. Professional carvers do not work this way, and this is as much a sign of confidence as the need to get the job finished.

The answer lies in *roughing out the form first*. This means that the lines will be removed – which is what unnerves students – and the carver must have a clear idea of what the form is going to be.

If I ask students where the edge of the leaf, or the stalk, will lie, they can invariably tell me: 'Oh, quite close to the background, rising up here and then dropping down there', and so on. If you can do this, then you are seeing the eventual form. Trust yourself and carve it. *Then* draw the new outline back in. *Then* ground out the now shallow depth required around it.

This is a much more fluid way of working: the form comes first, then the outline; not the other way round. It is also much more efficient because you are not undoing work and you maintain good access. As you become more confident this will be a much more 'natural' way to carve. See the methods I have presented in this book as good starting points, but use them intelligently and don't be afraid to adapt and innovate.

A simple depth gauge

Although the eye is a remarkably accurate instrument for judging depth, it is sometimes necessary to check and compare depths, especially when there are several planes or the carving is complicated.

A simple depth gauge is shown in Fig 6.17, made from a piece of straight hardwood, a nail, and a small screw. The wood is of a length to span between two points on the original surface. A masonry nail makes a good 'pointer', being narrow and truly straight; make it a tight fit in its hole. After the depth is set, lock the pointer with the screw.

Fig 6.17 *A simple depth gauge for measuring internal or enclosed grounds; the straight wooden strip can be any length.*

Fig 6.18 *Three-quarter front end view of our high relief carving: enough undercutting to give clear shadows and some 'lift' to the tail and fins, but not so much as to make these parts too weak.*

Undercutting

Other terms for undercutting are 'backing off' and 'backcutting'. It involves removing wood from behind a sharp edge (Fig 6.18) or beyond what I have called the 'form horizon'.

It is popularly thought that the more you can undercut some part of a carving, the higher the degree of skill shown by the carver, and the better the carving. This is only true if the technique has been used with discretion: it has both advantages and drawbacks.

Advantages

- Undercutting gives the effect of lightness and thinness to a carved element.
- The sense of detachment from the background – of relief – is increased.
- The undercut part is sharper, visually thrown forward towards the viewer, and this is useful where the carver wants a sense of depth and perspective.
- There is often a greater sense of reality (Fig 6.19).

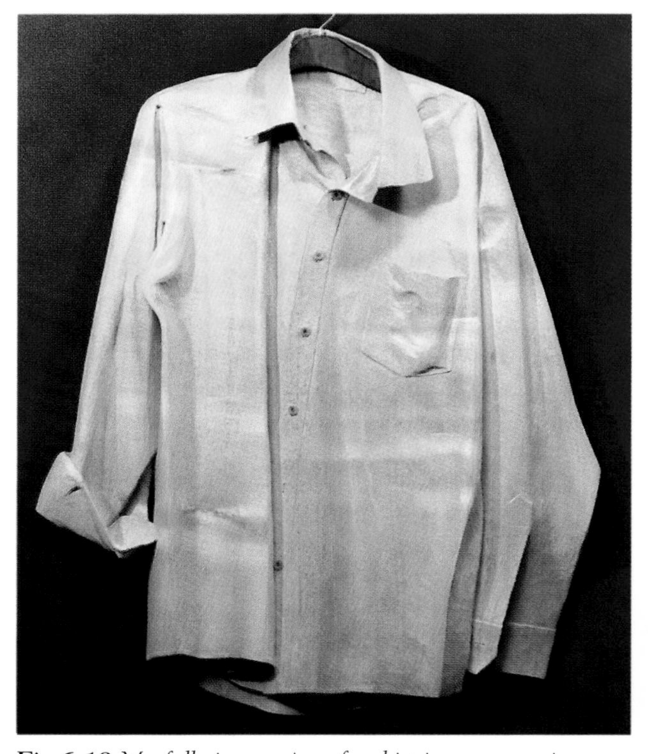

Fig 6.19 *My full-size carving of a shirt in sycamore is extensively undercut to give the realism I wanted, but is far stronger than it looks.*

- By creating stronger shadows the 'drama' of a subject is enhanced (Fig 6.20). The contrast with other, more solid, parts of the carving adds variety and interest.

DISADVANTAGES

- The strength of the undercut part is weakened.
- The position and depth of whatever is undercut are fixed.

These benefits and costs must be weighed up in each case.

Beginners usually have a strong tendency to start cutting under the outline as, or shortly after, it is set in. Sometimes this is due simply to not holding the carving tool vertically. But just as often it is because undercutting adds to the drama of a piece: the relief immediately looks stronger; there is a sense of getting on quickly with the job. In the projects you found me urging restraint in undercutting until towards the end of the carving, and students must be clear why this is so.

Whenever an edge – of the fish's tail, or a leaf or whatever – is undercut, the vertical depth becomes *fixed*. The edge cannot now be lowered without the outline changing. Remember, one can only carve wood, not space! Undercutting is fine as long as you are absolutely sure the edge is lying *exactly* where you want it, in three dimensions. Because all parts of a carving are relative to others, the form normally only 'settles down' as it is modelled. So it is towards the end of the carving that edges and form horizons are firmly in position and undercutting is completely safe. The undercutting almost seems to take care of itself. All too often students will undercut too early: when later they realize they need to take the undercut part deeper, they find the outline must be sacrificed. This might not be a problem; but, equally, it might be disastrous.

The other disadvantage to undercutting an edge is the loss of physical strength, especially where an undercut part has short grain (fibres). Not only is there the danger of breaking off the part while carving, but bear in mind that many carvings come within the reach of viewers who like to use the 'how-much-does-it-wobble' test for fragility.

Fig 6.20 *Detail from a carving by Gino Masero. The panache of the piece comes in part from the energetic toolwork, in part from the dramatic shadows that come from deep undercutting.*

So my advice always is to:

- run the grain (wood fibres) into the weakest parts, in the design stage;
- carve the form and definitive edges first;
- leave any undercutting until last;
- undercut as much as is necessary to give the effect, but not so much as to leave the edge unnecessarily weak.

The last bit of advice raises the question: how much does one undercut, and at what angle?

This depends really on the position from which the carving is to be viewed (Fig 6.21), and how much of the actual edge may be seen. You must really try to think of the level at which a relief carving will hang before you begin it (Fig 6.22). Different parts of a carving will normally need to be undercut to different amounts.

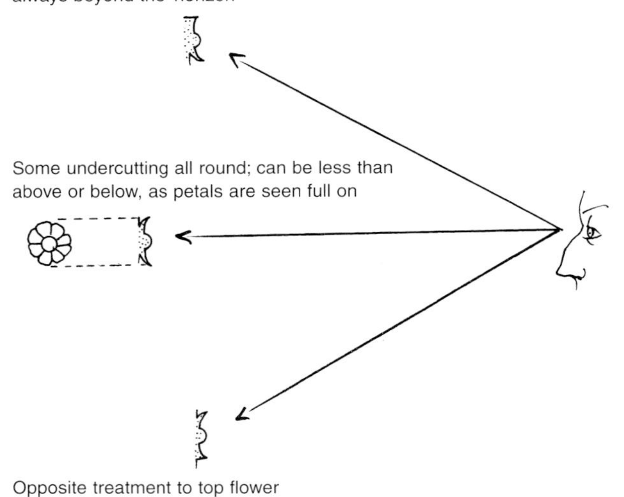
Lowest petals undercut extensively, as these edges are most visible from below; top petals only lightly undercut, as the areas behind them are always beyond the 'horizon'
Some undercutting all round; can be less than above or below, as petals are seen full on
Opposite treatment to top flower

Fig 6.21 *What undercutting is needed, and the extent of it, in any carving depends a lot on the point from which it will be seen. As a rule, only undercut as much as will give the effect, so as not to weaken the carving excessively.*

Fig 6.22 *This four-leaved boss was carved originally to be placed high up on the ceiling. Strong, simple carving is enough; undercutting is hardly necessary.*

Start at an angle of about 20–30° to the vertical and see what the effect is. From there you can pare the angle back to suit. It is not necessary to hollow-undercut (Fig 6.23), making the edge wafer-thin. The effect is all at the edge, so a straight cut will do, keeping strength and creating adequate shadows. You might even try a rounded undercut first if you want to maximize strength, flattening it to suit particular parts.

Techniques of undercutting were looked at in the relief carving projects. The more complicated the carving, the more adept the carver must be – but that is the challenge of carving, of course. Sometimes specific tools are needed (backbent gouges are often helpful where access is tight: see Fig 2.15, and *Woodcarving Tools, Materials & Equipment*, pages 35–8, 88–9), and on large carvings you might even find you can saw off some of the undercut waste.

Undercutting, like texturing, and like all toolwork in fact, is a technique in the carver's repertoire. Use it selectively and with discretion.

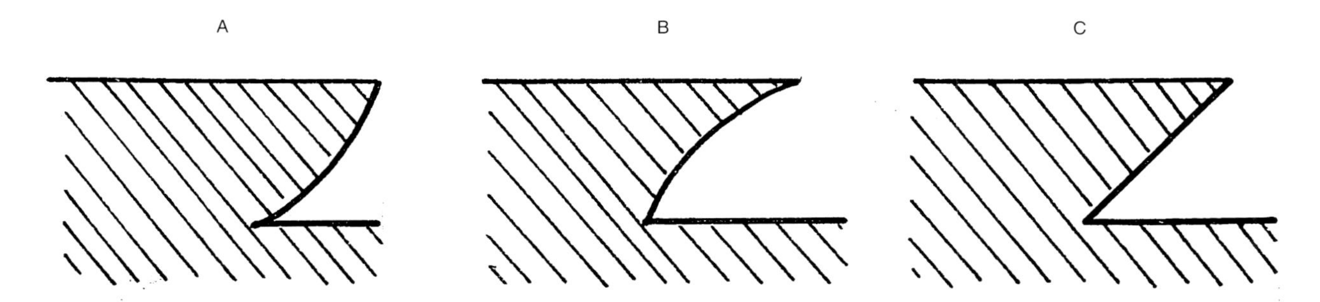

Fig 6.23 *Normally straight cutting back (**C**) is best. Rounded (**A**) is stronger, hollowed (**B**) is weaker.*

CHAPTER SEVEN

NEXT STEPS: RELIEF CARVING DESIGN

If you have successfully completed the exercise projects you will have acquired a lot of basic high and low relief carving skills, which in the future will usually be combined within any one piece of work. Many students find this hard to believe, despite the evidence! They mistake the fish itself – with which they may be unhappy – with the skills it took to carve it. Lists of some of the techniques which you have experienced appear on pages 75 and 112.

Following the fish carving, unless a student has burning desires otherwise, I advise students to undertake a relief carving of their own: to repeat the skills they have learned and gain further experience and confidence. The Gallery shows the relief carvings of a few students, which follow on directly from the fish projects – in other words, the students' first 'solo' carvings – and will give you some idea of what can be attempted.

In this chapter I want to make some clear suggestions for your next relief carving, and give you some thoughts on its design.

From the next solo carving, students tend to move into the work they have a particular interest in, including work in the round.

Because your next carving may well be more complicated than our simple fish, we also need to look at what additional tools you might need.

YOUR NEXT RELIEF CARVING

You have completed the low and high relief fishes. The suggestion and many features of the fish were mine. The next step must be to carve something from beginning to end which is entirely *yours*.

I say this to students and watch many a heart slowly sink. At this point I ask students to pause and remember that they have:

- successfully completed both a low and a high relief carving;
- been handling carving tools for a while now;
- followed the carving process through twice, from beginning to end;
- gained a lot of experience to build on, meaning that they have got through the worst part of the learning curve.

What is important to understand is that there are no great hidden skills they don't know about – nothing magical – or even much different, in what a more experienced carver does. All the experienced carver has is a lot of practice, and so experience. Oh yes, and a lot more practice …

It is my experience that *everyone* who has got so far has artistic and mechanical abilities enough to continue. The secret of successful progress is *not to design ahead of what you are capable of*.

Take your carving step by step, gradually progressing. Find subjects which interest and motivate you. Offer yourself a reasonable challenge without setting yourself up for failure.

For your first solo relief carving, which follows the fish, I suggest you:

- Make it simple – with one subject in a straightforward context. Have the main subject in high relief, with uncomplicated surroundings in low relief.
- Keep the depth somewhere near that of the high relief fish project – keep the wood thickness to a maximum of around 2in (50mm), using about $^{2}/_{3}$ to $^{3}/_{4}$ of this depth for the carving.

- Make the overall size large – around 16 x 12in (40 x 30cm), or A3 paper size (though it can of course be of entirely different proportions).
- Keep the wood rectangular or square. The piece will look something like a picture. Add a frame if you want to; straight frame edges are best carved with straight chisels.

The idea is to carve a simple, largish relief which will consolidate what you have learned and move you into your own designs. 'Simple' because you will probably find this challenging enough at this stage and you can introduce complexities as your experience grows; and 'largish' because larger is more impressive, a great boost to confidence, and tells everyone that a new carver has arrived!

You will need to find a large enough piece of wood, or have one joined up. Timberyards often offer this service, at a cost, as do joinery firms.

It must of course be something you are interested in – a subject which will stimulate your enthusiasm and energy, and maintain your patience. The next question is: what to carve?

WHERE DO IDEAS COME FROM?

If you treat ideas like apples, scattered around 'out there', waiting to be picked when you feel peckish, then there is always the chance that you may find the season gone, the apple wormy, or that you may really have fancied something different.

Better to treat them like seeds, from a wide range of favourite plants, which you continually sow: some flowers are growing while others are fading, but there is always something to pick, from a wide choice.

The crucial difference is between being passive (waiting until you find something to do), or active (generating a flow of ideas).

Most students start by being passive. They wait until they have finished a carving (which may have taken months), and only then begin to look for another one to start on. Sometimes, because of the pressure of having something to do in a class, they start something they are not really interested in but will do until something better comes along. This leads to frustration.

'The Idea' is probably the most important stage in carving, and I don't use the seed analogy lightly. A far better plan, one that gives ideas the importance they should have and is ultimately more satisfying to students, is to become active and sow lots of seeds.

Right from the beginning, start three books:

A scrapbook

Put in here cuttings from magazines, postcards, photocopies from books, or whatever, of things that interest you; other people's ideas, sources of inspiration.

A notebook

In here jot down themes that interest you; details of books you have read; carvings you have seen; techniques you have discovered; sources of wood; and so on.

A sketchbook

Your sketches need only be simple lines, enough to record an idea so you can work on it later. They could show, for example, how you might treat one of the ideas in the scrapbook.

As these books fill, you will see your interests developing and will never be at a loss either for the germ of an idea or a fully developed one.

All artists are like magpies, collecting shiny jewels into their nests. We are all – and carvers are no exception – stimulated by the work of others. In the early days many students start with ideas from something like a photograph, perhaps in a magazine, of (say) an animal or a plant. They may carve the design exactly, or eliminate small parts without changing much. But as their own ideas develop they will alter more, bring in more, combine ideas, and change the original into something new.

In turning your idea into a design you have to look at things from the point of view of the carver.

Fig 7.1 *Fairground carving from the museums at Wookey Hole Caves, Somerset (now dispersed). Many fine carvings by skilled artisans are found in odd settings; they don't have to be about anything 'real' at all.*

Fig 7.2 *Victory figures at the Befreiungshalle in Kehlheim, Bavaria. Architectural carving is a rich source of inspiration and instruction.*

Fig 7.3 Foliate Head and Viola: *found in Maine, USA, carver unknown. It is stimulating to stumble on carvings and useful to record them, and your thoughts. With this piece I felt the hollowness of the carving was at odds with the almost pregnant fullness I associate with the soundboxes of stringed instruments. The association of the two ideas is disturbing, but why not?*

Fig 7.4 The Banquet at Simon's *(1490–2) by Tilman Riemenschneider: one of the great masters of woodcarving, playing with depth and perspective. For me it doesn't quite work: my attention is continually drawn to the central chicken around which everything else orbits – perhaps there is a symbolism here of which I am ignorant? Nevertheless it shows a scale of possibilities in low and high relief carving.*

RELIEF CARVING DESIGN

The more you can work out in your mind before you begin carving, the more chance of success you have. So before you begin, consider the following points:

RESEARCH

What do you really need to know? You cannot have too much research, but you *can* have too little. One of the principal reasons why carvings fail for students is that they actually don't know what they are carving. Only when they are in trouble do they think it a good idea to find out what a rabbit (or a bit of a rabbit), say, looks like; by which time vital wood has been cut away.

Students don't do the research because 'it is not carving'. Carving actually starts long before steel meets wood, and time spent on research is *never* wasted.

DRAWINGS

Drawings are extremely useful, even the simplest of sketches – always start with them (Fig 7.5). However, drawings are only a way of helping to organize your ideas and approach. Whatever you draw on the wood, it will eventually disappear into the carving.

A drawing is *not* a relief carving. Drawings are not three-dimensional – you cannot look around the corners of a drawing. You need to think, to visualize, what the drawing hides that will be revealed as the subject is rendered more three-dimensionally.

Sometimes a quick model in clay or Plasticine will help you see problems and make decisions better than a drawing.

Fig 7.5 *Preparations for a large figure carving: working drawings, joined wood. Much needs to be done before any carving starts.*

DESIGN THOUGHTS

Design is a very involved and tantalizing subject. Forms, shapes, depth, mass, profile, colour, planes, light and shadow, rhythm, balance, movement: it is difficult even to talk about it!

A sense of design and an ability to express what you feel when you observe a carving comes with experience and practice. For the moment, here are a few points and suggestions which seem to come up regularly with students. They are not 'rules', just thoughts to start with; bear them in mind in your own designing and when you look at the Gallery carvings.

- Simplicity is usually best; this probably means a single subject or event.
- The carving must 'read' in a straightforward manner – no carver likes the response of 'Yes, but what is it?' or 'What's supposed to be happening?' from a viewer when the carving is not supposed to be a test, or an abstract. Which is not to say that it should reveal everything at the first glance.
- Give the relief a focal point. Be aware of how your eye moves around the design; whether its passage gets lost or blocked.
- Don't 'float' subjects in a void. Give them a context, even if only lightly 'drawn' into the background, to anchor them.
- Some relief carvings are simply studies. Others engage the viewer by having a sense of 'narrative': something happening which is intriguing. Several pieces in the Gallery show this.
- The silhouette of a subject is very important when it comes to establishing its identity (Fig 7.6). The change of plane which makes the principal outline should be strong compared with the changes of plane within the relief.
- If you don't know any of the rudiments of perspective, try artists' drawing books from the library. Perspective is a very useful tool (Fig 7.4).

Fig 7.6 *What's this? A strong silhouette or profile carries most of the information about what something is. In relief carving the silhouette should normally be the strongest change of plane.*

In terms of the mechanics of carving:

- Don't make trouble for yourself. It is easy to draw something which is a nightmare to carve! For example: overlap leaves rather than having large numbers of holes to excavate between them, or delicate stems stretching through space (Fig 7.7); the two floral compositions in the Gallery are good examples of this.
- If you feel there is something you cannot carve, don't include it! If you can't draw or carve hands, put them in the subject's pockets.
- Rounding over the edges in the fish carving made these parts appear more solid. 'Kicking up' an edge, as with the fish's tail, made it appear lighter – but being thinner it is also more fragile.
- A hard ('kicked-up') edge is more 'focused'; it comes forward in the design. A soft (rounded) edge is more 'unfocused' and tends to recede.
- Always make full use of what depth you have – otherwise you may as well use a thinner piece of wood.
- Usually there is ground to lower *within* a relief carving, besides lowering the ground at the edge: see Chapter 6, pages 119–22.

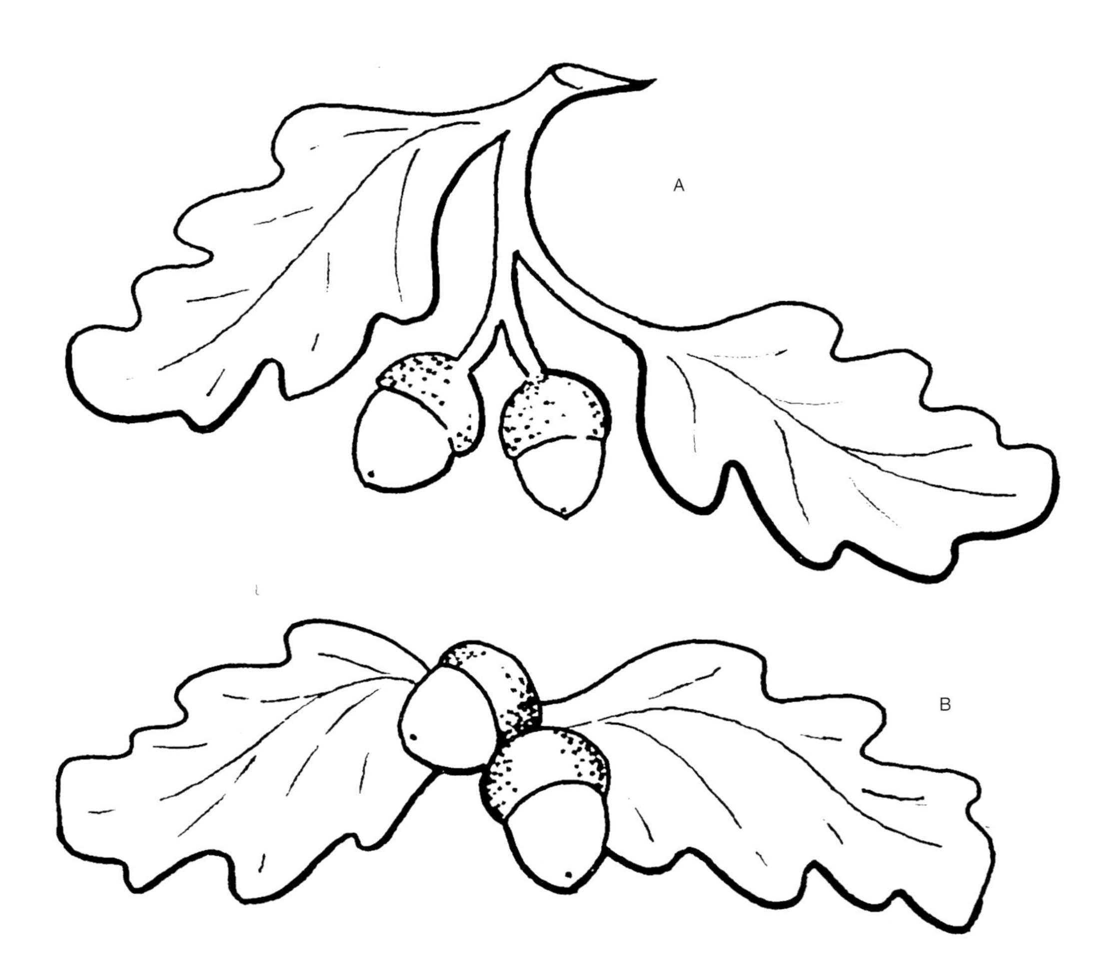

Fig 7.7 *Easy to draw might be difficult to carve. The leaves and acorns* (**A**) *have channels and weak cross grain that disappear with rearrangement* (**B**). *Thinking out beforehand and trying to visualize the carving can save much effort and heartache.*

- Your carving tools can be seen as having something of the pencil about them, in their ability to draw lines (Fig 7.8), as well as something of the paintbrush with which to texture surfaces (Fig 7.9).

Fig 7.8 *Detail from* Heron and Frog *by John Daines (see page 141): the V-tool has been used, pencil-like, to draw in feathers.*

Fig 7.9 *Detail from* Heron and Fish *by Glyn Jones (page 147): many tools have been used with almost paint-like effect to texture the background.*

Along with research and drawing, you must think in terms of *wood*: its strengths and weaknesses; how the design will work in your material.

- The principal point to think of is the length of the wood fibres: long fibres are stronger than short ones. So, the more long fibres ('long grain') run into a part, the stronger it is; and conversely, where the fibres within a part are predominantly short, that part will be weaker.
- On your drawing make a note of the direction you plan to have your grain (the wood fibres) run; normally this is vertical or horizontal. Check how the fibres run along or across vulnerable parts and see if you can alter the design or the overall grain direction to help.
- A stem which is narrow in width will also be narrow in *depth* and may be free from the background entirely (Fig 7.10). You can strengthen elements of a relief carving by tying them to the background or to some stronger element. The challenge is to do this while keeping the design looking natural.
- Think also about how you will hold the work, what tools, equipment, skills, time, energy you have at your disposal.

The important thing is to design to your own level of ability; stretch yourself a little at a time; carve regularly and as much as possible.

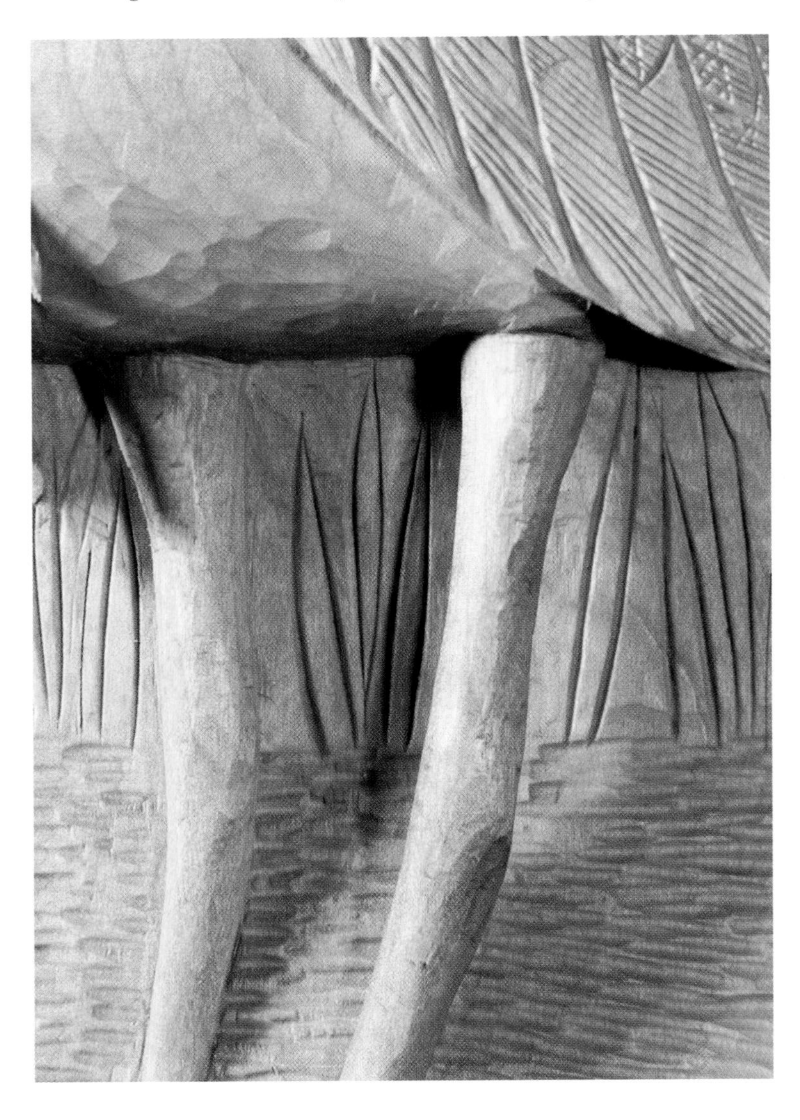

Fig 7.10 *Detail from* Heron and Frog *by John Daines (page 141): because the leg is narrower than the depth to which the ground has been taken, it must end up fully three-dimensional.*

ADDITIONAL TOOLS

The 11 tools with which we carved both the high and the low relief fishes are ones you will always find useful. However, it is unlikely that they will satisfy your needs for long. At some point you will realize that you need different shapes or sizes and that you are no longer content to 'make do'.

All students buy additional tools at some point, although when they do so varies considerably between individuals. There is a common pattern:

First, students find they want similar tools but larger, and smaller (Fig 7.11). You will find that once your relief carving gets larger, what once seemed to be a large tool, such as 3/4in (19mm), seems a lot smaller. Larger tools mean that both the grounding out and the smoothing of surfaces can be done very much quicker. Helpful tools would be:

no. 3 x 1in (25mm)

no. 6 x 1in

no. 9 x 1in.

Secondly, students get more interested in details. Perhaps there are small eyes to be carved, small recesses to get into. The tools need to be narrower:

no. 3 x 1/8in (3mm)

no. 6 x 1/8in

no. 9 x 1/8in.

Next, as the carvings get complicated students need to get deeper into recesses and between elements. The tool might be the right width and sweep, but the shank fouls the edge of the wood beyond a certain depth. Shortbent (spoon or spoonbit) tools are the answer, of which two points can be made:

Fig 7.11 *The middle three tools are the flat gouges recommended for the projects in this book. Most students choose larger (1in (25mm) plus) and smaller (1/8in (3mm)) tools, of flat, middle and deep sweeps, as their next requirements.*

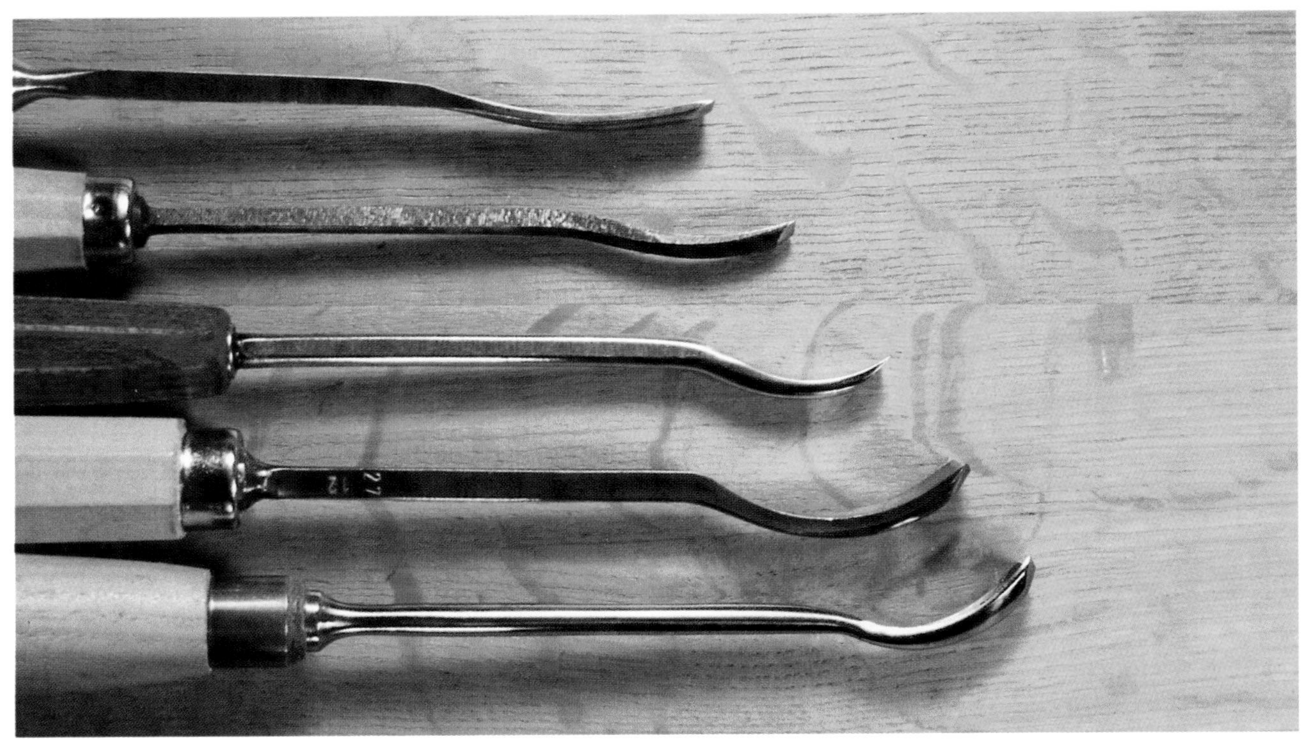

Fig 7.12 *These five shortbent or spoon gouges are of approximately the same width and sweep, but look at what different manufacturers offer by way of bend. The top two are hardly better than a regular straight gouge. Make sure you get a tool which actually does the job you want to do.*

Fig 7.13 *Grounding tools: the no. 3 (flattest) shortbent gouge (left) will clean recessed surfaces without digging in at the corners. The shortbent chisel (right) will dig in and is not to be recommended for relief carving.*

1 Manufacturers differ in the amount of bend they put on tools; some have so little as to offer no advantage over the straight version (Fig 7.12). Do look carefully at the amount of crank; after all, this is the feature of the tool that you really want.

2 Shortbent flat chisels are useless for grounding, even though they are sometimes referred to as 'grounders' – a relic of the furniture trade where grounds were stippled with punches. It is impossible to keep the corners clear of the wood and the result is a torn surface. Use shortbent flat gouges as grounders, finishing a surface in the way you would with a straight gouge (Fig 7.13).

In addition, try a few fishtail versions of the regular gouges (see Fig 2.16 on page 11; also *Woodcarving Tools, Materials & Equipment*, pages 27–30, 87–8). These are light and have a lovely feel about them, especially for light, finishing work.

Buy tools as you need them, by comparing with what you have and using the Sheffield List diagram (pages 150–1) and manufacturers' charts as guides.

CHAPTER EIGHT

GALLERY OF STUDENTS' WORK

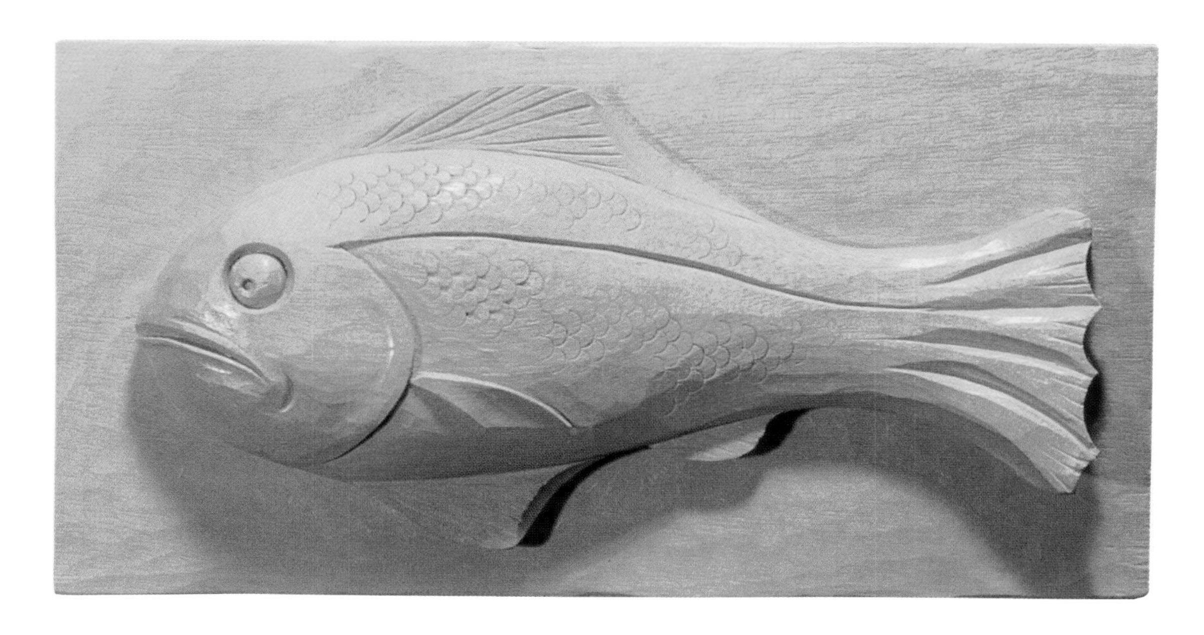

Vivien Wallace

Fish

Clematis *Limewood, 18 x 9½in (46 x 24cm)*

Eileen Kemp
Fish
Lion *Limewood, 14½ x 10in (37 x 25.5cm)*

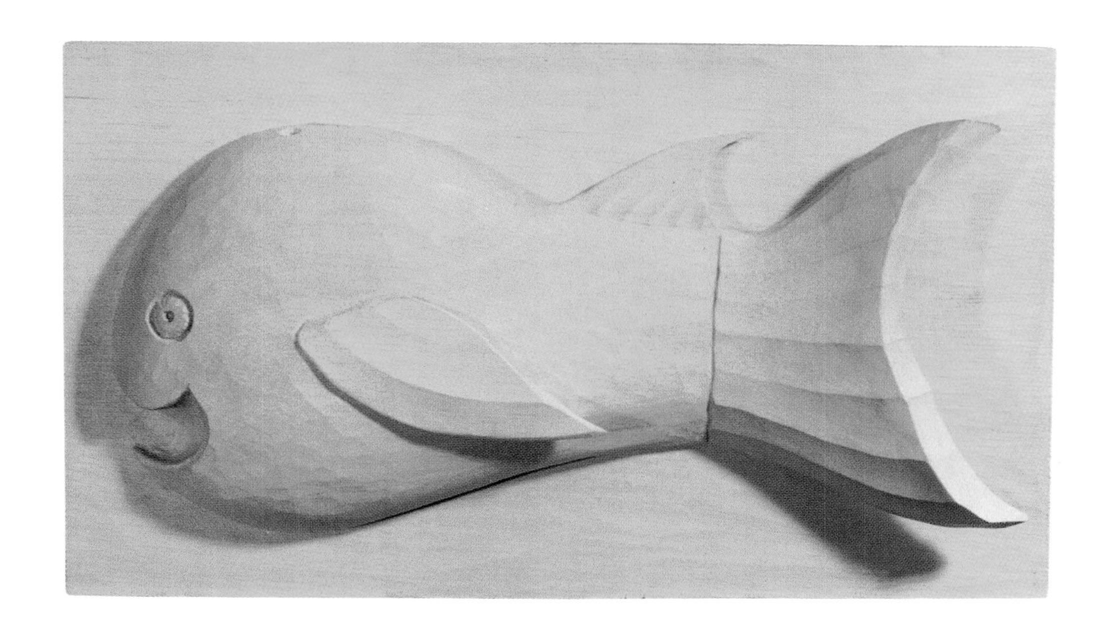

Mick Botten
Fish
Parrot over Tao Valley *Mahogany, 18 x 13in (46 x 33cm)*

Roger Pickford
Fish
Head of a Woman *English oak, 22 x 6½in (56 x 16.5cm)*

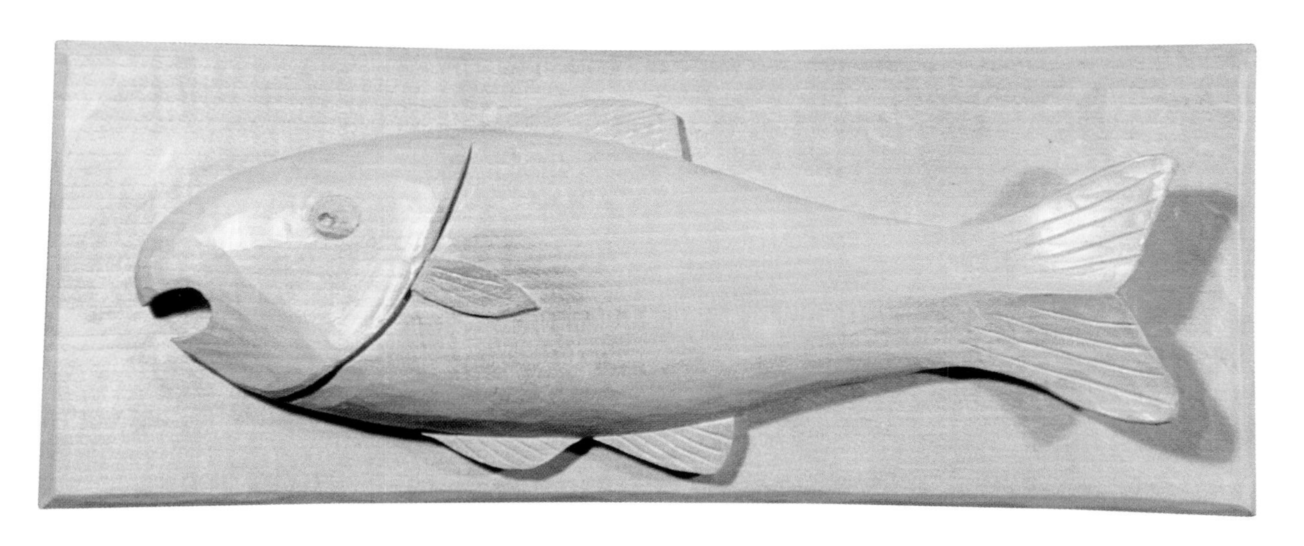

John Daines
Fish
Heron and Frog *Limewood, 25 x 14in (63 x 36cm)*

Beryl Thompson
Fish
Poppies *Limewood, 19 x 12in (48 x 30.5cm)*

Christine Tutt
Fish
Dragon *Limewood, 16 x 8in (40 x 20cm)*

Bill Grice

Fish

St Peter *taken from the Norman portico, Kilpeck church, Herefordshire. English oak, 30 x 6in (76 x 15cm)*

Ken Wilce
Fish
Screech Owl *Mahogany, 18 x 16in (46 x 40cm)*

Graham Alcock
Fish
Man Imbibing *taken from a pew end at the Church of St Winnallows, St Winnow, Cornwall. English oak, 25 x 13in (63 x 33cm)*

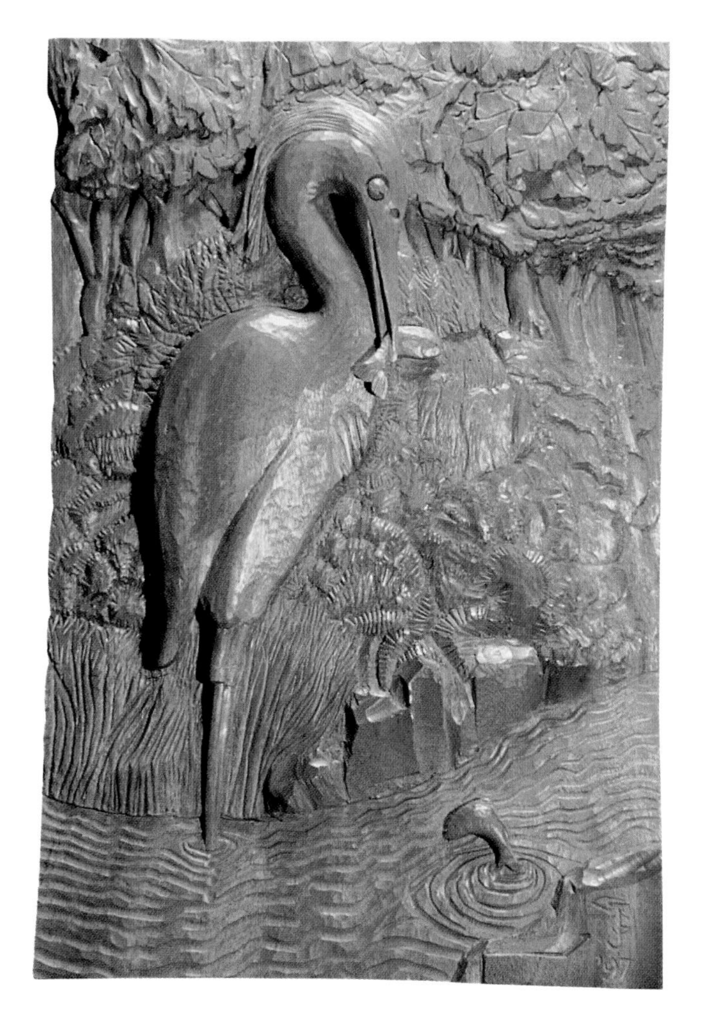

Glyn Jones

Fish

Heron and Fish *Mahogany, 20 x 15in (51 x 38cm)*

Geoff Tutt

Fish

King Offa *Sycamore, 40 x 13in (101 x 33cm)*

Detail of **King Offa**

Susan Locke
Fish
Angel *Mahogany, 17 x 18in (43 x 45.5cm)*

THE SHEFFIELD LIST OF WOOD

NUMBER — PROFILE OF

Straight Tools	Long Bent Tools	Short Bent Tools	Back Bent Tools	2 1/16	3 1/8	5 3/16	6 1/4	8 5/16	10 3/8	11 7/16	13 1/2	14 9/16	16 5/8	20 3/4	22 7/8
1	–	21	–												
2	–	22	–												
3	12	24	33												
4	13	25	34												
5	14	26	35												
6	15	27	36												
7	16	28	37												
8	17	29	38												
9	18	30	–												
10	19	31	–												
11	20	32	–												
39	40	43	–												
41	42	44	–												
45	46	–	–												

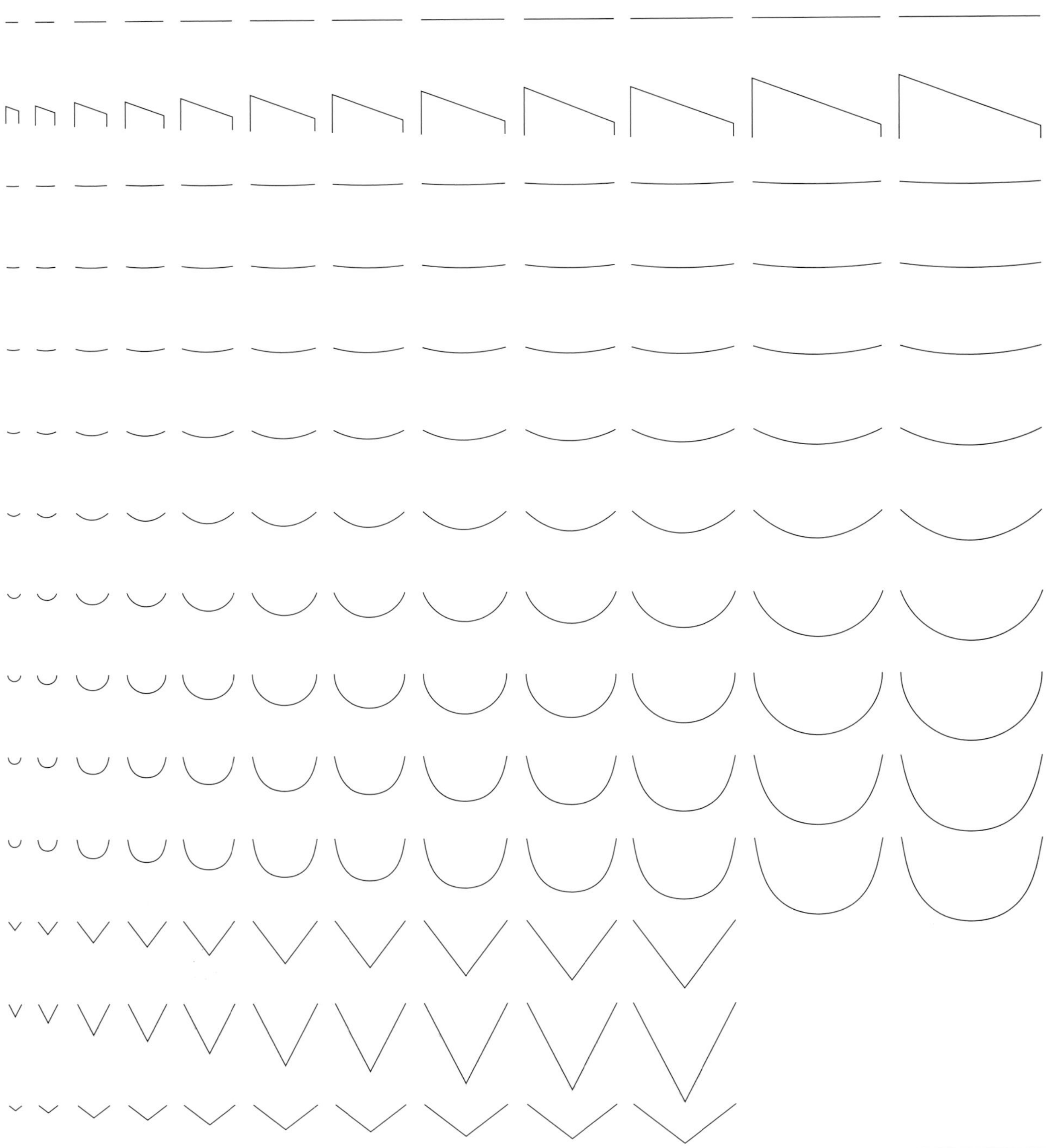

CARVING TOOL SHAPES & PROFILES

CUTTING EDGE

26	30	32	36	38	mm
1	1⅛	1¼	1⅜	1½	in

NB: Although this numbering is used by most British and many overseas manufacturers, exact shapes may vary considerably from one make to another. When ordering new tools it is important to consult the manufacturer's own chart, and to bear in mind that even this may be only an approximation.

GLOSSARY

backbent see **bent tools**.

background the plane against which the *whole* subject is placed. See **ground**.

bent tools have a curve or crank along their length, giving them a greater facility for getting into recesses. **Longbent** (salmon, sowback, curved) tools are bent along the whole blade length for shallower recesses; **shortbent** (spoon, spoonbit) tools have a long straight shank and a tight crank at the blade for getting into deeper hollows; **backbent** tools are reversed shortbents for use when the tool is to be presented to the wood 'upside down'.

bevel the wedge of metal between the **cutting edge** and the **heel**. It is normally flat, with an angle of about 20°.

bosting another word for the roughing out or 'sketching' stage of carving, where the underlying forms and flow of a subject are established.

concave hollow (like 'caves').

convex rounded.

cutting edge the extreme edge of a cutting tool, invisible to the naked eye, which leaves the final cut surface.

edge the hard end of an object seen in plan view.

facet small plane or surface left after a wood chip is removed; its actual contours depend on the quickness of gouge used. Facets can be made 'meaningful' and seen as ways of texturing the wood.

finishing may mean the last stages, 'finishing off' a carving; or the act of colouring, sealing, and/or waxing the finished piece.

fishtail (of a gouge or chisel), having a narrow bar of a shank, splaying out towards the cutting edge.

flat gouge one with the shallowest sweep (no. 3 in the Sheffield List); gouges become 'flatter' as their depth of cut decreases in proportion to their width. Amongst other uses, flat gouges are particularly effective in smoothing off surfaces to a finish.

flute/fluting a deep channel, groups of which may be gathered together in furniture legs, etc.

fluter a deep U-shaped gouge, used for running deep channels, sometimes as an alternative to the V-tool. It is used in a different manner from arc-based gouges because of its straight sides.

form a rather loose term meaning the external shape of something, the disposition of masses or parts – not the colour, subject-matter, or surface, more how the object is occupying space. See **shape**.

form horizon my own term for the apparent line where the surface of a soft form (such as a hill, ball, or the body of our fish) disappears from view. It seems fixed when drawn on paper as a line, but in reality there is no line, only a horizon which changes with viewpoint, unlike fixed, hard edges (such as the fish's tail) which remain relatively stable. It is important when moving from a two-dimensional drawing to a three-dimensional carving to know what lines represent and how the carver must deal with them.

ground differentiate this from **background**. A ground is the plane from which *any* part of the design is raised; so the body of the fish is a ground for the side fin. A ground is 'enclosed' if there is no free side from which to gain access.

grounding out (or simply **grounding**) the process whereby a **ground** or **background** is reduced to a specified level. It usually involves a rapid **lowering** stage followed by **levelling** to finish off the surface.

grounding tool or **grounder** a shortbent flat carving tool for finishing enclosed grounds. In the past flat chisels were often used, at a time when a lot of grounds in low relief furniture carving were punched or matted over (see **punch**), so that the torn grain left by the digging in of chisel corners could be disguised. Today the tool of choice is more likely to be a gouge of no. 3 (flattest) sweep, which will leave a smooth, flat ground while keeping corners clear.

heel the corner where the bevel meets the back of the blade proper. It should be polished so that it burnishes the facet after the cut.

high relief carving where the background is relatively deep compared with the width of the subject; as with **low relief**, the term does not refer simply to the *measured* depth. In our high relief fish the background depth was about a quarter of the fish's width. As a high relief gets deeper, so the subject approaches the full three dimensions.

incising literally 'cutting'. Any surface carving with gouge, V-tool, etc. which does not involve **grounding out**.

intaglio literally the 'engraving' of a surface. Any design in which the subject is incised, leaving the background untouched. A buttermould would be an example of intaglio carving.

in the round see **sculpture**.

junction the line where **wall** meets **ground**. This should always be left neat, as junctions often show poor toolwork more than surfaces; and people always look!

levelling the finishing off of the **background** to a smooth plane. The background need only *appear* flat and level – it is not necessary to be precise.

lining in outlining the subject prior to waste removal, normally with a V-tool or fluter. 'Outlining' is a good alternative, although the 'outline' is usually taken to be the principal one surrounding the whole subject.

longbent see **bent tools**.

lowering removing waste from a **ground** or **background** to a required level.

low relief a shallow, but arbitrary, depth of carving. It is defined not so much by the actual physical depth of the background as by the relationship of this depth to the size of the subject. The background of our low relief fish is about $^1/_8$in (3mm) in depth, which is about 1/30 of the full depth of a real fish, in the round. A huge Assyrian lion wall relief may be 20 times as deep, but still be classed as the same level of low relief because the ratio of depth of background to subject is the same.

mass is contrasted with **space**, both of which are present and sensed in a carving and must be considered of equal importance in a design. Carvers create space by removing the mass, but paradoxically it is space they work with. Mass *appears* to arise in the carving as the space is formed, even though it was really all there in the original block.

modelling the stage in which secondary and further forms are carved, after the principal underlying forms have been established and before proceeding to detailing.

parting tool an alternative name for the V-tool, which points to one of its principal functions: that of separating one part from another.

pierced relief relief carving in which the background is cut away, either completely or in parts.

plane a flat surface. In relief carving one can use 'plane' to mean a different level, as in a 'change of plane': a change of level between surfaces which may not be actually flat, but which have an integrity and are distinct relative to one another.

punch a small bar of metal with the end shaped for indenting wood, used either for cleaning and levelling the bottom of a small hole, for example, or for decorating a surface.

quick gouge one with a deep sweep (no. 8 or 9 in the Sheffield List); gouges become 'quicker' as their depth of cut increases relative to their width. The quickest gouge 'proper' (as opposed to U-gouges, which must be used in a different manner) has a semicircular sweep. Quick gouges remove wood more quickly, and so help in the roughing out stages of a carving, as well as serving to set in tight curves.

relief carving lies in its own world, somewhere between painting and sculpture. The depth dimension is compressed, and subjects are usually related to a virtual (original) surface plane and set against a background plane. See **low relief** and **high relief**.

rocking cut a short **sweep cut**, one of the principal techniques of woodcarving. The handle of the gouge is given a twist (rotated) as it is pushed forward, so the chip is sliced out. This gives much cleaner cutting than simply pushing the tool straight ahead.

running cut a long cut with a V-tool or a deep gouge, without rocking.

sculpture a term of wide interpretation. I use it here to mean carving which is fully three-dimensional ('in the round'), as compared with relief carving, where the depth dimension is less than in reality.

setting in precisely shaping the outline of a subject.

shape sometimes used as an alternative to **form**. I tend to use 'shape' as an aspect of form, to mean the configuration of an edge or area – how the surface of the three-dimensional object appears to the eye. So 'shape' is something more two-dimensional than 'form', even if actually moving through space.

shortbent see **bent tools**.

shoulder (or **bolster**) the prominent lump of metal between the blade and the **tang** of a chisel or gouge, which prevents the tang penetrating and splitting the handle.

slicing cut the gouge is given a sideways movement as it is pushed forwards. This may involve simply 'drifting' to the side – sometimes called 'sliding' – or rotating the handle a little (see **rocking**), or both. It can be done to the left or the right and is particularly effective with flatter gouges. See **sweep cut**.

slip/slipstone a small, shaped stone for working the insides of gouges or V-tools.

space see **mass**.

stop cut a short, stabbed cut which limits the extent to which wood fibres may tear up during a subsequent cut.

surface this is what you actually see in a carving, so it is a mistake and a lost opportunity not to make full use of it, and the qualities (texturing, tool marks, etc.) you, as a carver, can give it.

sweep the curvature of a gouge in cross section, being an arc of a circle. Gouges are identified by the amount of curvature, from **flat** (almost, but definitely not, a chisel) to **deep** (or **quick**, the quickest being a semicircle), with **medium** in between.

sweep cut (or **sweeping cut**) a **slicing cut** with an emphasis on rotating the gouge by the handle so that the cutting edge tracks along the **sweep**. It is particularly used with deeper (but not U-shaped) gouges, which can make full use of their perfectly shaped sweeps to set in clean outlines.

tang the sharp upper end of a carving tool's blade, which fits into, and should be in line with, the handle.

undercutting cutting from behind an **edge** or a **form horizon** to increase the sense of thinness or relief.

veiner a small (1/8in (3mm) or less) deep or U-shaped gouge.

wall the side of the subject, having a certain depth, and with which a **junction** with the **ground** is made.

wasting removing unwanted wood so as to approach the surface form or outline of a subject.

RESOURCES

The firms listed below produce useful and often very instructive catalogues. I suggest you phone first, as some are quite substantial and a charge has, reasonably, to be paid.

I would be pleased to hear from other carving tool and equipment suppliers for inclusion in future editions of this and other books.

Chris Pye
The Poplars
Ewyas Harold
Hereford HR2 0HU
Tel./fax: (01981) 240516

- Carving tools, wood blocks, and other equipment as used for the projects in this book. Please send a stamped, self-addressed envelope for details.

UK SOURCES OF CARVING TOOLS AND EQUIPMENT

Avery Knight and Bowlers
James Street West
Bath
Avon BA1 2BT
(01225) 425894

- Supply French Auriou woodcarving tools.

Axminster Power Tool Centre
Chard Street
Axminster
Devon EX13 5DZ
Tel. (0345) 585290
Fax (01297) 35242

- Supply Kirschen, Ashley Iles and Henry Taylor woodcarving tools; sharpening and accessory carving equipment; wide range of power tools including drill presses and routers.

BriMarc Associates
7–8 Ladbroke Park
Millers Road
Warwick CV34 5AE
Tel. (01926) 493389
Fax (01926) 491357

- Supply Tormek water-cooled grinding and sharpening systems, with jigs for carving tools.

Bristol Design (Tools) Ltd
14 Perry Road
Bristol BS1 5BG
(0117) 929 1740

- Supply their own make of carving tools; second-hand carving tools and other woodworking equipment; sharpening products.

Craft Supplies Ltd
The Mill
Millers Dale
Buxton
Derbys SK17 8SN
(01298) 871636

- Supply Pfeil carving tools as well as other carving, sharpening and finishing products.

Ashley Iles (Edge Tools) Ltd
East Kirkby
Spilsby
Lincs PE23 4DD
(01790) 763372

- Supply their own make of carving tools; some carving equipment; sharpening products.

Henry Taylor (Tools) Ltd
The Forge
Peacock Estate
Livesey Street
Sheffield S6 2BL
(0114) 234 0282

- Supply their own make of carving tools; sharpening products; punches; rifflers; knives; and adzes.

John Boddy's Fine Wood and Tool Store
Riverside Sawmills
Boroughbridge
N. Yorks YO5 9LJ
(01423) 322370

- Supply Henry Taylor and Ashley Iles woodcarving tools; carving and sharpening equipment; finishing products.

Tilgear
Bridge House
69 Station Road
Cuffley
Herts EN6 4BR
(01707) 873545

- Supply Pfeil woodcarving tools; full range of sharpening products; clamps, bench vices and holdfasts; finishing products.

Alec Tiranti Ltd
70 High Street
Theale
Berks RG7 5AR
(01734) 302775

also:

27 Warren Street
London W1P 5DG
(0171) 636 8565

- Supply Henry Taylor woodcarving tools; full range of sharpening products; carving equipment; frosters and decorative punches; strop-dressing compound.

US SOURCES OF CARVING TOOLS AND EQUIPMENT

Wood Carvers Supply, Inc.
PO Box 7500
Englewood
FL 34295–7500
Phone voice and fax: 941–698–0123
(24 hours daily)
Toll-free phone voice 800–284–6229
(US callers only, 24 hours daily)

- Supply a wide range of Lamp and Henry Taylor woodcarving tools; carving and sharpening equipment; 70-page catalogue free on request.

Woodcraft
210 Wood County Industrial Park
PO Box 1686
Parkersburg
WV 26102–1686
Phone 800–225–1153
Fax 304–428–8271

- Supply Pfeil carving tools and a variety of woodcarving and sharpening equipment.

OTHER SOURCES

Tormek AB
Box 152
S–711 23 Lindesberg
Sweden
Tel. (+46) 581 147 90
Fax (+46) 581 109 30

- Makers of water-cooled grinding and sharpening systems.

BIBLIOGRAPHY

Denning, A. (1994) *The Craft of Woodcarving*. London: Cassell.

Hasluck, P. (1911) *Manual of Traditional Woodcarving*. New York: Dover (reprint).

Norbury, I. (1987) *Relief Woodcarving and Lettering*. London: Stobart & Sons.

Onians, D. (1997) *Essential Woodcarving Techniques*. Lewes: Guild of Master Craftsman Publications.

Pye, C. (1994) *Woodcarving Tools, Materials & Equipment*. Lewes: Guild of Master Craftsman Publications.

Pye, C. (1995) *Carving on Turning*. Lewes: Guild of Master Craftsman Publications.

Pye, C. (1997) *Lettercarving in Wood*. Lewes: Guild of Master Craftsman Publications.

Schnute, W. J. (1985) *High Relief Woodcarving*. New York: Sterling.

Wheeler, W., and Hayward, C. (1963) *Practical Woodcarving and Gilding*. London: Evans.

ABOUT THE AUTHOR

A professional carver for over 20 years, Chris Pye's work has been almost all commissioned, and examples can be found in many private collections and various public buildings. It covers a broad spectrum: from lettering to heraldry; architectural carving to fine butterflies; restoration of large bedheads to personal sculpture; and from Green Men to Buddhas.

Chris Pye was originally a student of the late master woodcarver Gino Masero, and is the first to acknowledge the influence of this mentor on the way he works.

Chris has a City & Guilds Certificate in Further Education and has been teaching woodcarving for many years. He currently runs ongoing adult classes, both local and residential, at his workshops, and it is from these classes that the examples of students' work have been chosen. Chris also teaches woodcarving at the Centre for Furniture Craftsmanship, Maine, USA.

A regular contributor of articles, tool and book reviews to *Woodcarving* magazine, he also writes occasionally for *Furniture & Cabinetmaking* and *Woodturning*. His previous books are: *Woodcarving Tools, Materials & Equipment* (1994), *Carving on Turning* (1995) and *Lettercarving in Wood: A Practical Course* (1997), all published by GMC Publications.

Chris Pye has been a Buddhist for many years – which deeply affects his outlook and attitudes to life and work – and was ordained into the Western Buddhist Order in 1990.

He is married to Karin Vogel, psychotherapist and painter, to whom this book is dedicated. Together they run their large house as a Bed & Breakfast for visitors to the beautiful Golden Valley in Herefordshire, and Chris runs occasional residential courses for students of all abilities.

Photograph: David Lloyd

Chris Pye
The Poplars
Ewyas Harold
Hereford HR2 0HU
(01981) 240516

INDEX

Toymaking

Designing & Making Wooden Toys — *Terry Kelly*
Fun to Make Wooden Toys & Games — *Jeff & Jennie Loader*
Making Board, Peg & Dice Games — *Jeff & Jennie Loader*
Making Wooden Toys & Games — *Jeff & Jennie Loader*
Restoring Rocking Horses — *Clive Green & Anthony Dew*
Scrollsaw Toy Projects — *Ivor Carlyle*
Wooden Toy Projects — *GMC Publications*

Dolls' Houses and Miniatures

Architecture for Dolls' Houses — *Joyce Percival*
Beginners' Guide to the Dolls' House Hobby — *Jean Nisbett*
The Complete Dolls' House Book — *Jean Nisbett*
Dolls' House Accessories, Fixtures and Fittings — *Andrea Barham*
Dolls' House Bathrooms: Lots of Little Loos — *Patricia King*
Easy to Make Dolls' House Accessories — *Andrea Barham*
Make Your Own Dolls' House Furniture — *Maurice Harper*
Making Dolls' House Furniture — *Patricia King*
Making Georgian Dolls' Houses — *Derek Rowbottom*
Making Miniature Oriental Rugs & Carpets — *Meik & Ian McNaughton*
Making Period Dolls' House Accessories — *Andrea Barham*
Making Period Dolls' House Furniture — *Derek & Sheila Rowbottom*
Making Tudor Dolls' Houses — *Derek Rowbottom*
Making Unusual Miniatures — *Graham Spalding*
Making Victorian Dolls' House Furniture — *Patricia King*
Miniature Bobbin Lace — *Roz Snowden*
Miniature Embroidery for the Victorian Dolls' House — *Pamela Warner*
Miniature Needlepoint Carpets — *Janet Granger*
The Secrets of the Dolls' House Makers — *Jean Nisbett*

Crafts

American Patchwork Designs in Needlepoint — *Melanie Tacon*
A Beginners' Guide to Rubber Stamping — *Brenda Hunt*
Celtic Knotwork Designs — *Sheila Sturrock*
Collage from Seeds, Leaves and Flowers — *Joan Carver*
Complete Pyrography — *Stephen Poole*
Creating Knitwear Designs — *Pat Ashforth & Steve Plummer*
Creative Embroidery Techniques Using Colour Through Gold — *Daphne J. Ashby & Jackie Woolsey*
Cross Stitch Kitchen Projects — *Janet Granger*
Cross Stitch on Colour — *Sheena Rogers*
Embroidery Tips & Hints — *Harold Hayes*
An Introduction to Crewel Embroidery — *Mave Glenny*
Making Character Bears — *Valerie Tyler*
Making Greetings Cards for Beginners — *Pat Sutherland*
Making Knitwear Fit — *Pat Ashforth & Steve Plummer*
Needlepoint: A Foundation Course — *Sandra Hardy*
Pyrography Handbook (Practical Crafts) — *Stephen Poole*
Tassel Making for Beginners — *Enid Taylor*
Tatting Collage — *Lindsay Rogers*
Temari: A Traditional Japanese Embroidery Technique — *Margaret Ludlow*

The Home

Home Ownership: Buying and Maintaining — *Nicholas Snelling*
Security for the Householder: Fitting Locks and Other Devices — *E. Phillips*

VIDEOS

Drop-in and Pinstuffed Seats — *David James*
Stuffover Upholstery — *David James*
Elliptical Turning — *David Springett*
Woodturning Wizardry — *David Springett*
Turning Between Centres: The Basics — *Dennis White*
Turning Bowls — *Dennis White*
Boxes, Goblets and Screw Threads — *Dennis White*
Novelties and Projects — *Dennis White*
Classic Profiles — *Dennis White*
Twists and Advanced Turning — *Dennis White*
Sharpening the Professional Way — *Jim Kingshott*
Sharpening Turning & Carving Tools — *Jim Kingshott*
Bowl Turning — *John Jordan*
Hollow Turning — *John Jordan*
Woodturning: A Foundation Course — *Keith Rowley*
Carving a Figure: The Female Form — *Ray Gonzalez*
The Router: A Beginner's Guide — *Alan Goodsell*
The Scroll Saw: A Beginner's Guide — *John Burke*

MAGAZINES

Woodturning ◆ Woodcarving ◆ Furniture & Cabinetmaking ◆ The Router
The Dolls' House Magazine ◆ Creative Crafts for the Home ◆ BusinessMatters